W9-CCC-892

Frank H Prentiss

DESPERATE VENTURE

Also by Norman Gelb

DUNKIRK
THE BERLIN WALL
SCRAMBLE
LESS THAN GLORY
THE BRITISH
IRRESISTIBLE IMPULSE
ENEMY IN THE SHADOWS

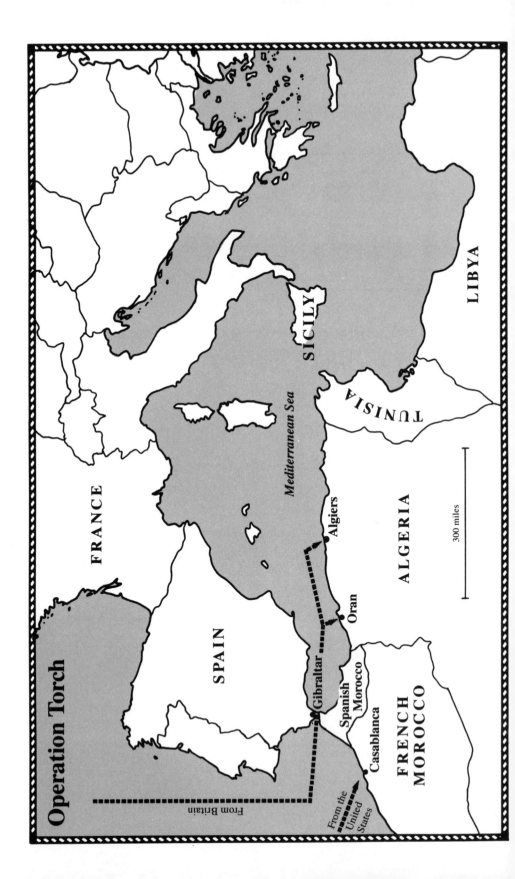

Operation Torch

FRANCE

SPAIN

Mediterranean Sea

SICILY

TUNISIA

LIBYA

ALGERIA

Spanish Morocco

FRENCH MOROCCO

Casablanca

Gibraltar

Oran

Algiers

From Britain

From the United States

300 miles

DESPERATE

★ ★ ★

VENTURE

THE STORY OF OPERATION TORCH, THE ALLIED INVASION OF NORTH AFRICA

Norman Gelb

William Morrow and Company, Inc.
New York

Copyright © 1992 by Norman Gelb

All rights reserved. No part of this book may be reproduced or utilized in any form or by any means, electronic or mechanical, including photocopying, recording, or by any informa- tion storage or retrieval system, without permission in writing from the Publisher. Inquiries should be addressed to Permissions Department, William Morrow and Company, Inc., 1350 Avenue of the Americas, New York, N.Y. 10019.

It is the policy of William Morrow and Company, Inc., and its imprints and affiliates, recognizing the importance of preserving what has been written, to print the books we publish on acid-free paper, and we exert our best efforts to that end.

Library of Congress Cataloging-in-Publication Data

Gelb, Norman.
    Desperate venture : the story of Operation Torch, the Allied invasion of North
      Africa / Norman Gelb.
          p.   cm.
      Includes bibliographical references and index.
      ISBN 0-688-09883-5
          1. Operation Torch. 2. World War, 1939–1945—Campaigns—Africa,
    North. 3. World War, 1939–1945—Diplomatic history. I. Title.
    D766.82.G379   1992
    940.54′23—dc20   92-13844
                                                                               CIP

Printed in the United States of America

First Edition

1 2 3 4 5 6 7 8 9 10

BOOK DESIGN BY BRIAN MOLLOY / CIRCA 86, INC.

MAPS BY ABLENE SCHLEIFER GOLDBERG

For Barbara

CONTENTS

⭐

. . . Torch was the most important decision taken during the war.

—LEWIS DOUGLAS
American ambassador to the Court of St. James's

DESPERATE
VENTURE

★ 1 ★

OPERATION TORCH

*The job I am going on is about as desperate a venture
as has ever been undertaken by any force in the
world's history.*

—GENERAL GEORGE S. PATTON, JR.

In the dark, early-morning hours of November 8, 1942, an armada larger and mightier than any ever before assembled took up positions at points off the coast of Northwest Africa. Its mission was to launch Operation Torch, the first massive Allied offensive operation in World War II. More than five hundred American and British warships, supply vessels, and troop transports were taking part. An invasion by more than 100,000 troops was to be the operation's opening phase. But Torch had a much broader objective—no less than to inaugurate the process that would lead to the destruction of Adolf Hitler's Third Reich.

The operation was an intricate, multifaceted undertaking. Aside from its military aspect, it wove together political intrigue, conspiracy, espionage, deception, and diplomacy. Involved, either directly or on the periphery, was a wide assortment of prominent figures, including Franklin Delano Roosevelt, Winston Churchill, Joseph Stalin, and Adolf Hitler. Also involved was the fledgling Office of Strategic Services (OSS), from which the CIA would in due course evolve, as well as a clutch of novice American diplomat-spies who had been learning their trade in the salons, cafés, and souks of Algiers, Oran, and Casablanca.

Washington and London were deeply apprehensive about Torch,

with good reason. Despite its significance and the size of the forces committed, this first combined American-British operation in the war had been hastily patched together. Half-trained, newly equipped troops, virtually none of whom had ever seen battle before, had been dispatched across thousands of miles of ocean infested with enemy submarines, to storm ashore immediately upon their arrival at their target destinations, with the possibility that they might meet stubborn resistance and that enemy action at their rear might leave most of them stranded.

The difficulties they encountered before Torch's objectives were fully achieved did indeed turn out to be formidable. Nevertheless, the operation proved a dramatic success, with momentous consequences for the Allies. It dictated their future strategy at a crucial moment in the war. And whatever reverses the Allies subsequently sustained proved only incidental to their final triumph over Nazi Germany.

However, questions remain about whether, in the last analysis, Operation Torch was a significant military achievement or a big mistake.

★ 2 ★

GENESIS

America has just come into the war, and there is no one but Winston to take her by the hand.

—SIR CHARLES WILSON

[The president] has been completely hypnotized by the British, who have sold him a bill of goods. . . . The Limeys have his ear, while we have the hind tit.

—GENERAL JOSEPH STILLWELL

On Sunday, December 7, 1941, Churchill was at Chequers, the prime ministerial country home in Buckinghamshire, an hour from London. It was there that he learned from a BBC evening radio report that the Japanese had bombed Pearl Harbor in Hawaii, plunging the United States into war. Within minutes, the prime minister was on the telephone to President Roosevelt at the White House in Washington. The spread of false rumors and misinformation had become so chronic in the war that he wanted to confirm that the BBC report was not mistaken. Assuming that it wasn't, he also wanted to wish the United States well in the global conflict into which it was now being thrust.

Churchill did not pretend to be sorry about the Japanese raid. It meant Britain would no longer stand alone in the war with Germany it had been fighting and losing for more than two years. The Germans were bound by treaty to Japan. The prime minister was certain they would now feel obliged also to go to war with the United States, whose formal neutrality had long been marked by an explicit pro-British bias. Hitler had given Tokyo personal assurances that his country "would promptly take part in case of conflict between Japan and America."

To the despair of many of his generals, Hitler did indeed declare war on the United States four days after the Pearl Harbor raid. In doing so, the German Führer performed for Roosevelt an unintended but much appreciated service. Despite the Japanese onslaught, the president and his advisers regarded Nazi Germany, with its military might, expansionist policies, and economic power, as a greater threat to American national security than Japan. Despite the isolationist sentiments of the American public, the White House, the State Department, and the War Department had concluded some time before that war between the United States and Germany was inevitable. By declaring war on America, Hitler relieved Roosevelt of responsibility for dragging the country into the bloody conflict in Europe, contrary to the wishes of a vast majority of the American people.

The United States was now also at war with fascist Italy. His fate bound to that of Germany, Italian dictator Benito Mussolini had declared war on America too. The United States and Great Britain—including its far-flung empire—were now wartime allies. They were allied as well to the Soviet Union, which had been invaded by Hitler's armies the previous June. They were also allied to China, large parts of which had been overrun by the Japanese. World War II had truly taken on a global aspect.

On the day the Japanese bombed Pearl Harbor, their warplanes also raided British imperial outposts in Asia. Hong Kong, Singapore, and Malaya were attacked and under threat of invasion. Having to fight in the East as well as the West placed additional strains on Britain's already overstretched resources. But Churchill knew the price was worth paying. The British and the people of the United States, the world's greatest industrial power, were now comrades in arms across the globe.

No American [Churchill later wrote] will think it wrong of me if I proclaim that to have the United States at our side was to me the greatest joy. . . . I knew the United States was in the war, up to the neck and in to the death. . . . So we had won after all. . . . We had won the war. England would live; Britain would live; the Commonwealth of Nations and the Empire would live. . . . We should not be wiped out. Our history would not come to an end. We might not even have to die as individuals. . . . I went to bed and slept the sleep of the saved and thankful.

18

Two days after Pearl Harbor had been bombed, in a message to President Roosevelt, Churchill invited himself and his senior military aides to Washington. He wanted to meet with Roosevelt to coordinate Allied strategy in the conflict. More specifically, he wanted to bring his influence to bear on strategic thinking in the United States at a time when Americans were still to emerge from the trauma of finding themselves at war, having already received a thrashing and about to suffer worse.

Roosevelt, who much enjoyed Churchill's company, was always pleased to see him. But neither he nor anyone else in Washington was anxious to receive a top-ranking British delegation at that time. Everyone there already had more than enough to do. Bad news poured in from the Pacific in a seemingly interminable cascade. Reports on the losses suffered at Pearl Harbor were still being received and generated ever-growing alarm. Clark Field in the Philippines, the major forward American air base in the Pacific, had also been bombed, and aircraft there, lined up in neat rows, had been destroyed on the ground. The Japanese had attacked Guam, Midway, and Wake islands. Communications were unreliable. There was no telling what other U.S. territories and bases were or soon would be under fire. Maybe Alaska. Maybe the Panama Canal. Maybe even California!

Congress wanted to know what had happened, what was still happening, and what the president and the armed forces were doing about it. Faultfinding and blame fixing were very much on the agenda. People across the country were asking why the Japanese had been able to mount their attack undetected and what urgent steps were being taken to prevent any further such raids from succeeding.

Contingency plans had to be trotted out. They had to be reviewed and implemented where advisable and possible, and updated where not. Steps had to be taken to transform peacetime America into an arsenal without delay. Security had to be tightened at military installations, war-supply factories, ports, airfields, bridges, and countless other locations across the country—and for the president as well. There was no way of predicting what an enemy, who had already demonstrated his audacity, ingenuity, and ruthlessness, might be up to. Secretary of the Treasury Henry Morgenthau, responsible for the Secret Service and Roosevelt's safety, wanted to ring the White House with armed troops and position light tanks at its entrances. Fearing to alarm the public excessively, the president vetoed that idea.

Called to Washington from his job commanding III Corps at Monterey, California, Major General Joseph Stillwell wrote to his wife that he found the capital a bedlam.

> My impression of Washington is a rush of clerks in and out of doors, swing doors always swinging, people with papers rushing after other people with papers, groups in corners whispering in huddles, everybody jumping up just as you start to talk, buzzers ringing, telephones ringing, rooms crowded with clerks all banging away at typewriters. "Give me 10 copies of this AT ONCE." "Get that secret file out of the safe." "Where the hell is the Yellow Plan (Blue Plan, Green Plan, Orange Plan, etc.)?" Everybody furiously smoking cigarettes, everybody passing you on to someone else—etc. etc. Someone with a loud voice and a mean look and a big stick ought to appear and yell "HALT. You crazy bastards. SILENCE. You imitation ants. Now half of you get the hell out of town before dark and the other half sit down and don't move for one hour." Then they could burn up all the papers and start fresh.

Emergency meetings were called at the White House, the War Department, and a multitude of other government departments and agencies—those responsible for the conscription of men into the armed forces, the shift to a war economy, the production of war supplies, shipbuilding, civil defense, counterespionage, the control of enemy aliens, labor relations, transport, and everything else that had anything to do with equipping the nation for security and combat.

Troops had to be moved. They, and those already positioned to take the brunt of the Japanese attack, had to be supplied with the tools of war, comparatively few of which were yet available. General Douglas MacArthur, the U.S. commander in the Far East—who had been responsible for leaving the planes neatly lined up at Clark Field after the Pearl Harbor raid—was left with fewer than seventy fighters and only seventeen heavy bombers to help repel the Japanese.

Americans were demanding that the nation get even, that the Japanese be halted immediately, hurled back and severely punished. Reflecting popular sentiment, the *Chicago Tribune* abandoned its long-held isolationist stance to declare that "an undivided people will go forward until they . . . have made Japan feel the consequences of what it has permitted its insane militants to do."

Panic was in the air. Lieutenant General John DeWitt, commander of the U.S. Fourth Army, trying to explain away a mistaken report from his headquarters that Japanese war planes had flown over San Francisco, warned people there that "death and destruction are likely to come to this city at any moment." Another mistaken false alarm—from Army intelligence no less—caused a stir with a claim that a secret Japanese airfield had been established not far from San Diego.

Lookouts were posted to spot Japanese mines in case they were laid in San Francisco Bay and other West Coast ports. Rumors told of Japanese warships steaming close enough to California for their big guns to shell targets there. Foreboding and precautions seemed justified when, soon afterward, a Japanese submarine surfaced off the coast of Southern California and lobbed some shells landward. They struck unoccupied ground near Santa Barbara and did no serious damage. But freighters were attacked by Japanese warships not far from the California ports of Santa Cruz and Eureka. Nightly blackouts were instituted as far inland as Boise, Idaho. A Seattle crowd smashed the illuminated show windows of stores that ignored blackout instructions, and took the opportunity to engage in some subsequent looting. The traditional annual Rose Bowl football spectacle was shifted from Pasadena to North Carolina. Exaggerated assessments of the dangers fueled the mood of fury and frenzy that was sweeping America.

Local officials telephoned the White House to warn that America's western seaboard was indefensible. Some urged that defensive positions be established well inland, in the western foothills of the Rocky Mountains, to stop Japanese invaders when they got that far after streaming ashore on the Pacific coast and forcing their way through coastal defenses.

A false report had hit Major General Joseph Stillwell "like a kick in the stomach." Before being summoned to Washington, Stillwell had been assigned the task of organizing the defense of the Southern California coast. The report he received told of a Japanese battle fleet spotted a mere 164 miles off San Francisco. The general shuddered at the thought "that our defenses were down, the enemy was at hand, and . . . we not only had nothing to defend ourselves with, but that Time was against us. . . . Had the Japs only known, they

21

could have landed anywhere on the coast, and after our handful of ammunition was gone, they could have shot us like pigs in a pen."

With so much happening and priority problems to deal with, it seemed the wrong time for the leaders of the United States to be bogged down in consultations on grand strategy with distinguished British visitors. Roosevelt suggested that perhaps such talks could be postponed a little while. But Churchill was able to persuade him that an immediate British-American conclave would be of great advantage to both nations. The pressing problems they faced, he told the president, "can best be settled on the highest executive level."

Churchill's sense of urgency was understandable. He had to know what sort of ally the United States was going to be. He told King George VI, "The whole plan of Anglo-American defense and attack has to be concerted in the light of reality," which meant reality as he interpreted it. His friend Field Marshal Jan Christiaan Smuts, prime minister of South Africa, then part of the British Commonwealth, would later tell Churchill, "Much of your time will have to be devoted wisely to guiding Washington in its war effort and not letting vital war direction slip out of our hands." Churchill knew that already. His doctor, Sir Charles Wilson, who was with him in the United States, noted in his diary that the prime minister "wanted to show the President how to run the war."

Going by sea was thought to be safer than flying. But Churchill's decision to cross the Atlantic at that time was nevertheless a daring, even reckless act. The British people had gone through the blitz and were enduring great privations as a result of the war. They had been hardened by their experience and their morale was mostly holding firm but the prime minister was very much in command of the country's war effort. Britain could boast no figure of comparable leadership qualities who might readily replace him if he was lost en route. Churchill's most likely successor was Foreign Secretary Anthony Eden, who was visiting Russia for previously scheduled consultations with Soviet dictator Joseph Stalin.

So both the prime minister and the man who would step into his shoes as leader of the nation at war would be out of the country at the same time despite Britain's precarious situation. All of its considerable imperial and Commonwealth interests in the Far East and the Pacific, and the substantial forces already committed to defending them, were in jeopardy. The country's armed forces had already sustained a string of serious military reverses. The Axis powers had virtual control of the Mediterranean Sea while wolf packs of German submarines roamed the Atlantic. The British merchant fleet had lost almost 8 million tons of shipping since the outbreak of the war in Europe and was still losing more than 300,000 tons a month. The Royal Navy was hard-pressed to keep Britain's lifelines, and the lifelines to its troops abroad, from being cut.

Things were going terribly wrong. Calls were being issued for the country's war command to explain and make good glaring shortcomings. The loss of Crete by British troops to half their number of German invaders seemed a worrying foretaste of what might be in store. When two of the Royal Navy's most formidable warships, the battleship *Prince of Wales* and the battle cruiser *Repulse,* were sunk by Japanese aircraft off the coast of Malaya, the London *News Chronicle* quoted an unnamed "high British authority" as describing the failure to provide aerial cover for those vessels as "an act of imbecility."

For reasons of public morale and national unity at a time of crisis, British newspapers mostly refrained from criticizing Churchill personally for the long list of military setbacks. But some grumbling was now heard in London about the prime minister "swanning off to America" when the nation and the empire were under grave threat. The mass circulation London *Daily Mirror* wanted to know what "made worth while the . . . absence of the head of state during some of the most critical days of the war." And the London *Daily Sketch* asserted, "We are entitled to ask those to whom the destinies of this great empire have been unreservedly entrusted to take themselves more seriously in hand."

The outlook for the Allies was not unrelievedly bleak. The British had recovered from earlier setbacks in Libya and appeared to have Axis forces there, commanded by General Erwin Rommel, on the run. With the onset of the fierce Russian winter, the Red Army, which had earlier seemed on the verge of disintegration, appeared finally, though probably only temporarily, to have halted the German army's drive deep into the Soviet Union. With the United States and its vast military potential now in the war, victory appeared ultimately inevitable.

But it was not immediately in prospect and Churchill's presence at the helm in London at such a worrying time, rather than in far-off Washington, appeared eminently advisable. However, the prime minister never neglected what he considered to be the central issue in any problem, and he was certain that at that moment "a complete understanding between Britain and the United States outweighed all else."

At stake was how America's enormous resources could be harnassed most profitably to the cause of victory. Churchill believed that only a personal meeting between himself and Roosevelt could quickly resolve possible differences and difficulties. In addition, U.S. military chieftains would benefit from Britain's war experience and expertise. Accordingly, he was to be accompanied on the journey to the United States by an impressive team of senior officers—Field Marshal Sir John Dill, Admiral of the Fleet Sir Dudley Pound, and Air Chief Marshal Sir Charles Portal. Minister of Supply Lord Beaverbrook was also along, seeking increased American material support for Britain's war effort. General Sir Alan Brooke, Chief of the Imperial General Staff, was left in London to mind the store.

On December 13, after having journeyed by train from London, the prime minister and his party boarded the battleship HMS *Duke of York* at the mouth of the River Clyde in Scotland to begin their transatlantic voyage. They were both hopeful and apprehensive. Immensely relieved to be allied with the industrial might and potentially massive military manpower of the United States, they nevertheless feared that the American approach to winning the war might be different from their own.

They had cause to be concerned. Demands that the full weight of American power—such as it was then—be brought to bear against the Japanese were growing in intensity across the United States.

> The official reports and Press summaries we had received [Churchill wrote] gave the impression that the whole fury of the nation would be turned upon Japan. We feared lest the true proportion of the war as a whole might not be understood [by the Americans]. We were conscious of a serious danger that the United States might pursue the war against Japan in the Pacific and leave us to fight Germany and Italy in Europe, Africa, and in the Middle East.

Indeed, the delivery of war supplies from the United States to Britain and other Allies was suspended while decisions were made on where those supplies would do the most good against the enemy. The shortfall in weapons for America's own armed forces was worrying. The War Department insisted that until the dust had cleared, whatever was available should be scrupulously conserved for America's own military buildup and to make up for the losses sustained in the Pacific.

The relationship between the United States and Britain had been transformed by what had happened at Pearl Harbor. The United States had suddenly been catapulted out of an uneasy neutrality into the role of senior Allied power, without whom the war could not be won. Just as abruptly, having earlier stood alone against Hitler's military machine, Britain found itself reduced to junior partner in this transatlantic alliance.

The British visitors to Washington would be required to adjust to the changed situation. It would, however, be difficult for them to mask their conviction that because of their wartime experiences so far—not to mention their country's long history as a global power—they understood the problems, priorities, and possibilities in the struggle against the enemy far better than their American hosts possibly could.

Their realization that they needed the Americans far more than the Americans needed them complicated things for them. Nor could they extract any comfort from the fact that the United States was unprepared for war emotionally, materially, and organizationally, as was symbolically demonstrated to the British upon their arrival in Washington. The officer responsible for arrangements for this critical Allied gathering failed to provide a room big enough to accommodate all the military luminaries and their aides who were to attend the opening session of the conference. Alternate arrangements had to be quickly made.

It was not an isolated bureaucratic bungle, nor was the impression it gave of American unpreparedness misleading. The situation was, in fact, far worse. After having had an opportunity to examine conditions in some detail, Field Marshal Dill would shortly report despairingly back to London, "At present this country has not—repeat not—the slightest conception of what the war means, and their armed forces are more unready for war than it is possible to imagine."

But to the relief of the British, upon arrival in Washington they found agreement on fundamental Allied strategy. The Americans made it clear at once that despite the popular clamor in the United States for vengeance against the Japanese, and the temptation to concentrate first on dealing with them quickly and conclusively, they still deemed Germany to be the primary threat and its defeat "the key to victory."

Years later, during the postwar witch-hunts Senator Joseph McCarthy led in his bizarre crusade against those Americans he declared to be Communists or Communist sympathizers, the senator attempted to smear U.S. Army Chief of Staff General George C. Marshall (later secretary of state) because of that decision. McCarthy insinuated that Marshall had revealed himself to be sympathetic to Communism when he chose to give priority to saving the Soviet Union from Nazi destruction when the defeat of Japan should have taken precedence.

In fact, the Germany First policy made military sense. At the time, Germany rather than Japan was the enemy that all three major Allies—the United States, Britain, and the Soviet Union—could conceivably subject to simultaneous, effective, and possibly decisive military pressure in the not too distant future (as in fact they did). If, however, the United States sought to defeat Japan first, Britain and the Soviet Union, already in serious trouble, might in the meantime be even more badly mauled by the Germans. The United States would then be left with enfeebled allies—or perhaps even none at all—when it finally could turn from the Pacific to winding up the war in Europe. Also, unless Germany was soon forced onto the defensive, it was conceivable that its armies would have fought their way through the Middle East and the Persian Gulf region to connect with the Japanese, perhaps on the Indian subcontinent. If such a linkup had been permitted to take place, the Axis powers would have been much more difficult to crush.

Besides, the Germans appeared to have far greater potential than Japan in productive power and scientific capabilities. Racial prejudice had made most Westerners think of the Japanese as undersized, buck-toothed, idiotically smiling, ever-apologizing caricatures, not really very clever. They were thought capable of triumph only over other Asians, whom they treated with barbaric cruelty, or when they resorted to pusillanimous sneak attacks like that at Pearl Harbor.

On the other hand, the Germans were known to be highly efficient and technologically creative. It was thought that if they were given time to develop their scientific and productive capacities during years of stalemate in Europe—while the United States was preoccupied in the Pacific—Hitler could "prove more difficult if not impossible to defeat." In fact, German scientists were then about to begin experimenting with the application of atomic physics to weaponry.

Churchill was the ideal Englishman to influence the development of American strategy for winning the war at a time when it was still being formulated. Roosevelt respected him and found him intellectually stimulating. He was personally popular with the American press, in which he was portrayed as the symbol of British defiance of Nazi bullying, aggression, and brutality. What was more, the prime minister did have considerable experience as a military strategist. He had served as First Lord of the Admiralty in both world wars and had been overseeing his country's military effort ever since he had succeeded Neville Chamberlain as prime minister in 1940 on the day the Germans thundered into the Netherlands, Belgium, and Luxembourg on their way to conquering France.

Nevertheless, while still en route to the United States aboard the *Duke of York,* Churchill received a warning from Harry Hopkins, Roosevelt's friend and adviser, about the forthcoming Washington talks. In a message relayed by Lord Halifax, the British ambassador in the American capital, Hopkins advised the British against seeming to instruct the Americans on how to fight the war. Acquainted with Churchill's irrepressible enthusiasms and take-charge habits, Hopkins warned that the U.S. Chiefs of Staff, facing up to the battering the Japanese were inflicting on the Americans, were unlikely to be overly receptive to preset advice from foreigners on how to go about defeating the enemy.

Nevertheless, as the *Duke of York* crossed the Atlantic, the members of Churchill's party, under the prime minister's leadership and direction, reviewed key points of grand strategy they wanted to propose to the Americans. By December 22, when their ship docked at Hampton Roads, Virginia, from which they were whisked by plane to Washington, they had produced an outline for how to go about defeating the Axis powers. Though Churchill was concerned not to give the impression that the British were "concentrating exclusively on our problems and ignoring those of America," he ignored Hopkins's warning, and the British plan was presented when the Washington conference—code-named Arcadia—began.

Preoccupied with trying to shore up U.S. defenses in the Pacific and not as accustomed as the British to engaging in such comprehensive consultations, the Americans had no comparable strategic overview to present. As a consequence, the British plan served as the basis for discussion on how the Allies should seize the initiative in the war. The British did most of the talking while the Americans did most of the listening. The British delegation was treated with the deference due to distinguished representatives of an Allied power that had gallantly resisted the common enemy for so long and as visitors who had been welcomed to Washington by their president. But, as Hopkins had warned, some at the War Department remained less than impressed with the British for having shown up with a set of ideas on how to win a struggle they had been losing, with hardly a respite, since the first shot was fired.

The underlying British strategy had a logical simplicity. The Western Allies would employ their strengths against Germany's weaknesses and avoid exposing their weaknesses to Germany's strengths. Though hard-pressed, the Allies had greater naval and maritime resources than the Germans. Churchill wanted Britain and the United States to exploit that advantage to compel Hitler to scatter his land forces, which were stronger for the time being. There would be a gradual "closing and tightening" of a ring around German-occupied Europe, with incursions and raids at its most vulnerable points, before the Allies moved in for the kill.

Churchill's views on how the war should be fought were dominated by ingrained acceptance of the fact that Britain, despite its global interests, was a comparatively small country. When it was confronted by a formidable adversary, it was logical for it to fall back on an approach based on the prudent use of the limited resources at its disposal. Recent history—horrific losses in World War I and the dismal experience just two years earlier of the British Expeditionary Force in France—had shown that when it did not do so, it paid a steep price. This time, however, by tightening and closing the ring around Germany, they would avoid repeating that error. The Germans would be forced to disperse and squander their own resources. No massive frontal assault on Hitler's Fortress Europe was to be undertaken until its success, without immense cost, was virtually guaranteed.

The American approach was fundamentally different. The United States was a huge nation with a large population and vast resources. Its basic attitude was: Whatever the job is, go out and do it without dragging things out or playing around the edges. At the War Department, that meant that whatever the initial cost, the sooner the Allies locked horns with the Germans, the sooner war-winning momentum would be established.

For America's military planners, Churchill's vision of closing the ring around Hitler made little sense. It seemed to be toying at the periphery of the war rather than going out to win it. It would consume resources better used elsewhere in operations that, even if successful, appeared unlikely to contribute much to ultimate triumph. The Americans were disconcerted by Churchill's seemingly cavalier suggestion of a hodgepodge of Allied amphibious operations—in Norway, Denmark, Holland, Belgium, France, Italy, possibly even the Balkans.

> The potential front of attack [would thus be] made so wide [Churchill said] that the German forces holding down these different countries cannot be strong enough at all points. . . . It need not be assumed that great numbers of men are required. If the incursion of . . . armoured formations is successful, the uprising of the local population, for whom weapons must be brought, will supply the corpus of the liberating offensive.

To launch his policy of closing and tightening the ring around the enemy, Churchill focused in particular on French territories in North Africa, across the Mediterranean from mainland France. He proposed that a campaign be launched within a year to gain a dominant presence in those territories. To that end, he said, "Plans should be set on foot forthwith." It was to be hoped that the objective could be achieved without bloodshed, that the Allies would be able to move into French North Africa with an "invitation" from French officers and officials there, anxious to redeem the honor of their country after its defeat by Germany. But preparations had to be made to use force if necessary, in the form of a major amphibious operation.

Churchill told Roosevelt that he had already earmarked 55,000 troops for Operation Gymnast, as his North Africa scheme was code-named. They were ready to be boarded and dispatched when the signal was given. He urged that United States forces take part in the operation too.

Roosevelt was greatly interested. However, the War Department recoiled at the idea. To General Marshall, Operation Gymnast would be no more than a distraction. It would tie down troops and resources in North Africa, where they would do little toward bringing the war to a victorious conclusion. Marshall also had grave doubts about the operation because of its likely complexities and hazards. It would be an amphibious exercise taking place far from any major Allied land base. Troops would have to be ferried great distances to assault territory to which the enemy had easier access. Marshall warned that a "failure in this first venture would have an extremely adverse effect on the morale of the American people."

Other senior U.S. officers were even more dismissive. They made their objections known in internally distributed War Department memorandums. Lieutenant General Lesley McNair, chief of staff at U.S. Army General Headquarters, suggested that Churchill was engaging in empty bravado. McNair cited a litany of British setbacks to emphasize his point.

> While the willingness of the British to take long chances in such expeditions shows admirable courage, the soundness of their judgment is not so apparent. A Gallipoli, Norway or Crete will not advance us far along the road to victory.

McNair thought so little of British military skills that if the United States did intend to embark on a North Africa campaign, his advice would be that it should do so "entirely independently of Great Britain. . . . We must take the offensive in our own way. . . ." He and some others at the War Department uncharitably imagined the impoverished British rubbing their hands in glee over the vast pool of American resources which they now thought they could draw upon at will as the grandiloquent Churchill went about mesmerizing Roosevelt with outlandish stratagems.

Major General Stanley Embick, one of the War Department's

most highly regarded strategic planners, warned that without promising much by way of reward, a North Africa operation would entail the heavy commitment of troop and naval resources in an area "far more favorable to the Germans than to ourselves," and "would prove a mistake of the first magnitude." Embick condemned the scheme as being "so irrational that it is fantastic." Like a number of other senior American officers, he was convinced that British overall strategy was devised not so much to defeat Germany as to preserve the British Empire, which Americans, if they thought about it at all, generally considered an iniquitous anachronism.

Even Roosevelt, despite his high regard for arch-imperialist Churchill, had strong feelings about that. The president believed that the British Empire, and the French Empire as well, would have to be dissolved after the war for reasons of social justice and to preserve the postwar peace. But when, during the Arcadia Conference, he presumed to ask Churchill about the possibility of eventual progress toward independence for India—the proverbial jewel in the British crown but subject to intense independence agitation at the time—the prime minister firmly indicated to him that it was none of his business.

That did not make Roosevelt any less interested in Churchill's thoughts about how the war should be fought. But suspicions about British motives persisted among a hard core of senior figures at the War Department. General Marshall was not one of them. His strong objections to British perceptions were purely strategic. He later said there was "too much anti-British feeling on our side [during the Arcadia conference].... Our people were always ready to find Albion perfidious." The British, Marshall said, were far less suspicious of the Americans but may have "just felt we weren't smart enough to cause them trouble."

Certainly the War Department, including Marshall, believed that Roosevelt was being taken in by Churchill's rhetoric and grandiose schemes. At Roosevelt's invitation, the prime minister had taken up residence at the White House during his Washington stay. He and Roosevelt conferred regularly, informally, enjoyably, and often alone. The U.S. Chiefs of Staff were not always told what they discussed or what conclusions they had drawn. To their chagrin, they sometimes only learned what had transpired between the two leaders from British officers who were regularly briefed by Churchill.

At one point during the Arcadia talks, Secretary of War Henry Stimson threatened to resign after word reached him of what had occurred at one those summit chitchats. Stimson learned that the president had impulsively indicated to the prime minister that some forces being sent to reinforce American troops falling back before the Japanese advance in the Philippines might, if they could not get there in time, be diverted to help the British in beleaguered Singapore. The idea was not outlandish. But the implication that U.S. resources might be so casually rerouted, and that they might be put at the disposal of the British when America's needs were critical, was infuriating. General Stillwell was particularly enraged by Roosevelt's interest in Churchill's North Africa scheme.

> [He] has been completely hypnotized by the British, who have sold him a bill of goods. . . . The Limeys have his ear, while we have the hind tit. Events are crowding us into ill-advised and ill-considered projects. . . . The Limeys want us in with both feet. So the answer is, we must do something *now,* with our hastily made plans and our half-trained and half-equipped troops.

But however ill-conceived the War Department considered Churchill's North Africa proposal to be, the president was impressed by the British leader's presentation of it. The American military, therefore, felt constrained from engaging their British visitors in vigorous debate about it at the conference. It was still early days; nothing final was yet being decided. Besides, the British military, more cautious than the prime minister and more closely attuned to how overstretched British resources already were, did not seem to share his zeal with regard to North Africa. However, rough initial estimates were drawn up on the resources that might be needed for Operation Super-Gymnast—as the plan was retitled now that U.S. involvement had become a possibility—and it was passed on to planning officers for closer study and operational recommendations.

North Africa was just one of the issues considered at the Arcadia Conference. Others included the importance of keeping the Soviet Union from being forced out of the war by the Germans, the dispatch of American troops to Britain, the security of essential lines of communication, and long-term equipment requirements.

An embryonic United Nations organization was created, consisting of the twenty-six Allied countries whose governments, some in exile, pledged to continue the war against the Axis powers until victory. There was little dispute on any of those matters. But controversy developed over a Combined Chiefs of Staff Committee that was to be established to coordinate the plans and operations of the Western Allies and oversee the direction of their war effort.

The Americans proposed that this committee be based in Washington. The British would have liked it to be based in London but realized the Americans would never accept that. Instead, they proposed that two such committees be set up, one in Washington, the other in the British capital. The Americans rejected that idea, maintaining that such duplication at so high a level would create a needless bureaucratic morass when efficiency and promptness in decision making were essential. They insisted that only one committee be established and that Washington had to be the place for it. The British Chiefs of Staff in London would be represented on it by senior subordinates who would be in continuous contact with Britain but permanently stationed in the American capital. That was where Allied strategic control would be exercised.

Grudgingly, the British acquiesced to the Washington arrangement. It was an acknowledgment that their country was the junior partner in the transatlantic alliance but nonetheless was accepted by some of them with bad grace. According to White House adviser Harry Hopkins, they "kicked up a hell of a row." Sir Charles Wilson noted in his diary, "The Americans have got their way and the war will be run from Washington, but they will not be wise to push us so unceremoniously in the future. Our people are very unhappy about the decision." Looking on from afar in London, General Brooke growled that Churchill and the members of his party had sold Britain's "birthright for a plate of porridge."

But the prime minister didn't much mind where the Combined Chiefs of Staff Committee was located. He knew the important decisions would be made by Roosevelt and himself and he had found the president largely receptive to the main thrust of his ideas.

A decision of far greater significance than where the Combined Chiefs would hold court was made by Roosevelt alone at the time of the Arcadia Conference. The Americans having confirmed their agreement to the Germany First strategy, the president informed his Chiefs of Staff he wanted that agreement acted on without undue delay. He instructed them to make certain that American troops would be in combat against the enemy in the European Theater of Operations within the next twelve months. The influence that order would have on the entire course of the war was not appreciated at the time.

The visiting British luminaries saw no reason to take issue with Roosevelt on the deadline he imposed—the Arcadia talks were for general planning rather than operational purposes. However, they tended to dismiss the president's gifts as a military thinker. Colonel Ian Jacob, the assistant military secretary to the British War Cabinet, who was with the Churchill party in Washington, wrote in his diary, "The President is a child in military affairs, and evidently has little realization of what can and cannot be done. He doesn't seem to grasp how backward his country is in its war preparations, and how ill-prepared his army is to get involved in large-scale operations."

Churchill was of course anxious to get the United States militarily committed in the European Theater as soon as possible. Besides, he had always been an advocate of offensive action against the enemy at the earliest possible moment, even sometimes when such action seemed inadvisable. It was widely believed in British military command circles that the prime minister succumbed too readily to the whims of his fertile imagination and that he had a "general dislike for those aspects of reality which impeded his grand design for victory."

General Brooke, Britain's top soldier, thought Churchill's "military plans and ideas varied from the most brilliant conceptions at the one end to the wildest and most dangerous at the other." "God knows where we should be without him," Brooke wrote in his diary, "but God knows where we shall go with him!"

★ 3 ★

AFRICAN PRELUDE

[We] dropped like so many Alices into the African wonderland.

—U.S. DIPLOMAT-SPY KENNETH PENDAR

General Stillwell and others at the War Department were wrong to believe the idea of a North Africa operation appealed to Roosevelt only because Churchill had mesmerized him with fine words and wild ideas. The fact was, the president needed no cajoling to share the prime minister's interest in such an undertaking. He had long before ordered the State and War departments to keep developments in France and French Africa under close examination for purely American reasons.

On June 14, 1940, a month after Hitler had dispatched his armies westward in a march of conquest and destruction across Europe, German troops had marched in triumph down the Champs-Élysées. The people of France were staggered by how quickly resistance to the invaders had crumbled, how the numerically inferior Wehrmacht had easily outmaneuvered, outgunned, and overwhelmed the French Army, whose generals had boasted that it was invincible.

Shortly before the Germans arrived in Paris, the government of Premier Paul Reynaud had abandoned the city and fled southwest to the city of Bordeaux, 580 miles away on the Atlantic coast. There, two days later, Reynaud acknowledged the hopelessness of his position and resigned. He was replaced as head of the French government by the eighty-four-year-old World War I hero Marshal Philippe Pétain, who had already made clear his belief that the war was lost.

One day later, Pétain rejected calls that the struggle against the German aggressors be carried on from France's North African territories and asked Hitler for armistice terms. He was acting in accordance with the wishes of most French people. Only comparatively few who had not been totally demoralized wished to fight on against the invaders. Even before armistice terms had been negotiated, countless French soldiers laid down their arms. Most officers who instructed their men to continue resistance were disobeyed.

French people seeking a way to justify their easy acceptance of national defeat were comforted by the reassuring grandfatherly figure of the esteemed Pétain. He was a symbol of France's former glory. The marshal would take the weight of the nation's plight on his own aged shoulders and relieve his people of their shame and despair. The following month, the French National Assembly, seeking similar relief, surrendered supreme political power to him. He assumed the position of head of state, with full executive and legislative authority.

Pétain set up his new French government in the sleepy spa town of Vichy in the south. It was intended as a temporary shift, lasting only until the situation was clarified. But Pétain's regime was to remain in Vichy until the Germans were driven out of France four years later. Vichy France, the region it was to administer once armistice terms were finally agreed with Germany, consisted of less than half the country but covered all the south, including France's Mediterranean coast. The rest of France was occupied by German troops and ruled by a German military government.

The country's willingness to accept subjugation was so widespread that the Wehrmacht could have overrun this hastily devised geopolitical fabrication without half trying. But for the time being, Hitler was prepared to tolerate the existence of Vichy France and its facade of independence, provided he could exercise ultimate control over its actions and policies. He wanted to consolidate his existing conquests as he prepared to seek new ones, and as he set about establishing a Nazi new order for Europe in which a fascist France could play a role.

He also wished to undermine the morale of the British. They had been shocked by the French military collapse and by the momentous setback suffered by their own forces. They had lost almost 70,000 men before being driven out of Europe and into the sea at Dunkirk. As the British grimly braced themselves for a follow-up German invasion of their homeland, Hitler hoped to demonstrate to them that with a less intractable government, they too might extract lenient peace terms from him, be spared further wartime pain and grief, and still remain independent.

The French-German armistice agreement was, however, hardly an inducement. The Germans retained a million and a half French prisoners of war as a guarantee that Vichy France would refrain from any act that might be contrary to German interests. Hitler also made it clear he was prepared to complete his brutal occupation of France if disobliged by a troublesome Vichy regime. That seemed unlikely to happen once that regime indicated its readiness to adjust to the Nazi new order by banning political parties and trade unions, establishing a fascist-style political police corps, persecuting Jews, and replacing France's traditional principles of Liberty, Equality, and Fraternity with an authoritarian ethic based on Work, Family, and Motherland.

In addition to the trappings of independence, Vichy retained administrative control of France's North African territories. A German-Italian Armistice Commission, staffed by intelligence officers and Gestapo agents, was assigned to keep an eye on the situation in those territories. An army of French and French colonial troops, a small French air force, and a portion of France's still powerful fleet were based there. Their existence, outside of direct German control, might have caused alarm in Berlin had it not been for an incident on the coast of Algeria two weeks after the French capitulation to Hitler.

Fearing that Vichy France's accommodating regime would be required to transfer French warships to German command, the British took action. On July 3, 1940, they launched a surprise attack on a portion of the French fleet anchored in the port of Mers el-Kébir near Oran. One battleship was destroyed, another battleship and a battle cruiser were disabled, and more than twelve hundred French seamen were killed. At the same time, French warships then in British ports were seized and their officers and men were interned.

These acts by France's former ally outraged Vichy leaders, who considered declaring war on Britain in response. The French military command was particularly bitter. It already believed that the British had treacherously abandoned France when their Expeditionary Force was evacuated en masse back to England from Dunkirk a month earlier, while the French were still fighting the Germans. With hatred of Britain now rife among Vichy's leaders and with those leaders subservient to Berlin, the Germans believed they had little to worry about in French North Africa.

For the United States, though neutral at the time of France's collapse, the European developments in the spring and summer of 1940 were traumatic. With France defeated and Britain's future uncertain, it was possible that an unprepared America would soon have to provide its own first line of defense. What was more, German influence had spread to South America, a region of strategic concern to Washington. Only sixteen hundred miles of ocean separated Dakar in Vichy-administered French West Africa from Brazil. Vulnerable mid-Atlantic islands were even closer. In a radio address, President Roosevelt warned the American people about the dangers the country faced even before the United States entered the war.

> They [the Germans] . . . have the armed power at any moment to occupy Spain and Portugal, and that threat extends not only to French North Africa and the western end of the Mediterranean, but also to the Atlantic fortress of Dakar and to the island outposts of the New World—the Azores and Cape Verde Islands. The Cape Verde Islands are only seven hours distant from Brazil by bomber or troop-carrying planes. They dominate shipping routes to and from the South Atlantic. The war is approaching the brink of the Western Hemisphere itself. It's coming very close to home.

Despite the president's warning, the American public continued to oppose both U.S. involvement in the conflict and any major effort to prepare for it. The attack on Pearl Harbor was then still more than a year off, and opinion polls continued to show that Americans were overwhelmingly determined not to repeat what they widely accepted to be their country's mistake in World War I. This time the Yanks would not be coming to help the ungrateful, fractious Europeans sort out their endlessly recurring bloody squabbles.

Despite American neutrality, Roosevelt tried to bolster the British, sending them fifty venerable destroyers and some arms. But Congress had put restrictions on what he could offer and he knew he was limited in what he could do to buck popular isolationist sentiment. Nevertheless, the president remained fearful that Vichy, through compulsion or voluntary collaboration, would let the Germans use French African territory as a springboard for intrusion into the Western Hemisphere.

He also had other grounds for anxiety about what the Vichy regime might do. Many years before, the president had been assistant secretary of the navy. Like Churchill, he had particular regard for the capabilities of the French fleet. It was largely intact even after the British raid on Mers el-Kébir. Most of its warships—including three battleships and eight cruisers—were at anchor at the French naval base at Toulon on the Mediterranean. Seized by Hitler, those ships could help him turn the Atlantic Ocean into a German lake.

That was a prospect Roosevelt could not tolerate with equanimity, not with much of America's own fleet based at Pearl Harbor and elsewhere in the Pacific in case of Japanese aggression. He acted accordingly. He abominated the quasi-fascist character of the Vichy regime but he instructed the State Department to establish diplomatic relations with it; the United States was to recognize Marshal Pétain's government as the legitimate successor to the previous French government. U.S. diplomatic representation in France was accordingly shifted from German-occupied Paris to Vichy.

That decision provoked a chorus of criticism in Congress. Newspaper editorials pointed to the glaring contrast between American acceptance of this shabby replacement of democracy in France and British recognition of the fledgling Free French movement* that Brigadier General Charles de Gaulle had established in London to continue the struggle against German aggression and oppression.

But American policy toward Vichy France was not based on

---

*De Gaulle's movement was soon renamed Fighting France but continued to be popularly called The Free French.

ethical considerations. It was designed to place diplomats in a position to press Pétain and the people around him to resist German pressure for France to join the Axis powers as a belligerent in the war and to persuade them to fend off German demands for the use of Vichy's territory and resources when such demands were made. Besides, it would have been absurd to break off relations with Vichy on moral grounds while retaining an embassy in Berlin.

When Roosevelt appointed his friend Admiral William Leahy as ambassador to Vichy in January 1941, eleven months before Pearl Harbor, his role was carefully spelled out to him at the White House.

> The President wanted me to be a "watchdog" to try to prevent France from extending any aid to Germany beyond what was required by the Armistice agreement. He knew that there were persons high in the Vichy Government who believed that an Axis triumph was inevitable and who for selfish reasons wished to be on the winning side. I was to repeat to all and sundry that an Axis victory would mean the dismemberment of the French Empire and reduce France to a vassal state. . . . I was to seek renewed pledges that under no circumstances would the [French] fleet fall into German hands.

While engaging in such tasks, U.S. diplomats in Vichy were to seek ways to draw France back into the war against Germany. Vichy at the time was home to a weird potpourri of political creeds. There was no room in its leadership and officialdom for anyone who believed in democracy or was openly anti-Nazi. But among those in official positions were some who, though admiring Hitler's domestic policies, had always hated Germans for chauvinistic reasons and now did so more than ever. There were also army officers who felt humiliated by France's military collapse and who longed to redeem their country's honor. Others were opportunists who, though they readily collaborated with the Nazis, would come to believe as the Allied position grew stronger that Germany could not possibly emerge victorious and wanted to be on the winning side.

Some, though authoritarian by political creed, were appalled by what that turned out to mean in practice—the reality of the police state Vichy became. Admiral Leahy's staff sought to cultivate such individuals. In due course, it did so with some success. Some Vichy officers and officials, notably a number attached to the Deuxième Bureau, the French Army's intelligence service, surreptitiously began feeding military and classified political information to American embassy personnel.

Pierre Laval was the senior French figure most determined to bring his country into Hitler's new European order. A wheeler-dealer, Laval was a former Socialist politician who, over the years, had shifted to the extreme right. He had served briefly as French premier and as foreign minister during the 1930s. After the government had fled from Paris as the Germans marched in, he had been a central figure in organizing the destruction of French democracy through the emasculation of the National Assembly and the establishment of the authoritarian Vichy state. When the Vichy regime was formed, Laval was appointed vice premier and deputy to Marshal Pétain. Hoping to gain favor with Hitler, Laval sought, even more assiduously than the Germans themselves, to determine in "what practical form our collaboration can serve the interests of France, Germany, and Europe."

However, his fawning and power-grasping exertions were too blatantly and crudely displayed. In December 1940, shortly before Admiral Leahy arrived in Vichy to take up his post as American ambassador, Pétain, who found Laval personally distasteful, removed him as deputy prime minister. The marshal, who in any case preferred a military man as his successor-designate, named Admiral Jean François Darlan in his place. Darlan effectively took over as day-to-day head of the Vichy government.

The admiral, sixty years old, short and swarthy, was more a politician than a sailor. A career naval officer, he was the first not born of aristocratic lineage to rise to the most senior rank in the French Navy, a position he held at the time of the German invasion of France. He was among the prominent French figures who favored an early capitulation to the Germans rather than fighting on from North Africa.

Darlan had developed a deep dislike of Britain well before the war. He considered the British raid on the French fleet at Mers el-Kébir to be proof that if Britain won the war, his country would be stripped of its navy and empire. It would, he believed, be left to exist as nothing more than a "second-class Dominion, a continental Ireland."

41

Darlan was not, however, especially pro-German. He was not prepared to be as slavishly submissive to Hitler as Laval. But like Laval, he believed Germany would win the war and that France should prepare to play a revived role in a new German-dominated European geopolitical structure. By collaborating with Hitler when pressed to do so, he believed Vichy France would be able to maintain its autonomy in the shadow of German preeminence and retain control of France's overseas territories. To that end, he granted a German request for military facilities in French West Africa and in the French protectorate of Syria.

Ambassador Leahy disliked and distrusted Darlan, considering him unscrupulous and "a complete opportunist." Nevertheless, Leahy had been sent to Vichy to establish cordial relations with its senior figures and he proceeded to do so with the admiral. "As one sailor to another," the ambassador said, "we 'talked shop' easily." Leahy tried to persuade Darlan that Germany was doomed to eventual defeat and that Vichy's collaboration with Hitler could have disastrous consequences for France. Darlan was not convinced. But he realized that the United States probably would be drawn into the war against the Axis before much longer and that its participation might ultimately be decisive. He told Leahy that when the Americans "have 3,000 tanks, 6,000 planes and 500,000 troops to bring to Marseilles, let me know. Then we shall welcome you."

While officials at the American embassy in Vichy did what they could to promote the Allied cause both before and after America's entry into the war, U.S. diplomatic personnel in North Africa were operating along different lines. In October 1940, more than a year before Pearl Harbor, Roosevelt had summoned diplomat Robert Murphy to the White House for consultations. Murphy, the affable American chargé d'affaires at Vichy, had established a friendly working rapport with prominent figures in the Vichy regime, whom he tended to view more charitably than Leahy did. Murphy believed that de Gaulle's London-based, anti-Vichy Free French movement was of minimal significance and could contribute little to the cause of the Western democracies. De Gaulle, in turn, considered Murphy "skillful and determined, long familiar with the best society and apparently inclined to believe that France consisted of the people he dined with in town."

Believing the entry of the United States into the war to be inevitable, Roosevelt wanted Murphy's expert assessment of whether Vichy's armed forces in France's colonial empire in Africa could be won over to the Allied cause and thereby kept out of German control. Perhaps a discreet approach could be made to General Maxime Weygand, who, though anti-German, had recently been appointed Vichy's senior official in France's North African territories—Algeria, Morocco, and Tunisia—with the title of delegate general. Murphy found Weygand receptive to establishing links with the Americans and negotiated a commercial agreement with him early in 1941. French funds frozen in American banks after France's capitulation to Germany would be used to buy badly needed nonstrategic American goods for the North African territories.

The agreement contained a clause permitting the United States to assign additional consular personnel to key locations there. Officially those individuals—holding the rank of vice-consul— were to supervise the implementation of the agreement. In fact, they were to establish an intelligence network—Sidney Bartlett, Franklin Canfield, Donald Coster, David King, Kenneth Pendar, and Stafford Reid in Morocco on Africa's Atlantic coast (America's prime area of interest in the region); John Boyd and John Knox in Algiers; Ridgeway Knight and Leland Rounds in Oran; John Utter and Harry Woodruff in Tunisia.

These Twelve Disciples, as they came to be known in Washington (some of whom would be replaced before the invasion), often found themselves in settings something like that portrayed in the movie *Casablanca,* dotted with casbahs, souks, gambling parlors, and outdoor cafés. The population of French North Africa was predominantly Arab and Arabized Berber but included a scattering of native Jewish communities, some of which dated back to Roman times. Most of the region's far more affluent European minority had been established there no more than two or three generations. But the Europeans now included an assortment of refugees from Nazi-occupied Europe, expanded French military and police forces, German and Italian Armistice Commission officials, and spies servicing various intelligence organizations.

The United States at the time had no experienced espionage agents. What little training the newly assigned Twelve Disciples had received hardly prepared them adequately for the clandestine operations in which they now engaged. One of them later observed, "I didn't even know how to pry open a desk drawer." German intelligence operatives on the spot were not slow in identifying these novices. After briefly observing them in action, they concluded they were nothing to worry about. One of them reported as much to Berlin.

> Since all their thoughts are centered on their social, sexual and culinary interests, petty quarrels and jealousies are daily incidents with them. Altogether they represent a perfect picture of the mixture of races and characters in that savage conglomeration called the United States of America, and anyone who observes them can well judge the state of mind and instability that must be prevalent in their country today. . . . Lack of pluck and democratic degeneracy prevails among them, resulting from their too easy life, corrupt morals, and consequent lack of energy. . . . They are totally lacking in method, organization and discipline. . . . We can only congratulate ourselves on the selection of this group of enemy agents who will give us no trouble.

So little did the German agents in North Africa think of these American spies that they informed Berlin that "the danger presented by their arrival in North Africa may be considered as nil. It would be merely a waste of paper to describe their personal idiosyncrasies and characteristics."

That may have been merely the excuse of a lazy bureaucrat with more pleasurable things to do in Algiers or Casablanca than shadow some novice adversaries. But Murphy himself wryly informed Washington, "One or two of us, with luck, might be able to distinguish a battleship from a submarine on a particularly clear day." And Pendar, a linguist who had been lifted from his job at the Harvard library to become a spy in Morocco, thought his own behavior at first, and that of his colleagues, would have been laughable in less serious circumstances.

> We control officers . . . were so anxious to be capable international sleuths that we produced many of the prize rumors in that rumor-rich land, and it was a poor week when we didn't turn in at least one report of an imminent German invasion. . . . We also turned in lists of pro-Germans and collaborators, most of whom later proved to be among our closest well-wishers and friends. Then we suffered from an absurd sense of rivalry among ourselves, like cub reporters on their first beats.

We jealously watched each other's pipelines among the French and natives. . . .

One of these neophyte agents almost immediately fell in love with and proposed to marry a Frenchwoman who turned out to have connections with members of the German-Italian Armistice Commission. Another was reported to be more inclined to accept the statements of the friends he made in "high society" as genuine and deny other sources. Others engaged in senseless squabbles with the professional U.S. diplomats, who resented their nondiplomatic activities, whose premises they shared, and whose intrigues in Morocco got Pendar shifted to Algiers. But despite their early fumblings, Murphy's Disciples settled down and got on with their assigned missions.

> We soon began to collect the best French military maps. Some of them came from our friends in the French Army, who would bring them secretly to our homes. Others we bought at a Casablanca bookstore where the proprietor, a handsome, dark-eyed Frenchwoman, would hide them for us in the cellar. . . . We also gradually accumulated . . . a mass of information of all kinds: the depth of ports, the best beaches for landings, the position of coastal defenses, the tides, the treacherous Moroccan currents, the strength and disposition of French warships, the position and sizes of Army regiments, the condition and direction of roads, [and] the location of bridges, tunnels and railways.

As historian Ray Cline has written, "For the first time . . . Americans listed as diplomatic officials found themselves competing for scraps of information in the cafés and casinos with foreign diplomats and assorted spies of all countries." By the time a North Africa operation by the Western Allies came under consideration at the Arcadia Conference in Washington, the United States had established a network of undercover agents to feed back a wide range of valuable military information about the region.

☆ **4** ☆

ALLIES AT ODDS

Allies are the most aggravating of people. They are so difficult to understand, so unreasonable; they approach quite straightforward problems from such extraordinary angles. Even when one agrees with them on common objectives their methods towards obtaining them are so queer, so very queer. They even introduce consideration of their own national politics and hangovers from their past history, none of which have the faintest bearing on the matter of immediate issue. Their most annoying characteristic, however, is that among all the arguing and haggling is the astonishing way they seem quite incapable of recognizing how sound, how wise, how experienced are our views; how fair, indeed how generous, how big-hearted we are. They even at times credit us with the same petty jealousies, narrow nationalistic outlook, selfish maneuverings, that sway them.

—FIELD MARSHAL WILLIAM SLIM

While in Washington, Churchill found his White House bedroom overheated and stuffy. Trying with some effort to open a stuck window late one night, he was stricken with chest pains and shortness of breath. His doctor diagnosed angina pectoris but realized the prime minister would never consent to the six-week rest period he would have liked to prescribe.

The attack was hushed up and remained a secret known to few until Churchill died twenty-four years later. He continued participating in the Arcadia Conference as if nothing had happened. When he left the United States for home on January 14, 1942, he was pleased with what he had achieved there. Not only were the Americans remaining true to the Germany First policy; they appeared to have accepted his strategy of closing and tightening the ring around German-occupied Europe. Despite the antipathy of the American military, Roosevelt had agreed with him in principle that the operation against French North Africa, code-named Super-Gymnast, should take place later that year. The Americans, the prime minister told his War Cabinet upon his return to London, were "not above learning from us, provided that we did not set out to teach them."

General Stillwell had earlier been assigned to examine the advisability of U.S. action against Dakar in French West Africa to keep it out of German hands. He was now reassigned to study the possibilities for Super-Gymnast instead. A close look failed to reverse Stillwell's initial objections to the operation. He did not need General McNair's urgings that he compile a list of "65 reasons why we should not do Gymnast." Nor did other senior American officers with whom he discussed it change their minds about its chances: "All agree that the means are meager, the transport uncertain, the complications numerous, the main facts unknown, the consequences serious. A few lucky hits [against troop transports] will jeopardize the whole affair."

American doubts about the scheme were heightened by what was happening in the Libyan desert. The day before Churchill and his entourage left Washington, Rommel had halted his retreat there. A week later, he went over to the offensive and was once again driving the British Eighth Army back toward Egypt. Churchill's suggestion during the Arcadia talks that Rommel's retreating forces would be trapped by the proposed Allied landings in French North Africa now seemed a pipe dream. It made the Americans even more skeptical about what the British might propose and what they could deliver.

In any case, relentless Japanese advances in the Pacific and on the Asian mainland appeared to make Super-Gymnast a nonstarter. The United States, upon whose participation it would depend, was very much preoccupied with difficulties in the East, as were the British, who also had Egypt—effectively a British protectorate—to worry about. Instructed nevertheless to keep the North Africa operation under review, British and American planners concluded that for the moment at least it would be no more than "an academic study and should be treated as such."

Meanwhile, Japan's continuing successes aroused much alarm.

47

As Churchill was winding up his visit to the United States, Japanese troops pressed ahead with their occupation of Burma, Malaya, and the Dutch East Indies. On January 22, they broke through an American-Filipino defensive line on Bataan Peninsula in the Philippines. On February 3, they bombed Port Moresby in New Guinea. On February 8, they established a bridgehead on Singapore. A week later, Singapore and its garrison of 85,000 men fell to them—"The greatest disaster to British arms which our history affords," Churchill called it.

In Washington, the War Plans Division drew a line on the map of the Pacific—Alaska-Hawaii-Samoa-Australia—beyond which the Japanese would not be permitted to advance. But there was no certainty that the line could be held. Warnings issued by some in the American military hierarchy that the Germany First strategy was insane were proving increasingly persuasive. The press expressed doubts as well. *Time* magazine wanted to know, "Was this some kind of private war, Winston Churchill and Franklin Roosevelt against Adolf Hitler?" Many Americans were coming to believe that unless the United States left it to Britain to hold the line in the European Theater and concentrated first on the Japanese peril, the war in the Pacific might lurch out of control. Indeed, four divisions of U.S. troops that had been earmarked for dispatch to Britain were instead rushed off to strengthen Pacific outposts.

General MacArthur, commander of American forces in the southwest Pacific, wanted much more than that. MacArthur had no doubt that the Germany First strategy was a catastrophic mistake. He vigorously pressed the War Department to shift its priorities and concentrate on the defeat of Japan. Vain and arrogant, MacArthur—who had access to prewar U.S. basic contingency war plans and should have known better—believed that the decision not to do so was part of a plot by his enemies in Washington to undermine his career.

Admiral Ernest J. King, who was about to succeed Admiral Harold Stark as Chief of U.S. Naval Operations, also favored switching to a Japan First strategy. The navy had so far taken the worst of the beating the United States was suffering at the hands of the Japanese and it wanted its revenge. Besides, the navy was likely to have a far greater war-winning role to play in the Pacific than in the European Theater.

However, Roosevelt, Secretary of War Stimson, and General Marshall refused to be shifted from their conviction that Germany was potentially the more dangerous foe and had to be vanquished first. That was also the view of Brigadier General Dwight David Eisenhower, who had arrived in Washington five days after Pearl Harbor to join the War Plans Division as deputy to the division's chief, Brigadier General Leonard Gerow. Within a few weeks, Gerow was shifted to a field command and Eisenhower was named to succeed him as head of the planning division.

Throughout his long army career, as he climbed through the ranks, Eisenhower had been highly regarded by the officers under whom he had served. He had established a reputation for decisiveness, competence, and finely developed organizational skills. What was more, his composure under pressure, affability, and apparent lack of unseemly vanity made him well liked as well as respected.

Eisenhower had never had a battlefield command. He had graduated from West Point in 1915, and when the United States entered World War I two years later, he was assigned to a base in Pennsylvania where troops were trained for the fledgling U.S. Army Tank Corps. He had just received orders to go overseas when the war ended. Between the two world wars, Eisenhower held a series of largely administrative positions in the army. From 1935 to 1940, he was chief of staff to General MacArthur in the Philippines, helping prepare the Filipino armed forces for the independence of their country. Shortly before Pearl Harbor was bombed, he had made a strong impression as chief of staff of the Third Army based in the American Southwest.

His assignment when he arrived at the War Plans Division— soon to be renamed the Operations Division—was to deal with the grim developments in the Pacific in general and the Philippines in particular. He quickly realized that the situation in that part of the world was beyond immediate repair. Like most senior officers at the War Department, he concluded that the Germany First strategy that Marshall was stubbornly defending was correct.

But the Pacific and continuing Allied reverses there could hardly be neglected. Eisenhower's days at the Operations Division were long and filled with a succession of emergency meetings during which quick and sometimes far-reaching decisions on the deployment of forces, shipping, and supplies had to be made to cope with critical developments. He was endlessly presented with pressing demands for men and material and was anguished by how they obstructed the formulation of a comprehensive, calculated approach to winning the war.

> The struggle to secure the adoption by all concerned of a common concept of strategical objectives is wearing me down. Everybody is too much engaged with small things of his own. We've got to go to Europe and fight—and we've got to quit wasting resources all over the world—and still worse—wasting time. If we're to keep Russia in, save the Middle East, India and Burma, we've got to begin slugging with air at West Europe; to be followed by a land attack as soon as possible.

Eisenhower's impatience was a reflection of general frustration at the Operations Division over resources being gobbled up by requirements in the Pacific Theater and Asia with nothing to show for it but further setbacks. Eisenhower said, "We can't win by sitting on our fannies giving our stuff out in driblets all over the world." The way the situation was developing, it would be a painfully long time before the Allies would be able to seize the initiative in the war. That could not be tolerated. The Allies had to go over to the offensive, and soon. Having agonized over the desperate shortage of ships to supply vulnerable defensive positions in the Pacific, Eisenhower concluded that the most prudent attack on the enemy in the European Theater would be the one that would place the minimum strain upon shipping while offering "the shortest route to the heart of Germany." That ruled out French North Africa. He advocated a different approach:

> We should at once develop, in conjunction with the British, a definite plan for operations against Northwest Europe. It should be drawn up at once, in detail, and it should be sufficiently extensive in scale as to engage, from the middle of May [1942] onwards, an increasing portion of the German Air Force, and by late summer an increasing amount of his ground forces.

Despite the pressures to the contrary, the Joint Chiefs of Staff agreed and formally ordered that U.S. forces in the Pacific should be restricted to "current commitments." It would mean that many exposed positions defended by American troops or their Allies were likely still to be lost to the Japanese and that the United

States's posture in the war against Japan would be strictly defensive for the foreseeable future. In Europe, however, the initiative was to be seized. The Joint Chiefs expressed their support for an early invasion of the European continent by American and British forces—a frontal assault—possibly to take place before the year was out.

The British believed that was a wildly optimistic assessment of the possibilities. To Churchill and the War Office in London, it appeared to confirm the view that Britain's allies did not fully understand the situation. A senior British liaison officer in Washington concluded, "The American is a wonderfully naïve person. He reminds me of the small boy who says he has killed hundreds of Red Indians in the shrubbery!"

Churchill wanted to know whatever had happened to "closing and tightening the ring" around Hitler to which the Americans appeared to have agreed at the Arcadia conclave. To the British, prospects for an early Allied campaign in Europe were distinctly gloomy. Allied forces that would be available for such an operation would be very limited and the enemy resistance they could expect to meet would be formidable. The British Chiefs of Staff were convinced the Americans simply did not appreciate the dimensions of the operation they were proposing, nor the consequences of likely failure if it was undertaken prematurely. They agreed that consideration might be given to an Allied landing in France the following year rather than in 1942, but *only* if the enemy had by then been "weakened in strength and morale."

Planners were set to work trying to reconcile the differences between the Allies. But the War Department in Washington was baffled by the British reaction and more than a little annoyed. The Americans were anxious for vigorous, appropriate action to be taken to keep the Soviet Union, whose forces were being severely mauled by Hitler's armies, from being knocked out of the war. In addition, they understood that the Germany First policy to which they adhered despite their difficulties in the Pacific meant that Allied forces were to go on the attack against the enemy in Europe as soon as possible. That was the way to begin the process of demolishing Hitler's armies and bringing the war to an end without delay. Now it seemed the British were suggesting that the

Western Allies wait until the Germans were already practically beaten before launching a major offensive against them. There was no predicting when that would be.

Barely had the view of the British been digested in Washington than a proposal was made there to nudge them into line. On March 25, Eisenhower issued a memorandum urging that unless a definite American-British plan was adopted for an attack soon on Germany through Western Europe, "we must turn our backs upon the Eastern Atlantic and go, full out, as quickly as possible, against Japan!" Coming from the chief of operations at the War Department, the proposal for such an ultimatum demonstrated the level of exasperation in Washington. It was a refrain that would be sounded repeatedly during the following months. Neither the Joint Chiefs nor the Operations Division intended to permit American resources to be frittered away while waiting for the enemy to offer the Allies victory on a plate.

Neither did Roosevelt, as he made clear to Secretary Stimson and General Marshall when they lunched with him at the White House on the day Eisenhower's memorandum was received. Proposals for an invasion of the European continent to begin the march toward victory intrigued the president. But he also continued to contemplate an operation in North Africa instead, or possibly the Middle East. He was exploring the options. To Stimson's consternation, he seemed to be "going off on the wildest kind of dispersion debauch."

Anxious to prevent that from happening, Stimson and Marshall pressed their argument that only an early invasion of occupied Europe would be consistent with the priority objective of defeating Germany as quickly as possible. Roosevelt was impressed by their forceful presentation and called for an outline of a plan along the lines they suggested. Champing at the bit, Eisenhower's Operations Division quickly produced one which, with minor modifications, Stimson and Marshall presented to the president.

In addition to stressing the need for urgent action, the Marshall Memorandum, as it was called, stressed the reasons for targeting Western Europe as the scene of the first major Allied offensive.

> It is the only place in which a powerful offensive can be prepared and executed by the United Powers in the near future. . . . It is the only place

52

where the vital air superiority over the hostile land areas preliminary to a major attack can be staged by the United Powers. . . . It is the only place in which the bulk of the British ground forces can be committed to a general offensive in cooperation with United States forces. . . . Successful attack in this area will afford the maximum of support to the Russian front. . . . The element of time is of the greatest importance. We must begin an offensive on a major scale before Russia, now practically alone, can be defeated and before Vichy France, Spain, Portugal and Turkey are drawn into the ranks of our enemies.

The American plan involved three operations, code-named Bolero, Round-Up, and Sledgehammer. Operation Bolero was to be a massive American military buildup in Britain to include one million troops, 3,250 combat aircraft, and the appropriate equipment for a major British-American invasion of France for which the British would be expected to supply eighteen divisions of troops (about a quarter of a million men) and 2,550 combat aircraft.

Operation Round-Up was the code name given to that projected invasion of France. It was to occur between Le Havre and Boulogne and was tentatively scheduled to take place twelve months later, in April 1943.

Operation Sledgehammer—a lesser landing on the northwestern coast of France—would be launched in the autumn of 1942, just six months away, but only under extreme circumstances. It would be undertaken only if German control over Western Europe appeared to have been so critically weakened that a Soviet advance into the heart of Europe became a real possibility, or "as a sacrifice" act, to draw German forces from the Eastern Front if the Soviet Union appeared to be on the verge of being forced out of the war. If implemented, Sledgehammer would, of course, satisfy Roosevelt's insistence that U.S. troops be in action in the European Theater before the year was out. But a decision on all three proposed operations had to be made without delay in view of the extensive preparations that would be required.

Roosevelt was impressed. Finally things could begin to move on the far side of the Atlantic. The British had to be consulted immediately. At Hopkins's suggestion, the president instructed Marshall *not* to submit the plan to Washington-based British personnel on the Combined Chiefs of Staff Committee though the committee had been established at the Arcadia talks specifically to examine such grand-strategy schemes. It would only be bogged down in protracted debate and "be pulled to pieces and emasculated." Instead, Marshall and Hopkins were to hand-carry it immediately to London, where they were to seek top-level British agreement for an early assault on Hitler's European fortress.

☆ 5 ☆

COUP IN THE MAKING

If you learn anything in Africa of special interest, send it to me.

—FRANKLIN DELANO ROOSEVELT

The American decision to press the British to agree to an early cross-Channel invasion pushed the plan for an operation against French North Africa deeper into limbo. Preoccupied with developments in the Pacific, Asia, the Middle East, and now a possible invasion of France, Washington and London devoted little attention to North African possibilities in the months following the Arcadia Conference. However, having long before been activated, espionage activities in the French North African territories related to a projected Allied military campaign there remained operational and continued to develop.

As in mainland France, some officers, officials, and other prominent figures in Algeria, Morocco, and Tunisia had not been reconciled to the defeat and humiliation of their homeland by the Germans. They longed for the day when France would be free and united again. It was taboo for them to appear to cooperate with the British, their former allies but now the object of their resentment and bitterness. But the United States was generally admired by the French. French-American friendship dated back to the American Revolution when the French had helped the Americans gain their independence from Great Britain and had been much strengthened twenty-five years earlier by the arrival of U.S. troops in France at a crucial moment during World War I. Anti-Americanism, which flourished in some French circles after the United States emerged as a postwar superpower, had not yet surfaced.

Operating under diplomatic cover, newly arrived American agents had been able to establish links with the clandestine insurgent movement that had sprung up in North Africa with the aim of ultimately participating in the liberation of occupied France. The movement drew support from most strata of European life in the French North African territories—businessmen, professional people, civil servants, workers, intellectuals, junior army officers, and a few of higher army rank. There were conservatives, socialists, Gaullists, and royalists among the conspirators and even some who had been associated with prewar French fascist movements. They also included leaders and members of the Chantiers de la Jeunesse, the state-sponsored semi-military youth work group. The largest single group among the conspirators in Algiers—the main city in French North Africa—consisted of young men from the local Jewish community whose members had seen their French citizenship rights revoked by the anti-Semitic Vichy regime. Drawn together in physical-fitness clubs, they formed themselves into cells of a few members each to prepare to contribute to the Allied cause.

The conspirators were in continual danger. Through informers and German intelligence operatives, the authorities and pro-Nazi French associations were made aware of some of their activities. A number of activists were murdered. Others were imprisoned.

Despite agreement on basic objectives, this diverse, incipient resistance movement lacked a sense of cohesion. Missing was a distinguished figure to lead it and knit it together. Allied hopes that General Weygand, with whom Robert Murphy had negotiated the commercial deal for North Africa, would assume that role were dashed when Pétain was compelled by German pressure to remove Weygand from his post as Vichy's delegate general in the region. The Germans had intercepted American messages implicating the general in activities of which Berlin disapproved. Weygand subsequently decided to retire from public life and a search had to be launched for another possible pro-Allied insurgency leader for North Africa.

Five individuals were particularly active in attempting to organize the insurgency. Jacques Lemaigre Dubreuil was a wealthy businessman whose background and political connections led many to believe he was actually a fascist sympathizer turned opportunist. Jean Rigault was a conservative former newspaper editor. Colonel A. S. Van Hecke was regional director of the Chantiers de la Jeunesse. Jacques Tarbe de Sainte-Hardouin was a diplomat, and Lieutenant Henri d'Astier de La Vigerie, serving in the French army intelligence service, was a royalist officer from a distinguished family.

The Five, as these men came to be known, sought to lay the groundwork for a pro-Allied coup in North Africa as a first step toward the liberation of France. They hoped to receive from the United States the financial support and arms that would be needed for the coup when the proper moment arrived. Robert Murphy, who shared their conservative political leanings, considered them an ideal instrument for implementing Allied policy. Their activities brought them in touch not only with him and his corps of diplomat-spies, but also with the secret operatives of a newly established U.S. agency, the Office of Strategic Services.

Unlike Britain and Germany, the United States government previously had boasted no seasoned intelligence-gathering service. The American attitude toward espionage had been strongly influenced by the views of men like Henry Stimson, who, as secretary of state in 1929, undermined the existence of his department's code-deciphering bureau with the observation that gentlemen do not open each other's mail. As war neared, the Americans had to make do with the limited, unsophisticated efforts of the intelligence branches of the army and navy and with the burgeoning, brash investigative empire of FBI director J. Edgar Hoover. But it was apparent well before Pearl Harbor that such a jumble did not suffice.

In June 1941, Roosevelt appointed Colonel William Donovan to head the Office of Coordinator of Information (COI). "Wild Bill" Donovan was a much-decorated World War I veteran, a high-powered Wall Street lawyer, and a prominent Republican, whose strength of character and proposals for daring espionage schemes impressed the president. Roosevelt was also pleased with the way, after a visit to England during the Battle of Britain, Donovan had vigorously challenged the forecast of Joseph Kennedy, the American ambassador, that Britain's morale and defenses would crumble under German hammering.

On another pre–Pearl Harbor visit to England, Donovan, known in London to be both a supporter of Britain and influential in Washington, was introduced to the intricacies and procedures of coordinated wartime espionage and secret war operations. This was done through the intercession of people in high places and the courtesy of the British Secret Intelligence Service (SIS), which appreciated the contribution American resources might make when the United States was drawn into the war. Sir William Stephenson, coordinator of British intelligence services in the United States, cabled London, " . . . we can achieve infinitely more through Donovan than through any other [American] individual." Donovan was accordingly briefed on training methods, secret communications methods, operational techniques, and administrative control of operations.

When he reported to Roosevelt, his dynamic approach and grasp of what might be done convinced the president that he was the man to galvanize America's intelligence operations. The established American intelligence bureaus fumed at the emergence of this intruder as he set about organizing a staff and establishing operating procedures.

Though officially only coordinator of information, Donovan had no intention of confining himself to gathering and coordinating data.* He was a firm believer in vigorous secret war exploits, including activities behind enemy lines and in other places where the enemy could be undermined. So was Roosevelt, and six months after the United States entered the war, the Office of Coordinator of Information was transformed into the Office of Strategic Services, the OSS, from which the CIA would later evolve.

Donovan's inspiration was Sir Stewart Menzies, code-named "C," director of the SIS and the man upon whom author Ian Fleming would later base spy chief "M" in his James Bond fantasies. Aware of the contrast between his inexperienced recruits and the seasoned espionage operatives of European intelligence

---

*Donovan's mistaken belief that the Germans were planning to invade French North Africa had stoked Roosevelt's interest in Churchill's proposal for a North Africa operation at the Arcadia Conference.

organizations, Donovan accepted an invitation from Britain to send a group of his agents to England to observe operations there and further their understanding of their new craft. Writer Malcolm Muggeridge, then a British agent, recalled Donovan's men "arriving like jeunes filles en fleur straight from finishing school, all fresh and innocent, to start work in our frowsty old intelligence brothel. All too soon they were ravished and corrupted, becoming indistinguishable from seasoned pros who had been in the game for a quarter century or more."

In North Africa, the job of Donovan's men was to soften up the region for possible military action. They were to build networks of local activists and informants, establish clandestine communications links for espionage purposes, arrange to neutralize enemy communications at the appropriate time, and store arms that might be used by friendly insurgents. North Africa was to be the first testing ground for the OSS.

British intelligence was reluctant to hand this strategic region completely over to these American novices. Agents of Britain's Special Operations Executive (SOE) liaised closely with OSS counterparts in Gibraltar and Tangier. And the British received a steady flow of data from an independently established secret Polish espionage network in North Africa that was reporting to London.* But British intelligence felt it necessary to agree that to avoid operational overlap, the Americans would be responsible for Allied espionage activities in Vichy France and French North Africa. The diplomatic links and cordial relations that the United States, unlike the British, maintained with Vichy provided them with useful diplomatic cover and resources, though some officious U.S. career diplomats sternly objected to such misuse of diplomatic privilege on their patches. At least one OSS agent, masquerading

---

*"Agency Africa" was organized and headed by Rygor Slowikowski, a Polish army intelligence officer who fled to France after the invasion of Poland and then went on to North Africa, where, acting on instructions from officials of the Polish government in exile in London, he recruited and ran an extensive espionage network. Though little has been publicized about his contribution to the Allied war effort, it was considered significant enough to earn him an Order of the British Empire and for him to be made a member of the Legion of Merit by the United States. Much of the information he and his agents acquired was channeled to London through the American consulate in Algiers. That led to subsequent claims that some of the great amount of intelligence data U.S. agents were credited with acquiring was actually gathered by Slowikowski's network.

as a diplomat, was forbidden by the consulate from which he operated to place CD identification plates on his car.

Neither Murphy's nor Donovan's agents had a firm idea of exactly how much weight they carried or how far they could go in their dealings with local people. Murphy was a State Department man but Roosevelt, in a rush of enthusiasm over North African possibilities, had offered him direct access to the White House. "If you learn anything in Africa of special interest, send it to me," he had told him. "Don't bother going through State Department channels." That gave Murphy exalted status—which, however, proved to be less than that when he started stressing the urgency of the North Africa situation when the president was preoccupied with other matters, which was most of the time.

As for the OSS, which was supposed to be accountable to the Joint Chiefs of Staff, Donovan had his own thoughts about how the agency should be run. The Joint Chiefs soon discovered that he paid little attention to the established chain of command. They complained so vigorously to the president about his cavalier unaccountability that Roosevelt was said to be looking for a way of putting Donovan "on some nice, quiet, isolated island where he could have a scrap with some Japs every morning before breakfast" and thus be kept "out of trouble. . . ."

That didn't happen. Roosevelt thought too much of Donovan's imaginative drive and of the contribution the OSS might make toward victory to want to hobble him with bureaucratic constraints. Such restrictions would hardly have suited Donovan's two key agents dealing with the North Africa situation—U.S. Marine Colonel William Eddy and U.S. Army Lieutenant Colonel Robert Solberg.

Eddy, the son of missionaries, was an Arab-speaking intellectual and man of action. He had been born in Syria and had been a military intelligence officer in World War I. He had subsequently headed the English Department at the American University in Cairo and still later had become president of Hobart College in New York State. Shortly before Pearl Harbor, while serving as U.S. naval attaché in Cairo, he had been recruited into the OSS by Donovan and, posing as U.S. naval attaché at the International Zone of Tangier, became the OSS station chief covering all of northwest Africa. His assignment was to stimulate and coordinate the activities of Murphy's diplomat-spies and establish a network of his own, and he did so zealously.

There was, however, a danger he and his operatives might be overzealous in their schemes and plots. From the American consulate in Tunis came a plan to enlist the support of the family of the Bey of Tunis, the Arab leader of the country, to have the pro-Vichy French resident-general replaced with a pro-Allied figure. Donovan liked the idea and made $50,000 available for the necessary bribe. But Murphy reacted in horror because meddling with the "native population" and possibly stirring up the Arabs was certain to alienate his French contacts. "Nothing," he believed, "would have enraged our French colleagues more than this kind of monkey business, or been more ruinous of our chances of obtaining the support of French military forces." And the War Department feared that stirring up the Arabs might lead to a Christian-Muslim conflict.

Nevertheless, Eddy did not refrain from employing Arab and Berber contacts. In particular, OSS agents Carleton Coon, who would later gain international renown as an anthropologist, and Gordon Browne, a businessman with extensive experience in Morocco, established a working relationship with leaders of the restive tribesmen in Morocco. They generally avoided Arab nationalist intellectuals, who, Coon later wrote, "however honorable they might be and however worthy their ambitions and ideals, were not men of action. They were great talkers and mystics. . . . We would do much better to confine our attention to the men from the hills, the men who knew how to handle not the inkpot but the rifle. . . . We . . . left the dreamers alone."

Washington was told that the OSS could bring ten thousand armed Arabs to the Allied side at the appropriate time. Whether it actually could was in doubt. Even the men of action among the tribal leaders were interested primarily in independence from France. They did not intend to commit themselves until they could see which side was likely to win the war.

Though inexperienced, OSS agents in North Africa displayed much imagination and ingenuity. On a scouting expedition through Morocco, one of them looked for stones on the roads to ship back to London so that British intelligence could manufacture similarly innocent-looking booby traps for enemy vehicles. He came across very few stones but "mule turds were to be found in great abundance." Some were packed and sent to England with a warning that "the full, rich horse dung of the British countryside would not do in Morocco; it was the more watery, smaller-bunned mule type that passes there without suspicion. Also, it was important to have it a deep sepia color, sometimes with greenish shades, the product of straw and grass, not of oats and hay."

While his operatives engaged in their secret war exploits, Colonel Eddy established close contact in Algiers with Lemaigre Dubreuil and other members of The Five. They were increasingly anxious to proceed with preparations for the coup that would produce a pro-Allied regime in North Africa and thus start the process of bringing France back into the war against Germany. Eddy was informed by them that the French colonial army was ripe for such a move but they would need American guns and equipment, including planes and tanks, with which to arm the rebels.

Lemaigre Dubreuil provided considerable detail on how a coup would be organized and executed. He convinced Eddy this was an opportunity the Allies would be insane to pass up. Eddy informed Donovan, "We will not find such leaders elsewhere and we dare not lose them now." But despite pleas from Murphy, as well as from OSS officers in Washington, the idea was turned down there by the War Department. Not only had attention shifted from North Africa to plans for a cross-Channel invasion, but the requested equipment was in short supply. There was also no guarantee that it would not end up in German hands. Reports that a German invasion of French North Africa might be imminent, and that the would-be insurgents had to be armed without delay, did not change any minds in Washington. The War Department was not about to be panicked into backing a coup that looked like being no more than the fantasy of one of "Wild Bill" Donovan's unaccountable hotshots.

Donovan's other key agent in the region, Lieutenant Colonel Robert Solberg, was an exotic personality with an exotic background. Born in Poland, the son of a Polish general in the army of Czar Nicholas of Russia, he had himself been wounded while serving as an officer in the czar's cavalry during World War I. After recovering, he had been sent to New York to serve with the Russian World War I military purchasing mission. When the Communist revolution occurred, he stayed on in the United States, applied for and received American citizenship, and joined the U.S. Army. He subsequently left it to join an American steel company as an executive and then as managing director of the company's operations in France and Britain. While in that job, Solberg established contact with British intelligence, filtering to it information he gathered on his European business travels.

A year before Pearl Harbor, while retaining his business cover, Solberg enrolled in U.S. Army intelligence and began spending much time in French North Africa. He was subsequently recruited by Donovan to be chief of OSS special operations. He was sent to Portugal, ostensibly as assistant American military attaché, to establish and run what would become an OSS bureau in Lisbon, one of the busiest espionage crossroads in Europe. He was instructed to work in conjunction with British intelligence in developing and promoting contacts in the resistance underground in North Africa.

Solberg was, however, forbidden to travel to North Africa. It was believed that the Germans had identified him as an American agent and that potentially useful links forged with French military officers and the resistance movement would be compromised. But Solberg had no intention of bowing to what he considered this example of bureaucratic myopia. Anxious "to prepare the ground for an invitation to be issued to us by the French when the time comes for military intervention," he ignored the order that he stay out of North Africa.

He went in June 1942 first to Tangier and then to Casablanca, where a message from Donovan caught up with him, telling him to leave at once for London to report on what he was up to. Solberg replied that he could not do so because of the importance of the mission that had taken him to North Africa. Donovan nevertheless instructed him to return to Lisbon. Believing his mission too important to be dropped, Solberg proceeded to Algiers anyway. There he met with Lemaigre Debreuil, who informed him of a crucial development. The long-sought leader for a French revival had been found. That man was the highly respected General Henri Giraud, who was living in apparent retirement in Vichy France but who was anxious to rejoin the struggle against the Axis.

Instead of being delighted as Solberg thought he would be, Donovan was furious, as was British intelligence. Delicate relations were being established in North Africa with disgruntled

French officers and others. The presence of a roving American operative, well known to German intelligence, could have awkward consequences. Donovan was professionally embarrassed as well as angry. It made him vulnerable to persisting demands from the Joint Chiefs of Staff that the apparently happy-go-lucky OSS be taken over by an existing military intelligence agency over which they could maintain unquestioned control. When Solberg returned to Washington to report in person on what he considered his great success in identifying the French leader the Allies needed, he was reprimanded for the damage he might have done and unceremoniously dismissed from the OSS. But though Solberg was out of the picture, Giraud definitely was not.

During the spring of 1942, an important change had taken place in the political situation in Vichy. In April, as Marshall and Hopkins prepared to set off from Washington to seek British agreement for an early cross-Channel invasion of France, German pressure had compelled Marshal Pétain to restore Pierre Laval, their compliant underling, to the second most senior position in the Vichy government. He was to replace Admiral Darlan, who was, however, to stay on as Commander in Chief of Vichy's armed forces.

With the United States now in the war, Darlan, bitter about this demotion, wavered in his belief that the Germans were bound to win the war. He began to ponder the course of action he should follow in the changing situation. Washington had recalled Ambassador Leahy from Vichy in protest at Laval's return to power, but through intermediaries in Algiers, including his naval officer son, Alain, Darlan discreetly indicated to Murphy that under the proper circumstances, he might be prepared to collaborate with the Americans.

The prospect of Darlan's switching from collaboration with Hitler to collaboration with the Allies was not easy to digest in Washington or London. The war in Europe was an anti-Nazi and anti-German crusade. What the Allies needed on their side was an untainted senior French figure around whom the people of France could be persuaded to rally and who could lead them as they rejoined the war against the Axis foe. Darlan was not at all suited for that role. He may not have been as servile to the Germans as Laval, who would be executed for treason after France was liberated, but he was nevertheless besmirched by his own dealings with the Nazis.

A man who carried no such stigma and who was already striving to lead the cause of French redemption was the towering, proud, immensely dignified Charles de Gaulle. But there was little fondness for the Free French leader among French officers in North Africa from whom some eventual support for the Allies was hoped and expected. A comparatively junior officer, de Gaulle was widely considered by them to be an insubordinate, self-serving upstart. He had been promoted from his permanent rank of colonel only shortly before he had established the Free French movement in London. He had subsequently been demoted back to colonel by the French Army command and placed on the retired list for presuming to claim to speak for France. Most senior French officers considered de Gaulle a traitor because of a botched, British-backed Free French attempt in 1940 to seize Dakar from Vichy control and for backing a successful British operation against Vichy-ruled Syria in 1941. Besides, the French in North Africa considered his Free French movement to be a creation of the British—which, to a great extent, it was.

Churchill would have preferred to throw British backing behind a more senior French figure to rally anti-Nazi French resistance. Few people had heard of de Gaulle before the war, even in France. But he was a dynamic, charismatic figure and no more prominent French personality had come forward to promote the Allied cause with the same degree of vigor and determination. Churchill decided to make do with what he had and helped de Gaulle establish the Free French movement, providing him with public recognition, accommodations, start-up funds, authorization to recruit into a fighting force other Frenchmen who had fled to Britain, and BBC broadcast time to bring to France his message: "Whatever happens, the flame of French resistance must not and shall not die."

Given wide press coverage, the defiant de Gaulle quickly became a popular figure in Britain during the days when it stood alone against Hitler. He was a symbol of a France that would rise again to help defeat the Nazi ogre and preserve Britain's independent survival. People sent money and jewels to his Carlton Gardens London headquarters to help finance his movement. He was eulogized in the press. King George offered his personal acclaim.

But by the time Allied plans for an invasion of North Africa were being made, almost two years had passed since the establishment of the Free French movement and doubts were being raised about it. The War Office questioned how substantial a military contribution it could make to the Allied cause. The movement had been convulsed by internal intrigue, much of it resulting from the impression that de Gaulle treated it as his personal fiefdom. He maintained that he represented the soul and spirit of France and began referring to himself as "we," which made some who had to deal with him suspect that he was more determined to further his own interests than contribute to the Allied war effort.

Nevertheless, he remained enormously popular in England, retained many admirers in the British establishment, and was determinedly committed to the defeat of Nazi Germany. Whatever his faults, Churchill would have been pleased to see him lead a North Africa insurgency, but he realized there was no chance of that. Not only was there insufficient backing for de Gaulle in the French African territories but the Americans wanted nothing to do with him. His efforts to cultivate relations with Washington had been snubbed. Roosevelt considered him an eccentric and pompous adventurer. The president was told that de Gaulle believed he heard "voices" like Joan of Arc—the general believed no such thing—and that he hoped to make himself ruler of France after the liberation. Roosevelt was resolved not to "help anyone impose a Government on the French people." Secretary of State Cordell Hull dismissively called the Gaullist movement the "so-called Free French."

"So-called" or not, as far as the United States was concerned, there was no question of de Gaulle's emerging as the man to take the lead in reviving France's honor and fighting spirit. However, General Giraud, nominated by insurgency organizers in Algiers, seemed ideally suited for that role.

Henri Honoré Giraud, sixty-three years old, tall, slender, and dignified, was a man of action and looked it. He was a full general of long standing, far superior in rank to de Gaulle, and therefore could be expected to command considerable influence in Vichy's armed forces. What was more, he was also "clean." Although Giraud had not shone in the defense of France when it was overrun by the Wehrmacht—few French generals had—unlike several of his fellow senior officers, he had not been disgraced then either. He had been captured by the Germans soon after they had overrun northern France and imprisoned by them in a fortress at König-stein in Saxony which had been turned into a detention center for French generals.

He escaped in April 1942 by lowering himself down the wall of the fortress on a rope smuggled to him in prisoner-of-war pack-ages. He made his way to Switzerland despite an intensive effort to recapture him. The Swiss, who took him into custody, were pressed by the Germans to surrender this fugitive to them. But they ruled that because Giraud officially was a retired officer, no pris-oner-of-war claim could be made against him. He was released and found his way to Lyons in Vichy France, where he took up his life as a free man though he was kept under surveillance by both the Vichy police and the Gestapo.

Giraud's daring escape from the Königstein fortress—he had been captured by and escaped from the Germans in World War I as well—was seized upon by many French people as a badly needed injection of national pride. Once Pétain had received from him an assurance that he would refrain from political activity, the marshal felt able to resist demands from Berlin for his return to German custody.

Giraud did not have to be recruited to the Allied cause. Soon after he had settled in Lyons, he had visited other senior generals in southern France to enlist their support for an effort to free France from German occupation. He was unable to convince them of its chances of success. But contact was established between him and American "consular" personnel in Vichy and with the Algiers conspirators, including Lemaigre Debreuil and Brigadier General Charles Mast who had been a fellow prisoner of Giraud's at König-stein and who was now chief of staff of a French army corps in Algeria.

Ironically, though prepared to lead France's return to Allied ranks, Giraud was not overly interested in an Allied campaign in French North Africa. While incarcerated by the Germans, he had drawn up a crusade scheme of his own. It involved the emergence of resistance movements throughout German-occupied Europe, their guerrilla operations synchronized with an uprising by what remained of the French army in Vichy France—the so-called Armistice Army. All of that was to be coordinated with an invasion of mainland France by American and British forces. To the extent that it contemplated immediately challenging the forces of Nazi

Germany in Europe itself, the idea was not totally remote from the plan being concurrently proposed by the U.S. War Department.

But Giraud made certain stipulations to which, he maintained, the Western Allies would have to agree. French prewar continental and colonial borders would have to be guaranteed, and he himself, he insisted, would have to be supreme commander of any Allied operation in which French forces participated. The second of those conditions was bound to generate much misunderstanding and exasperation in the months ahead.

★ 6 ★

PRETENSE OF HARMONY

I had to work by influence and diplomacy in order to secure agreed and harmonious action with our cherished Ally, without whose aid nothing but ruin faced the world.

—WINSTON CHURCHILL

The year before, in 1941, during some of their darkest hours in the war, the British had created a unique planning unit, the Combined Operations Staff. Its role was to harmonize the input of Britain's three military services in amphibious operations. When General Marshall and Harry Hopkins arrived in London on April 8, 1942, to seek British approval for the American cross-Channel invasion proposals, Admiral Lord Louis Mountbatten had recently graduated to the command of that unit.

Mountbatten was an innovative strategic thinker, an immensely charming individual, and a cousin of the king. If he had not been so well connected, he probably would not have reached so elevated a position. He was adventurous and imaginative in a way that conventional senior officers generally found outlandish, dangerous, and unacceptable. He was, as Hopkins pointed out, "somewhat addicted to freakish schemes involving all manner of weird contraptions." Some proved workable; others, including a landing craft made out of shatterproof ice, did not.

Soon after taking over Combined Operations, Mountbatten had suggested that American officers be sent across the Atlantic to work with his staff and see how it functioned. Senior among those officers was Brigadier General Lucian Truscott, Jr. Truscott and the Americans who accompanied him were impressed by the eagerness of the Mountbatten team to come to grips with the enemy. They were even more impressed by how well traditional service rivalries, so entrenched in the American armed forces, had been submerged in its deliberations and planning.

Truscott soon became aware of the belief held by some of Mountbatten's junior officers that the British Army was "dominated by a defensive and defeatist attitude" and that "few had much stomach for continental operations." However, Marshall and Hopkins saw little of that upon their arrival in the British capital. They were warmly received by Churchill, with whom they conferred their first evening there.

The prime minister responded with unqualified approval to the proposals they brought for an American military buildup in Britain, a full-scale invasion of France in 1943, and an assault on France later in 1942 if the Russians appeared on the verge of collapse or if the German position suddenly was substantially weakened. The British leader called the proposal for a cross-Channel invasion "momentous." It was, he said, an example of the "classic principle of war—namely, concentration against the main enemy." Marshall outlined the American plan to the British Chiefs of Staff the following morning.

> Western Europe is favored as the theater in which to stage the first major offensive by the United States and Great Britain. By every applicable basis of comparison, it is definitely superior to any other. . . . Through France passes our shortest route to the heart of Germany. . . . Decision as to the main effort must be made now. . . . A major attack must be preceded by a long period of intensive preparation. . . . Our proposal, more fully outlined later, provides for an attack, by combined forces of approximately 5,800 combat airplanes and 48 divisions, against Western Europe as soon as the necessary means can be accumulated in England—estimated at 1 April 1943, provided decision is made now and men, material and shipping are conserved for this purpose.

Despite the warmth of Churchill's initial reception for the American scenario, now that some of the details were being filled in, British qualms became apparent. The prime minister and his generals had no doubt that an invasion of France would have to be undertaken eventually. The question now was whether, as the British believed, that invasion should be delayed until the Germans had been fundamentally weakened by setbacks elsewhere—whenever that might be.

There was an additional complication in understanding between the Allies. Aside from presenting the British with a forceful argument in favor of Round-Up, Marshall placed exaggerated emphasis on Operation Sledgehammer, although that lesser assault on northwestern France was to be undertaken later in 1942 *only* if extreme circumstances warranted. He deliberately overstated Sledgehammer's possibilities, giving the impression that he favored its implementation in a few months' time, emergency or not.

His purpose was to block persisting efforts by Admiral King and General MacArthur to promote a greater commitment of U.S. resources to the war against the Japanese. Also, if agreement in principle could be extracted from the British on Operation Sledgehammer in 1942, it would, Marshall hoped, guarantee that the forces and resources required for the full-scale invasion of France in 1943 would not be scattered about in Churchillian sideshows, even if Sledgehammer was later abandoned.

This subterfuge was, understandably, not explained by Marshall, and its significance escaped the British. They believed that the Americans, in their haste, zeal, and inexperience, wanted the Allies to crash helter-skelter into France within the next six months, regardless of circumstances prevailing at the time or the resistance that was likely to be met. Making the idea even more outlandish was the fact that few American troops would by then have arrived in Britain. Though British forces were already overstretched, Sledgehammer, as proposed by the Americans, would have to be largely a British operation.

The British had of course also examined possibilities for an early major assault on the French coast, from which their Expeditionary Force had been expelled under fire by the Germans in 1940. Proximity and experience had made them do so in even greater detail than the Americans had. As a result, General Brooke was appalled by what struck him as the shallowness of the thinking that appeared to have gone into U.S. operational planning.

He believed the Americans had not allowed for appropriate margins of error in their attack calculations and that they had no idea of the complexities of a large-scale amphibious operation against a strongly defended coast, or of essential follow-up requirements. A quick-witted, strong-willed, sharp-tongued man, fiercely intolerant of what he believed to be the failings of others, the British Chief of Staff wrote in his diary that Marshall's plan "does not go beyond just landing on the far coast. Whether we are to play *baccarat* or *chemin de fer* at Le Touquet . . . is not stipulated. I asked him . . . Do we go west, south or east after landing? He had not begun to think of it." Brooke believed, "[I]t was unlikely that we could extricate the forces if the Germans made a really determined effort to drive us out." He conjured up a vision of a replay of Dunkirk, from which he himself had been evacuated, except that this time the evacuation of the trapped troops would not succeed:

> They [the Americans] have not begun to realize all the implications of this plan and all the difficulties that lie ahead of us. The fear I have is that they should concentrate on this offensive at the expense of all else.

At that moment, "all else" had the British High Command deeply troubled. The Japanese were sweeping through Burma, threatening India, and could conceivably link up with the Germans who were advancing into the Middle East. Three quarters of a million British and British Empire fighting men could be cut off. Iraqi and Persian oil fields were at risk and might fall to the enemy. "With the situation prevailing," Brooke said, ". . . it was not possible to take Marshall's 'castles in the air' too seriously. . . . We were hanging on by our eyelids."

American diplomatic trouble-shooter Averell Harriman reported to Roosevelt that reliable sources in London believed it was only a matter of a few months before Churchill's government would fall because of Britain's plight. The mood was grim in London. Military as well as political figures there had begun to question the competence and resolution of British troops.

General Sir Archibald Wavell believed, "[W]e have lost a good deal of our hardness and fighting spirit." Major General Sir John Kennedy groaned that British troops "had not fought as toughly as the Germans or the Russians, and now they were being outclassed by the Japanese." Sir Alexander Cadogan, permanent undersecretary at the Foreign Office, gloomily feared that the British Army had become "the mockery of the world." Churchill angrily asked Brooke, "Have you not got a single general . . . who can win battles, have none of them any ideas?"

With despair rife in London, the prospect of engaging in Operation Sledgehammer—of dispatching the handful of infantry divisions Britain could spare at the time across the English Channel to carry virtually all the burden of confronting the Germans entrenched there—was more than alarming. Compounded by the belief that the Americans would be able to provide little help for Sledgehammer and didn't really know what they were talking about, it was terrifying. It was little wonder that the British Chiefs of Staff received American cross-Channel invasion plans with little show of enthusiasm. No matter how hard General Marshall pressed his case, they could not be shaken from their conviction that no such invasion should be attempted until the Germans were reeling.

As far as they could judge, other matters had to take precedence. Having once feared that the United States might concentrate too heavily on defeating the Japanese, the British now urged their American visitors to provide assistance for their forces in Asia trying to halt the Japanese advance. Aid was also needed to break the German offensive in Libya, which, if not stopped, would soon find the enemy in Cairo, en route to even richer pickings farther east.

But the Americans had not come to London to strew U.S. military resources around the world. Marshall was dismayed at how, when examining Allied offensive options, the British seemed to keep "returning to a concept of scatterization or periphery-pecking, with a view to wearing down the enemy, weakening it to a point which would permit almost unimpeded or undisputed invasion of Fortress Europe by our forces." Marshall warned that scattering Allied resources would leave plans for a war-winning invasion of occupied Europe reduced to the status of an impoverished "residuary legatee."

The British were in a difficult position when conferring with their American visitors. General Brooke was not only dismayed by American determination to hurtle blindly, as he saw it, across the Channel; he was also not greatly impressed by Marshall, though the U.S. Army Chief of Staff's rugged face and quiet, commanding presence seemed to support his reputation for unshakable integrity and superb leadership qualities. Marshall was revered by his subordinates at the War Department and much respected by Roosevelt and Churchill. To Brooke, however, he seemed only " . . . a pleasant and easy man to get on with, rather over-filled with his own importance. . . . I should not put him down as a great man."

Whether Marshall was a great man or not, the Chief of the Imperial General Staff and his colleagues had to reconcile themselves to the fact that in the last analysis the contribution of American resources in men and matériel was essential if Britain was not to go down to defeat. No matter how misconceived they seemed to be, the American proposals had to be treated with deference. A cable from Roosevelt to Churchill made it clear that they were being hand-carried by his personal emissaries.

> What Harry and Geo. Marshall will tell you . . . has my heart and *mind* in it. Your people and mine demand the establishment of a front to draw off pressure on the Russians . . . [who] are today killing more Germans and destroying more equipment than you and I put together. Even if full success is not attained, the *big* objective will be. Go to it!

To add to the pressure on the British, the day after Marshall and Hopkins had arrived in London, Bataan Peninsula in the Philippines had fallen to Japan. Twelve thousand starving U.S. troops were among the 76,000 Filipinos and Americans taken prisoner. It was a painful and humiliating setback, the worst defeat in the U.S. Army's history. At that moment, the Americans were particularly unlikely to take kindly to being trifled with by the junior partners in the alliance. Churchill was "still fearful that [Roosevelt] might be driven by public clamor to concentrate on the war with Japan."

Hopkins, recognized as Roosevelt's most trusted confidant, made doubly sure of a sympathetic reception for the American proposals.

> I made it very plain [to the prime minister] that our military leaders had, after canvassing the whole world situation, made up their minds that [the cross-Channel invasion plan he and General Marshall presented] was the one of all considered that was by far the most advantageous from a strategic point of view. I impressed as strongly as I could on Churchill that he should not agree to this proposal on any assumption that we do not mean business.

The prime minister got the message as did the British Chiefs of Staff. They were not about to enthuse over a strategy they deemed dangerously mistaken but they felt constrained to tone down what-ever openly stated objections they made to it.

The result was a communications breakdown during the London talks. To the visiting Americans, the British, while agreeing on generalities, seemed suspiciously "adept in the use of phrases or words which were capable of more than one meaning or interpre-tation." Marshall noted that they were not without "reservations regarding this and that" and that great firmness would be required to see that the agreed plans would not be sidetracked. Neverthe-less, it appeared to Marshall and Hopkins that they had got what they wanted. The British agreed to the Operation Bolero buildup of U.S. forces in Britain. They agreed in principle to the Operation Round-Up invasion of France in 1943, though, despite Churchill's outspoken enthusiasms, they had great doubts about the proposed timing. And they refrained from rejecting out of hand the proposal for an emergency Sledgehammer operation against France in 1942 despite their belief that it would be a huge mistake.

Churchill told his visitors how pleased he was that everything had been sorted out and that Britain and the United States would "march ahead together in a noble brotherhood of arms." The prime minister told Roosevelt that he and his Chiefs of Staff were in "entire agreement in principle with all you propose" and that Sledgehammer "met the difficulties and uncertainties [of 1942] in an absolutely sound manner." Hopkins told the president there had been a "real meeting of minds" in London. On hearing what appeared to have been achieved there, Eisenhower, at the Opera-tions Division in Washington, was greatly relieved.

> I hope that—at long last, and after months of struggle—we are all definitely committed to one concept of fighting! If we can agree on major purposes and objectives, our efforts will begin to fall in line and we won't just be thrashing around in the dark.

Churchill gave assurances that "nothing would be left undone on the part of the British Government and people which could contribute to the success of the great enterprise" on which the Allies were about to embark. He was still being less than candid. Despite his enthusiasm for Round-Up to take place eventually, he remained determined to tighten a ring around the Germans before daring to clash with them head-on in France as the Americans wanted to do. Unlike the Americans, he had his eyes firmly fixed not on France across the English Channel but on the periphery of occupied Europe—Norway perhaps, French North Africa most definitely. Like his service chiefs, he remained convinced that the American strategy of early frontal assault against the enemy was a recipe for catastrophe. He was prepared to deceive the Americans for what he considered their own good, as well as Britain's.

> I was almost certain [Churchill later wrote] the more [Sledgehammer] was looked at the less it would be liked. If it had been in my power to give orders I would have settled upon "Torch" and "Jupiter" [his proposed Norway operation], properly synchronized for the autumn, and would have let "Sledgehammer" leak out as a feint through rumor and ostentatious preparation. But I had to work by influence and diplomacy in order to secure agreed and harmonious action with our cherished Ally, without whose aid nothing but ruin faced the world.

This was the sort of stratagem Churchill recommended to de Gaulle when the general was exasperated by Washington's refusal to recognize him or his Free French movement. "Don't rush things!" he advised de Gaulle. "Look at me, how I yield and reassert myself in turn."

Major General Sir Hastings Ismay, deputy secretary of the War Cabinet, later came to believe that the deception practiced by the British against the Americans had been a blunder. Ismay said they should have been more frank in expressing their views, perhaps telling the Americans something like the following:

> We have not yet had time to study your proposals in detail, but you will doubtless wish to hear our first reactions. We agree in principle with Round-Up, but would not as yet like to commit ourselves to so early a date as September 1943. On the other hand, we regard Sledgehammer as an extremely doubtful proposition, and wonder whether you have given sufficient weight to its immense difficulties and embarrassing implications. The landing would be very hazardous; and if it failed, the result would be catastrophic. Even if it were successful, the maintenance of a bridge-head would be a terrible strain on our resources, and might cripple all other future enterprises, including Round-Up. Nor is it at all certain that it would draw off a single division from the Rus-

sian front. However, we will immediately examine all the possibilities, and if there is a reasonable prospect of success, we will do our share faithfully.

But at the time, the British, deeply worried about developments on various battlefronts, feared such frankness would not be appreciated by the Americans, especially in view of the call of the Pacific. They took comfort from the belief that when details of the proposed invasion operations were examined and their prospects for success assessed, the Americans would realize how misconceived they were. Agreement would then be reached on a more practicable approach to begin the process of defeating Germany, and no damage would be done to the alliance.

"Our Americans friends," Ismay observed, "went happily homeward under the mistaken impression that we had committed ourselves to both Round-Up and Sledgehammer. This misunderstanding was to have unfortunate results. For, when we had to tell them, after the most thorough study of Sledgehammer, that we were absolutely opposed to it, they felt that we had broken faith with them."

A new British study of Sledgehammer's possibilities, undertaken by three senior officers, was ordered soon after Hopkins and Marshall left for home. It proved to be little more than a formality. Two weeks were spent reaching the conclusion the British High Command had already reached—that an invasion of France in 1942 was a possibility only if Germany was faced with a military crisis that crippled its ability to resist effectively. In other words, it should take place only if the circumstances it was designed to create were already there. Battlefront communiqués and intelligence reports continued to show that was not about to happen. But the British still refrained from informing Washington that they believed Sledgehammer was a fantasy.

Mountbatten thought that a dangerous error. He feared that unless Britain's objection to Sledgehammer was made unmistakably clear before preparations for it were begun, "we might be ordered to carry it out." Churchill had no such concerns. He was confident he could sway Roosevelt at the appropriate time and that Sledgehammer would never take place.

* * *

The situation for the Soviet Union had all the while grown increasingly perilous. German armies that had stormed across Soviet borders the previous year had quickly plunged deep into the country. Their advance had been virtually unobstructed until fierce winter weather had forced them to halt. With the onset of spring, they were on the move again. Despite their fierce resistance, the Soviets were beaten back clear across the battlefront. They showed no sign of being able to stop the German rampage.

The Kremlin issued desperate pleas for the Western Allies to open a second front in Europe and compel Hitler to withdraw some of the 284 divisions he had on the Russian Front and shift them westward. The pleadings and demands to Washington and London were dressed with hints that unless such a second front was opened soon, the Soviets might feel compelled to sue for peace, pull out of the war, and permit the Germans to shift their attention and the bulk of their forces from the Eastern Front. That was what the Bolsheviks had done with devastating consequences for the Allies in World War I at the time of the Russian Revolution.

Massive Soviet reverses made such a development seem a genuine possibility. Eisenhower warned that Russia "must not be permitted to reach such a precarious position that she will accept a negotiated peace, no matter how unfavorable to herself, in preference to continuation to fight." Roosevelt told Secretary of the Treasury Morgenthau, "The whole question of whether we win or lose the war depends on the Russians." Popular and press pressure built up, particularly in Britain but in the United States as well, for a second front in Europe as soon as possible—a Sledgehammer type of operation.

The plight of the Soviet people and their often sacrificial resistance to the Nazi invaders was widely reported. It had great influence on public thinking. Churchill was so alarmed by popular Second Front Now pressure that he instructed Minister of Information Brendan Bracken to rally newspaper support against it.

An agitation in the British Press to invade the Continent ... would certainly lead to the loss of many British lives through the improved preparations and fortifications made against it, should such an operation ever be undertaken. ... Surely points like this can, with your authority and influence, be put to the [newspaper] proprietors and editors.

Desperate as the position of the Soviets was, Churchill did not believe they were about to succumb. Hitler had declared the eradication of Bolshevism as one of his primary objectives and had scorned Slavs as subhuman. Special German *einsatz* military extermination units were already indulging in orgies of slaughter of Soviet civilians. Both the Communist leadership and the Soviet people had too much to lose if they capitulated.

However, just as Churchill declined to reveal to the Americans his true feelings about early cross-Channel operations, so he kept the Soviets in the dark about his preferred strategic objectives, giving generalized assurances that all that was possible would be done to ease the Soviet Union's plight.

A second front in Europe was not the only demand Stalin was making of the Western Allies. Shortly before the German armies had invaded his country, the Soviet Union had annexed Latvia, Estonia, and Lithuania. The Soviet dictator now pressed Britain and the United States to recognize formally that those countries were henceforth inseparable parts of the Soviet Union.

Churchill had previously opposed granting recognition to this forcible extension of the Soviet borders and the extermination of independent nations. But he had come to believe that in view of Britain's own plight, it would be unwise to antagonize the nation that was doing most of the fighting against the common enemy. It would be for the sake of a principle which, at that moment, was irrelevant because the disputed regions were under Nazi occupation. For the sake of Allied harmony, the prime minister was prepared to extend diplomatic recognition to the sovietization of the Baltic states.

Roosevelt was not. Partly because of the objections of interested American ethnic groups and partly because he knew that Stalin was in no position to demand anything, the president declined to follow Churchill's lead on this or to be nudged into any long-term decision on territorial rights while the heat of battle distorted perspective.

However, the president recognized it was important not to humiliate Stalin at a time when the Soviet people were making immense sacrifices. To compensate for refusing to give way to

Moscow on the issue of the Baltic annexations, he informed the Soviet leader that he had "in mind a very important military proposal involving the utilization of our armed forces in a manner to relieve your critical western front." He suggested that Soviet Foreign Minister Vyacheslav Molotov be sent to Washington to discuss the matter.

Ever suspicious, Stalin was not so easily wooed. He first dispatched Molotov on an earlier planned trip to London, which he knew was more susceptible to pressure on the annexation issue and capable of influencing America's views on the subject. He also realized that if there was to be a second front in Europe soon, it would have to be largely a British affair because not enough American troops had yet arrived in Britain to participate in an early invasion.

When Molotov reached London on May 20, 1942, he did not concern himself overly much with British acquiescence over the Baltic annexations. The Soviet military situation was deteriorating alarmingly. The outskirts of Moscow were under assault. Leningrad was under siege. The Germans had driven deep into the Crimea and the Ukraine and were advancing elsewhere along the front. A Soviet counteroffensive had been crushed by German armor. Accordingly, the Soviet foreign minister largely confined his energies to pressing still more vigorously for the Western Allies finally to open the second front and draw off some of the German divisions the Red Army was failing to repel.

He achieved nothing. The visitor from Moscow was able to extract from Churchill no more than assurances that the Western Allies were in the process of preparing to go over to the offensive. Churchill declined to be browbeaten into military action contrary to his perception of how the war had to be fought. He was pleased to sign a previously blueprinted treaty of friendship with the Soviet Union and to give it wide publicity. It served to avoid giving the impression that the British and the Soviets were seriously at odds about what should be done.

However, the visit provided the British with an insight into the level of trust they inspired among their Soviet guests. When Molotov and his party stayed at Chequers, Churchill's country residence, staff there who managed to gain entry to their otherwise locked rooms found that they kept pistols under their pillows.

When he went on to Washington, Molotov fared better than he

had in England, though he still kept a pistol under his pillow in the room in which he had been installed in the White House. The Soviet foreign minister succeeded in convincing Roosevelt that the situation in his country was so desperate that emergency Western military assistance could not be long delayed. The week before, two Soviet armies had been caught in German armored pincers near the city of Kharkov. Seventy thousand Soviet troops had been killed; 200,000 had been captured.

Molotov told Roosevelt that the next general German offensive could send the Red Army scrambling back in headlong retreat all along the front. Moscow could fall and the Germans could overrun all of the Ukraine and the Caucasus, giving them access to vast supplies of oil and raw materials for war production. That had been one of Hitler's primary objectives from the start of the war and would have grave implications for the future course of the conflict. The Soviet Union might have to seek an armistice regardless of how harsh Hitler chose to make it. The United States, still gearing up for global conflict, would face an adversary enormously more formidable than it was already.

Having received daily accounts of how critically the Soviet situation was developing, Roosevelt needed little persuading. When Molotov asked for a straight answer to the Kremlin's request for a second front, the president was far more forthcoming than Churchill had been. He told him that the Russians could expect it to be opened "this year." A public statement to that effect announced: "Full understanding was reached with regard to the urgent task of creating a Second Front in Europe in 1942."

General Marshall now reversed the stance he had assumed in his talks in London. He tried to persuade Roosevelt to refrain from committing the United States to a 1942 deadline for an invasion of occupied Europe. Round-Up in 1943, not Sledgehammer, remained his primary interest. But the president refused to hedge on that point. It was true that he had not specified that the second front would take the form of a cross-Channel invasion from England. But the Soviets were convinced the president had indeed promised them a major assault on German-occupied Europe.

Roosevelt subsequently cabled Churchill that he was anxious for an offensive operation in the European Theater to be undertaken within the next four months. Whatever qualms his military advisers had about the availability of the necessary troops, supplies, and particularly shipping, the president was now more determined than ever that American troops should be in action against Hitler's forces before the end of the year, preferably before late-autumn weather closed in.

His reasons were as much political as strategic. The Philippines had fallen to the Japanese. The aircraft carrier *Lexington* had recently been sunk by them. Domestic pressure to concentrate on defeating Japan in the Pacific was relentless. That's where American young men were already fighting and dying. That's where, as newspapers reported, some of them were desperately holding out against the odds. That's where American warships were being sunk. That's where American installations were being attacked.

The war with Germany aroused little popular excitement in towns and cities across the United States, except among politically committed anti-fascists, people whose ancestral homelands had been ravaged by the Germans, and Jews, who had already been persecuted by the Nazis in Germany for many years. Roosevelt knew that until American troops were actually in combat in the European Theater, calls to junk the Germany First strategy and turn with full force against the Japanese would grow more insistent. Despite Roosevelt's warnings about the fundamental Nazi threat to American security, public-opinion polls indicated that some Americans thought it would not be a bad idea to try to extricate the United States from its conflict with Hitler through negotiations before American and German troops clashed—so that full attention could then be paid to defeating Japan. If many people came to think similiarly, the war-winning strategy backed by the president would be at risk.

Congressional elections were to take place in November. The Democrats hoped to retain control of both houses of Congress. The American people had to be kept from concluding that Roosevelt, the Democratic Party leader, was bungling his guidance of the country's war effort. Many people already did believe that. When Roosevelt told Molotov there would be a second front in Europe before the year was out, he meant it sincerely. For their own good, as well as his own political needs, he was determined to focus the attention of the American people more strongly on the war with Hitler.

(Later, when Marshall briefed Roosevelt about plans for the Torch landings in North Africa, which were expected to produce an easy triumph, the president "held up his hands in an attitude of prayer and said, 'Please make it before Election Day.' " However, he did not exert pressure to accelerate things when the military planners decided that the invasion would not take place until four days after the congressional balloting.)

On his way back to Moscow, Molotov passed through London again where he flaunted the second-front assurance he had extracted from Roosevelt. If the Americans could offer the Soviet Union such a promise, he wanted to know why the British could not do so as well. Churchill made it clear to him that as far as Britain was concerned, a second front depended on military conditions being favorable for such an operation.

Molotov was told, "We are making preparations for a landing on the Continent in August or September 1942. . . ." That was the Sledgehammer operation the prime minister knew would not take place. He added, "It is impossible to say in advance whether the situation will be such as to make the operation feasible when the time comes. We can therefore give no promise in the matter."

Once again the Americans were left believing that an emergency cross-Channel attack on France within the next few months remained, at worst, a possibility for which preparations were to be made. Once again the British refrained from making clear their belief that such an operation was totally unthinkable. Indeed, soon after Molotov's departure for home, Churchill cabled Roosevelt that "preparations are proceeding ceaselessly on the largest scale." He did, however, suggest that there might be some difficulties with regard to Sledgehammer and, at the same time, urged that the possibility of a North Africa operation should not be permitted to "pass from our minds."

☆ 7 ☆

GATHERING PACE

The British will never go into Europe except behind a Scotch bagpipe band.

—ADMIRAL ERNEST J. KING

The buildup of U.S. forces in Britain as a prelude to an invasion of France had been expected to proceed expeditiously in the weeks following the Marshall-Hopkins visit to London. Instead, it was dragging along sluggishly. A British-American communications breakdown on the buildup appeared to be largely responsible. Major General James Chaney, the commander of U.S. forces in Britain, was supposed to be providing on-the-spot liaison. But cabled exchanges between Chaney in London and the Operations Division in Washington provided few clues to what was going wrong. Marshall dispatched Eisenhower to Britain at the end of May 1942 to examine the situation. What he found there worried him.

The British appeared to be backing away from what the Americans thought was the agreement to launch an early cross-Channel invasion if emergency circumstances warranted. Eisenhower could find no sense of commitment to the operation and no sense of urgency in preparing for it. British planners with whom he spoke informed him discouragingly that it would take up to three months to secure a bridgehead in France and that a serious offensive could not be launched until after that had been achieved. Their attitude appeared to have important implications for agreed operations the following year as well.

In his report to Marshall upon his return to Washington, Eisenhower asserted that something had to be done to deal with the situation. He said, "It is necessary to get a punch behind the job or we'll never be ready by spring 1943 to attack. We must get going." He told Marshall that one of the problems was the absence of a credible senior American military officer in London. The British did not appear to hold General Chaney in high regard. That was perhaps because Chaney was not senior enough in rank, though after seeing the leisurely fashion with which the general ran his command—his staff took weekends off—Eisenhower had doubts about him too.

He urged that an officer be appointed to assume command of all U.S. forces in the European Theater of Operations. He suggested Major General Joseph T. McNarney, Deputy Army Chief of Staff, a highly respected military administrator, for the job. But to his surprise, Marshall chose Eisenhower himself, promoting him to the rank of lieutenant general so that he would be of sufficient rank to command the respect of senior British officers with whom he would have to deal. He had been chief of operations at the War Department for less than five months but war was an accelerating process.

Eisenhower arrived in England on June 24 to take up his post and speed up arrangements for the American military buildup in Britain that was to precede an invasion of France. He soon discovered that he was to play a completely different role.

Churchill had been kept informed of prevailing thoughts and moods at the U.S. War Department. Field Marshal Dill, who was permanently stationed in Washington, had established a warm personal relationship with General Marshall and had also gotten to know other senior officers well. Dill reported back to London that the Americans were growing unhappy because of the apparent lack of British enthusiasm for the agreed early cross-Channel operation. Once more, the call of the Pacific was being strongly felt both within the U.S. military establishment and among the public at large. The U.S. Navy's triumph in the Battle of Midway early in June, when Japan's fleet of aircraft carriers was crippled, generated a let's-finish-the-job mood in the country. Churchill realized that British-American differences on strategy in the European Theater, which he had so far successfully muffled, had to be resolved before the level of misunderstanding got out of hand and the Americans, in their exasperation, actually did raise defeating Japan to the top of their list of priorities.

The prime minister had already dispatched Admiral Mountbatten to Washington to begin the process of explaining to Roosevelt why an invasion of France within the next few months was out of the question. Charming and persuasive, Mountbatten was much respected and liked by American officers with whom he had already been in contact. He was cordially received by the U.S. Joint Chiefs but his meeting with Roosevelt aroused deep suspicion at the War Department. "Now," General Albert Wedemeyer wrote, "we had an extremely articulate Britisher endeavoring to raise bogies about the hazards of a cross-Channel operation."

That was exactly what Mountbatten did. He did not take issue with the proposed 1943 invasion plan, which he, unlike some of his colleagues in London, firmly backed. But he argued that because of the comparatively few landing craft that would be available for Sledgehammer, it stood no chance of succeeding in its purpose of drawing German troops away from the Russian Front. He told Roosevelt that Allied troops invading France in 1942 would stand little chance against the twenty-five German divisions stationed there. Hitler, he said, would not have to draw a single unit away from the Russian Front to deal with them.

Mountbatten also did not reveal to the president—perhaps he did not yet know—that Britain's Joint Intelligence Committee had concluded only a few days earlier that of seventeen German divisions clearly identified as being in France, none could be described as high-quality units. Five other unidentified divisions were described as "certainly not of higher category than medium." The remaining three divisions were in training in eastern France and were due to be transferred to the Russian Front by August, as were elements of other divisions.

Though certainly not to be discounted, German defenses in France were not as strong as Mountbatten suggested, but the Americans, with few intelligence resources of their own in Europe at the time, were unable to challenge his figures. It didn't make much difference. At that stage, a dispute about the balance of forces would have been irrelevant. The War Department still considered Sledgehammer in 1942 a contingency plan to be implemented only if essential to keep the Soviets from being totally overwhelmed by Hitler's war machine. Preparations for it were, however, to be jealously guarded to ward off attempts to fritter away the resources that were to be accumulated for the 1943 invasion on peripheral "nitpicking" operations.

No senior American officers were called in to attend Mountbatten's meeting with Roosevelt. Marshall was therefore in no position to take issue with what this persuasive visitor had to tell the president even though it made an impact on the president's perception of operational possibilities. Roosevelt told Mountbatten it was still American policy that a "sacrificial landing" in France might be necessary if the Soviets appeared to be about to go under but he was encouraged by his visitor to contemplate alternative operations.

Mountbatten's presentation softened the president up for what Churchill had to tell him when the prime minister, accompanied by Generals Brooke and Ismay, followed Mountbatten across the Atlantic in late June to make certain that Roosevelt was disabused of any idea that an early cross-Channel operation was possible. According to Sir Charles Wilson, he "set out to educate the president" on the harsh realities of the proposed enterprise. Other important matters also had to be discussed, including the atom bomb, then in its early stage of development.

In journeying to the United States once more, Churchill realized that the Americans—and Roosevelt in particular—could not be permitted to believe that the British were simply backing cravenly away from a difficult undertaking to which they had previously agreed. He had to counter mutterings about British double-dealing that rumbled through the offices and corridors of the War Department. There was talk there of how, when speaking to senior American officers, the prime minister commended U.S. proposals, but how he had less flattering things to say about them when conferring with Roosevelt. Wedemeyer, who it was said no longer would confer with a British officer without a witness in attendance, later described what he called "a prime example of British cleverness in influencing American strategical decisions":

> The Prime Minister would work on Hopkins and Roosevelt. Meanwhile, the British military representatives would talk to their American opposites. . . . In the course of discussions about strategy, the Americans would reveal their objections or affirmations concerning certain pro-

posals. This information would be immediately transmitted by the British military to Mr. Churchill, who then would be in a position to work on Hopkins and Roosevelt [who did not bother to maintain such intimate liaison with American military planners]. . . . In this one-sided way, American military opinion was conveyed to Roosevelt mostly through British eyes, ears, and expression. It was given the spin, the twist, which Churchill wished to impart to it.

Whatever the twist or spin, the prime minister assured Roosevelt that Britain was not reneging on its agreed obligations. He indicated that Operation Sledgehammer was still very much in the works, that arrangements were being made to deposit "six or eight divisions" across the English Channel in France before the end of the summer if circumstances made such a move advisable. He said that if a detailed Sledgehammer plan could be devised that offered a reasonable prospect of success, "His Majesty's Government will cordially welcome it, and will share to the full with their American comrades the risks and sacrifices."

But now the prime minister finally laid his cards on the table. He told Roosevelt the British government could not favor an operation that was certain to lead to disaster and that was what Operation Sledgehammer looked like to him and his advisers. "No responsible British military authority," he said, "has so far been able to make a plan for September 1942 which had any chance of success unless the Germans become utterly demoralized, of which there is no likelihood."

Like Mountbatten, Churchill insisted that Hitler's Atlantic Wall defenses would be too difficult to penetrate with the forces the Allies would have available for that task within the next few months. There weren't enough landing craft, nor enough planes to provide adequate air cover. He said that if implemented, Sledgehammer could jeopardize the chances of success for the massive invasion of France in 1943 that everyone agreed was the one that really mattered. While Secretary of War Stimson and General Marshall had been telling the president that an invasion of France was the only way to bring the war to a triumphant conclusion as quickly as possible, Churchill maintained that only through a premature attempt at such an invasion could the war be lost. Yes, he agreed, France had to be invaded; but not until more favorable conditions existed for such an undertaking.

Nevertheless, Churchill said, the Allies could not remain idle in the European Theater. Indeed, the time had come to look very closely at the possibility of some other offensive operation in 1942, one offering the prospect of success. Such an operation was required to show all concerned that the Allies were on the road to victory and, more immediately, it would directly or indirectly relieve German pressure on Russia. For that purpose, he said, French North Africa, which he knew had long aroused Roosevelt's interest, was eminently worthy of renewed consideration. An operation against North Africa would be far less hazardous than Sledgehammer. As had previously been suggested, the Americans might actually find themselves arriving by invitation of the French there.

It was very tempting. The prospect of an easy victory, to begin the march toward final triumph over Nazi Germany, could not be disregarded by the president, especially in a congressional election year. Once more, American strategic planners believed the president was being bamboozled by Churchill. A memorandum for the president was hastily drawn up at the War Department challenging the prime minister's casual assessment of the comparative risks involved in France and North Africa. "If disaster," it asked, "is to be expected in an operation [across the Channel] supported by the entire British Air Force based in the U.K. and a large increment from the United States Army Air Force, what chance can any other operation without such support have?" It went on to say that even if successful, an Allied invasion of North Africa "probably will not result in removing one German soldier, tank, or plane from the Russian front."

The Americans were not alone in their concern about Churchill's revival of Operation Super-Gymnast as a credible undertaking. Though enjoying his first visit to the United States, General Brooke was also worried by what the British and American leaders might be "brewing up together." He remained aghast by the idea of a catastrophic early invasion of France but was anxious also about developments in the Libyan desert where the British Eighth Army was still on the run, and about German U-boats still taking a heavy toll of Allied shipping in the Atlantic. Under the circumstances, Brooke dismissed a diversion of resources for a North Africa operation as "not possible."

But Churchill's mind was made up. He had successfully shaken Roosevelt's confidence in Sledgehammer, even as a standby emergency operation. However, the impression he made at the White House was undermined by a crisis elsewhere. While Churchill was conferring with Roosevelt, the president received and passed to Churchill a message that had just come in reporting that Tobruk, the key British outpost in Libya, had fallen to Rommel's forces and that 33,000 troops had surrendered. Rommel had been running very short of supplies, including fuel, but he had now captured vast quantities of it. The prime minister was badly jolted, angry and humiliated. His doctor described Churchill's reaction when alone with him shortly after the news had been received.

> "I am ashamed. I cannot understand why Tobruk gave in. More than 30,000 of our men put their hands up. If they won't fight . . ." The P.M. stopped abruptly. He forgot all about me, and kept crossing and recrossing the room with quick strides, lost in thought.

And Churchill himself later wrote, "Seasoned soldiers had laid down their arms to perhaps one-half their number. . . . I did not attempt to hide from the President the shock I had received. . . . Defeat is one thing; disgrace is another."

If his Eighth Army was being pummeled by Rommel's troops in northeast Africa, his argument for landing Allied forces in northwest Africa lost much of its persuasiveness. No longer could the prime minister project a picture of Axis forces being trapped between the Eighth Army advancing from the east and the Allied invaders advancing from the west. Instead, Alexandria, Cairo, the Suez Canal, and the Middle Eastern oil fields were now under threat. Despite Marshall's reluctance to scatter badly needed equipment about, with Roosevelt's approval he immediately made arrangements to provide three hundred Sherman tanks and one hundred self-propelled guns to reinforce the British in the region and bolster their position there.

Churchill was touched and grateful for this selfless and generous act. As he knew, the Sherman tanks were only just rolling off American production lines and were in great demand by U.S. units elsewhere. Nevertheless, never one to reel from a setback, he used the crisis that had developed for his forces in the Libyan desert to try to convince Roosevelt that an early invasion of France was definitely out of the question. But in view of this latest setback for his troops, there were limits to which he felt he could go in pressing the president to reject the advice of his own senior military advisers.

Once more he felt obliged to resort to guile in dealing with the Americans. He granted that preparations for an invasion of France later in the year should be "pushed forward with all speed, energy and ingenuity. . . ." But he added, "If, on the other hand . . . success is improbable, we must be ready with an alternative." The alternative he had in mind was, of course, French North Africa.

Once again, no hard-and-fast notice had been served by Churchill that an early cross-Channel invasion was off the agenda. When Eisenhower arrived in England a few days later to take up his post as commander of U.S. Army forces in the European Theater, he was still under the impression that if emergency circumstances warranted, Operation Sledgehammer would take place before autumn weather set in. He had crossed the Atlantic in June with the understanding that he was to prepare American forces to take part in it alongside the British. He had no qualms about that. After all, the plan for Sledgehammer had been devised by the Operations Division of which he had been chief until a few days before.

Churchill emerged from World War II with a reputation as the greatest wartime leader in British history and probably its greatest prime minister as well. But during the summer of 1942, that was hardly the image he projected in political circles at home. He was the butt of criticism and had been for some time. It could hardly be otherwise when British forces had been suffering setbacks just about everywhere they had engaged in combat.

Just a few months earlier, in January 1942, Churchill had felt it necessary to subject himself to a vote of confidence in Parliament because, as he told the House of Commons, "things have gone badly [in the war] and worse is to come." It had been a time of crisis then also, and the appearance of national unity had to be maintained. Consequently, only one vote had been cast against him.

For a time, questioning of his government's leadership was muted, only to become more pronounced when, as he had predicted, the outlook for Britain had grown even more bleak. Singapore had fallen in February. Much of Burma had been lost in March. In India, also threatened with a Japanese invasion, the independence movement was intensifying its agitation. German U-boats continued to send great numbers of British ships to the bottoms of the Atlantic and the Mediterranean. And now, a promising offensive in the Libyan desert had turned to dust. The British forces bent on crushing Rommel's army were themselves in danger of being crushed.

Churchill's absolute confidence in ultimate victory and his grandiloquent oratory lifted sagging national morale from time to time. But, as English historian and diplomat Harold Nicolson noted in his diary, the country was "too nervous and irritable to be fobbed off with fine phrases." Upon his return to London from Washington in late June 1942, just after the Tobruk debacle, the prime minister faced a barrage of criticism in both the press and Parliament for his supervision of Britain's war effort.

Most vitriolic was William Connor, who wrote under the name "Cassandra" in the mass-circulation London *Daily Mirror.* Connor regularly poured scorn on the quality of the war leadership. Much of it was described by him as consisting of "incompetents, fools, log-rollers and time servers" and "blimps, bullshit and brass-buttoned boneheads." The effect of the fall of Tobruk was made worse by the emphasis in official reports shortly before on how well the desert battle had been going. People across Britain now asked if anyone knew what was really happening and wondered whether they were being hoodwinked by their leaders.

Questions were raised about the qualities of the generals in command. A joke making the rounds told of "Some good news at last! Five of our generals were captured at Tobruk." Inevitably questions were asked about the most senior figure in the government—Churchill himself. Some believed he had developed a habit of whisking off to the United States whenever Britain was "faced with a major crisis," such as the one it now confronted.

The Middle East suddenly appeared to be within Hitler's grasp. Rommel's forces had driven into Egypt and were within sixty miles of the port of Alexandria. British ships at anchor there were ordered to put to sea to avoid the risk of capture. At Cairo, forty miles farther east, British government offices burned classified documents. Civilian dependents were evacuated to safety and many other civilians fled the city for fear of a German takeover with all that implied during Nazi times. Officers at the American military headquarters in Cairo fled south to Khartoum. Mussolini prepared to ride a white stallion in triumphal procession with Rommel through the Egyptian capital. In London, *The Times* warned Churchill that public opinion demanded "radical changes" in how the war was being managed.

On July 1, 1942, the House of Commons began its consideration of a vote of censure against Churchill. The motion, to be debated over three days, paid "tribute to the heroism and endurance of the Armed Forces of the Crown in circumstances of exceptional difficulty" but maintained that there could be no confidence in the central direction of the war. The motion was introduced by a prominent Conservative, Sir John Wardlaw-Milne, chairman of the powerful House of Commons All-Party Finance Committee, whose usual tasks included the study of administrative waste and inefficiency. But the fact that Wardlaw-Milne was leading an attack on the leader of his own party did not necessarily mean a great deal. Many prominent Conservatives had never trusted or liked Churchill because of his earlier history of maverick political behavior. Many had been dismayed when he had become prime minister and were considerably less than awed by his performance so far at Britain's helm.

Before the debate began, Wardlaw-Milne offered to withdraw his motion questioning Churchill's leadership, for the sake of national unity. Churchill turned him down. He knew that avoiding a vote would only encourage most of his critics to intensify their sniping each time British forces suffered a setback. "Considering," Churchill later wrote, "that for nearly three weeks the whole world, friend or foe, had been watching with anxiety the mounting political and military tension, it was impossible not to bring matters to a head." The debate was duly held.

A major criticism of Churchill was his decision to serve both as prime minister and minister of defense. It was said that he had taken on more than he could handle and that as a result Britain had "suffered in both fields." He was said to be doing both too much and too little, interfering with the military direction of the war, which otherwise would be more efficient and effective, and at the same time, missing important military opportunities because his time and energies were so fully stretched that he could not concentrate on seizing those opportunities when they arose. Leslie Hore-Belisha, a former Conservative secretary of state for defense, pointed out that Churchill had repeatedly been mistaken in forecasting battle victories in various corners of the world.

> [W]e may lose Egypt or we may not lose Egypt . . . but when my right honourable friend the Prime Minister, who said that we would hold Singapore, that we would hold Crete, that we had smashed the German army in Libya . . . when I read that he had said that we are going to hold Egypt, my anxieties became greater than they otherwise would have been. . . . How can one place reliance in judgements that have so repeatedly turned out to be misguided? . . . In 100 days we lost our Empire in the Far East. What will happen in the next 100 days?

Sir Herbert Williams told the Commons, "The public are angry, disquieted, above all, bewildered" by what was happening. He and others took Churchill to task because his government was not giving the public more—and more accurate—information about the quality of the equipment supplied to the troops and about war developments generally. The result had been a gradual accumulation of distrust.

Senior Labour party figures refrained from attacking Churchill. Their leader, Clement Attlee, was Churchill's deputy prime minister and shared responsibility for the government's shortcomings. But Labour Party left-winger Aneurin Bevan did not feel bound by the same restraint. Bevan, as stirring an orator as the prime minister, declared that Churchill "wins debate after debate and loses battle after battle." He charged that Britain's military services would have been able to perform much more effectively if they were not so thoroughly riddled with class prejudice that prevented gifted soldiers of lowly social status from rising through the ranks. "If Rommel had been in the British Army," Bevan told the House of Commons, "he would still have been a sergeant."

In insisting that the debate take place, Churchill knew that those in the House of Commons who found fault with his leadership would be far outnumbered by his admirers and supporters. Among them was Captain John Profumo, a serving officer who represented the constituency of Kettering and who declared that it was right to be concerned about the military situation but that there should be greater concern at the antics of "habitual critics who, after every reverse or setback, like hungry dogs smell around for a bone to pick. . . . This," Profumo declared, "is the moment for supreme unity." Flight Lieutenant Robert Boothby told the House of Commons that Churchill had " 'stood when earth's foundations fell.' " Boothby saw no reason to doubt that he would "see us through again."

Churchill himself did not pass up the opportunity to display his declamatory skills in a point by point defense of his direction of Britain's war effort. He did so to the usual good effect, winding up his response to his critics on the floor of the House of Commons with the inevitable appeal for national unity that was meant also to make an the impression far beyond Britain's shores.

> All over the world, throughout the United States . . . in Russia, far away in China and throughout every subjugated country, all our friends are waiting to know whether there is a strong, solid Government in Britain and whether its national leadership is to be challenged or not. . . . If those who have assailed us are reduced to contemptible proportions and their Vote of Censure . . . is converted to a vote of censure upon its authors, make no mistake, a cheer will go up from every friend of Britain and every faithful servant of our cause, and the knell of disappointment will ring in the ears of the tyrants we are striving to overthrow.

As before, Churchill got what he wanted from Parliament. The motion against him was defeated 475 to 25. National unity was preserved. Among those who refrained from voting against him were some members of the House of Commons who felt that the prime minister was not above serious criticism and who believed the direction of Britain's war effort needed to be substantially improved. They supported him nevertheless because they felt that there was no other figure of sufficient stature to replace him as leader of the British nation at that fateful moment. Even Admiral of the Fleet Sir Roger Keyes, who had seconded the motion of censure against the prime minister, believed, "It would be a deplorable disaster if he had to go."

Once the parliamentary challenge to his leadership had been successfully put behind him, Churchill could again devote his full attention to the prosecution of the war. One of the first things he did was act to resolve American-British differences on offensive strategy. Conflicting perceptions about Operation Sledgehammer could not be permitted to drag on any longer. After the fall of Tobruk, he had felt obliged to promise Roosevelt that he would again examine prospects for the operation. Now he intended to report his findings and use his influence with the president to bring the controversy to an end.

On July 8, he cabled Roosevelt: "No responsible British general, admiral, or air marshal is prepared to recommend Sledgehammer as a practicable operation in 1942." He said that his Chiefs of Staff had reported to him that the conditions that would make an invasion of France that year a sound, sensible undertaking were very unlikely to develop. He again maintained that if it was attempted, the drain on resources would mar if not completely ruin the possibility of mounting the major invasion of France the following year. Now was the time to opt instead for the dormant North Africa operation.

The prime minister was no longer toying around the edges of his argument. His long-suspected intention to hijack the direction of Allied strategic policy from the senior partner in the alliance was finally out in the open. He tried to persuade Roosevelt that a North Africa campaign had been the president's preference from the beginning. "This," he cabled him, "has all along been in harmony with your ideas. In fact it is your commanding idea. Here is the true second front of 1942." It offered "by far the best chance for effective relief to the Russian front."

Churchill knew very well that an operation against North Africa was not Roosevelt's "commanding idea." The president was very much interested in it and had been ever since he first began fearing that the Germans might use defeated France's African possessions to threaten the security of the Western Hemisphere. The activities of William Donovan, Robert Murphy, and their various agents had further whetted his interest, as had Churchill's arguments. But he was not so easily swayed on a matter he realized could have far-reaching consequences for the course of the war. His commanding idea at that moment was for American troops to be usefully in action in the European Theater before the end of the year to prevent the American people from being distracted from the importance of defeating Germany first.

The question for the president was whether the invasion of North Africa would be "the safest and most fruitful stroke that can be delivered this autumn" as Churchill maintained it was. The prime minister insisted that Operation Round-Up, the proposed cross-Channel invasion the following year, would not be preempted or forestalled by it. But Stimson, Marshall, and the War Department planners were convinced that if he got his way, the strategy the Americans had formulated would be completely discarded. Round-Up as well as Sledgehammer would be abandoned. Taking its place would be the reverse of the central focus of the War Department's strategic thinking. Allied military strength would be scattered about to nibble at the enemy's fringes rather than concentrated for a head-on, war-winning clash.

Stimson was infuriated by the British turnabout on an agreement that had been "so laboriously accomplished." Marshall, who did not often allow himself open displays of anger or bitterness, was also enraged by "these . . . decisions which do not stay made" and wondered whether it had ever been the intention of the British to stick to them. Chief of U.S. Naval Operations Admiral Ernest J. King had no doubt that despite their earlier protestations of agreement, the British had never been "in wholehearted accord" with operations proposed by the United States.

The top echelon of America's military establishment did not intend to let Churchill's maneuverings go unchallenged. With Stimson's encouragement, Marshall and King urged Roosevelt to stand fast on the strategy to which the British had previously indicated their support or unilaterally seek a totally different alternative.

If the United States is to engage in any other operation than forceful, unswerving adherence to Bolero plans [that meant no Churchillian distractions in North Africa or anywhere else], we are definitely of the opinion that we should turn to the Pacific, and strike decisively against Japan; in other words assume a defensive attitude against Germany, except for air operations; and use all available means in the Pacific.

Admiral King meant it. Not for a moment had he been distracted from his wish to concentrate on defeating the Japanese before turning to the task of trouncing the Germans. But Marshall still believed in the Germany First strategy. By now suggesting otherwise he was trying impress Roosevelt with the unanimous strength of feeling of America's top military men about what they considered Churchill's dangerous and costly fantasies.

97

But Roosevelt was not easily intimidated and called their bluff. Two days after receiving their memorandum, on the morning of Sunday, July 12, he ordered that a comprehensive plan for operations in the Pacific be submitted to him *that afternoon.* The implication was that if the country's senior military men were pressing for an early major offensive against the Japanese, they must surely have a blueprint for it ready for his inspection. The plan, he informed them, was to list the number of troops, ships, and planes that would have to be involved, as well as estimated times of operations. Also to be included were details of the withdrawal of resources for the Pacific operations from the Atlantic and the European Theater and assessments of how the military situations in the Middle East and the Soviet Union would be affected.

No such comprehensive plan existed, and Roosevelt suspected as much. One was hastily and inadequately patched together to meet his deadline but Marshall acknowledged that no adequate Pacific blueprint had yet been devised. It would not have made any difference if one had. The president remained convinced that the Germany First policy was correct and that the United States would have to pay a much heavier price in war losses if it changed its basic strategic approach.

Fearing the argument on strategy was being lost, Stimson maintained a vigorous rearguard assault on Churchill's military perceptions. He told Roosevelt that the British leader had been coming up with "half-baked" schemes ever since World War I, often with disastrous consequences. His latest ideas sounded like more of the same. The president was not convinced. A comparatively easy Allied takeover of France's North African territories, American troops soon in action in the European Theater, elimination of the danger of a German military presence on Africa's Atlantic coast, and possibly bringing France back into the war against Germany— all of that probably on the cheap—were temptations difficult for him to spurn. And if it could be made to happen before the November congressional elections, so much the better.

Whatever decision was to be reached, details had to be worked out without further delay if the Allies were to mount any sort of offensive operation within the next few months. Despite the Arcadia Conference, despite the establishment of the Combined Chiefs of Staff in Washington, despite the visit by Marshall and Hopkins to London in April and Churchill's trip to the United States in June, no one knew for certain what was supposed to happen next in the European Theater. On July 15, Roosevelt instructed Hopkins, Marshall, and King to go to London to lift Allied strategy out of the limbo of discord and indecision into which it had fallen.

In an effort to show his military men they did not have an adversary in the White House, he instructed his emissaries to press for British agreement on Operation Sledgehammer "with utmost vigor." But Roosevelt wanted no Sledgehammer ultimatum to be issued to the British despite Secretary Stimson's contention that one might be needed to "get through the hides of the British."

> If Sledgehammer cannot be launched [Roosevelt said] then I wish a determination to be made while you are in London as to a specific and definite theater where our ground and sea forces can operate against the German ground forces in 1942.

Aware of exasperation at the War Department's Operations Division, Field Marshall Dill cabled a warning to London from Washington. He urged that the British show their American visitors that their determination to advance quickly toward victory over the Germans remained firm; that they were anxious to initiate an attack on occupied Europe at the earliest possible moment; and that they would not insist on any operation that might shift resources away from the main effort. Dill cautioned that unless the Americans could be persuaded that the British were not backtracking, "everything points to a complete reversal of our present agreed strategy and the withdrawal of America to a war of her own in the Pacific, leaving us with limited American assistance to make out as best we can against Germany."

Dill did not appreciate how determined Roosevelt was not to abandon the Germany First strategy or how effective Churchill had been in impressing the president with his views. The prime minister knew he had won his argument on the perils of a premature cross-Channel invasion. All that was left for him to do was to get his visitors to accept that fact so that agreement could be reached on an alternative offensive operation with a minimum of hard feelings. He was prepared to employ all his considerable charm and persuasiveness to that end.

However, Marshall and King had no intention of rushing to expose themselves to the prime minister's blandishments and rhetoric. They had work to do. When they arrived in Britain, they spurned Churchill's invitation to a weekend at Chequers in the Buckinghamshire countryside. They went instead to confer first with Eisenhower, who was by then firmly ensconced in his London headquarters and who also favored Operation Sledgehammer rather than any peripheral distraction.

So did other senior London-based American officers—U.S. Eighth Air Force commander General Carl Spaatz and U.S. II Corps commander General Mark Clark, though Admiral Harold Stark, now commander of U.S. naval forces in Britain, was impressed by British warnings that Channel waters were treacherous in the early autumn, the earliest Sledgehammer could be launched.

Churchill was furious that the visiting Americans hadn't called on him first to discuss the situation. He "raised holy hell," telling Brooke that Marshall was trying to usurp Roosevelt's position as Commander in Chief of the U.S. Army. He protested that his behavior was a violation of protocol. It didn't really matter. The American buildup in Britain was now beginning to accelerate, but the fact remained that a cross-Channel attack before the end of the year would have to be largely a British operation. Aside from U.S. Air Force personnel, only one division of American troops had so far arrived in the United Kingdom. If the British wanted no part of Operation Sledgehammer, it simply could not take place—unless the Americans were able to compel the British to agree by threatening to shift their military emphasis to the Pacific, and Roosevelt had ruled that out.

When he arrived in England, Marshall was encouraged by a report from General Truscott, who had been seconded to Mountbatten's Combined Operations Staff to observe how the various British services cooperated in amphibious missions. Truscott said that unlike their seniors in the British military establishment, some of Mountbatten's people had not been caught in a rut of diversion and distraction. He said that despite Churchill's insistence to the contrary, they believed the Allies had the capability not only to seize a bridgehead on the coast of northern France in 1942—on the Cotentin Peninsula—but to hold it as well until Round-Up was launched the following spring to start the big push into the heart of Germany.

That was consistent with the revised presentation Marshall put before the British Chiefs of Staff in his desperate struggle to save

100

Sledgehammer from abandonment. The operation was no longer to be thought of as a sacrifical gesture, to be implemented only to save the Soviets from calamity. The British were told Sledgehammer could in itself be an important step along the road to victory, though that was highly unlikely in view of the limited forces that would have been available for it. It is hard to see how the operation could have been anything but a debacle.

Marshall was acting in desperation. His anxiety to prevent wasteful distraction from the main task appeared to cloud his normally sober assessments of what was possible. One of his advisers subsequently maintained that it was a ploy, never to be acted on, and that the American position all along was that Sledgehammer "was to be executed only under dire emergency conditions." And, indeed, he may have been pressing for it while planning to have it abandoned once he had thereby managed to preempt the expenditure of resources on peripheral operations.

Whatever Marshall's thoughts, Churchill and the British Chiefs of Staff stood their ground. They insisted, as they and Mountbatten had earlier, that even if a Sledgehammer beachhead could be attained, the German forces deployed in France were sufficient to contain it without having to withdraw a single division from the Russian Front for the purpose. In addition, the diversion of aircraft to cover the operation would sharply curtail the intensifying bombing campaign against German cities designed to disrupt Hitler's war industry and transportation network. What was more, the inevitable loss of much shipping in the operation would ruin the chances for an invasion of France in 1943 to which Churchill, to Marshall's growing doubts, still asserted he was unqualifiedly committed.

After three days of sometimes heated discussion between the military leaders of the two nations, it was apparent that no agreement on Sledgehammer was possible. Roosevelt was informed. It came as no surprise to him. He told his emissaries the time had come to forget about an invasion of France that year. The following year would do well enough. Meantime, they were immediately to explore with the British an alternative operation in which American troops could be deployed against the enemy in the European Theater before the year's end.

The abandonment of Sledgehammer was a particularly heavy blow to Eisenhower. Establishing himself first as chief of opera-

101

tions in Washington and then as commander of U.S. forces in Europe, he knew of British doubts. But he had proceeded on the assumption that a cross-Channel operation in 1942 was nevertheless at the top of the Allied agenda. That was what he believed belonged there, rather than some irrelevant distraction. He now felt that most of the work he had done for the better part of the previous seven months had been wasted and dreaded the consequences. He shared Marshall's belief that the cancellation of Sledgehammer meant Operation Round-Up was in danger as well. He believed that July 22, 1942, when the decision against Sledgehammer was made, might turn out to be "the blackest day in history."

Once an early invasion of France across the English Channel had been ruled out, a decision was quickly made on what was to take its place. Three major possibilities were considered—sending American troops to reinforce the British in the Middle East, an attack on German-occupied Norway, and, of course, the long-gestating operation to seize French North Africa.

Deliberations on the first two were brief and dismissive. Marshall recoiled against the Middle East proposal, which, like so many of Churchill's ideas, suggested to him a potentially endless drain on resources that could be better deployed elsewhere. As for the Norway scheme, the British Chiefs of Staff, having tasted humiliation on Norwegian soil at the beginning of the war, when British troops were forced to withdraw by the Germans, who had gotten there first in greater strength, were as put off as the Americans by its complications. That left an invasion of French North Africa. To the frustrated Marshall it appeared to be "the least harmful diversion."

Churchill was delighted. Accord had been reached on the lines he had intended all along. The capture of French North Africa would be the first objective of the combined forces of the Allies in the (expanded) European Theater of Operations. The danger of another slaughter of British troops in the mud of France had been averted. "All was . . . agreed and settled," Churchill later observed, "in accordance with my long-conceived ideas and those of my colleagues, military and political." "A very trying week," General Brooke, now reconciled to the North Africa plan, wrote in his diary, "but it is satisfactory to feel that we have got just what we wanted out of U.S. Chiefs."

Partly to put the fuss and fury of the Sledgehammer controversy behind them and partly for security purposes, the planned invasion of French North Africa was renamed. What had been Operation Super-Gymnast now became Operation Torch. A great believer in the power of stirring words, Churchill had proposed that more evocative code name. But though its new designation may have been meant to give the illusion of a fresh start, Marshall had not yet completely given up his efforts to thwart it. He had been obliged to acquiesce to Torch. But he clung to a belief that circumstances —perhaps an imminent collapse of Russian resistance—might still force Roosevelt and Churchill to see the error of their ways.

He extracted an agreement from the British that though Sledge-hammer was officially canceled, preparations for it should continue well into September. He argued that such preparations would help deceive enemy intelligence on where the Allies planned to strike. However, Roosevelt's mind was made up. The president was loyally represented in London by Hopkins, who well understood what Marshall was up to. He advised the White House that if there was to be no more shilly-shallying, a deadline for the implementation of Torch had to be set. Roosevelt immediately responded by declaring that Torch "was now our principal objective" and that it should be launched no later than October 30, a few days before congressional elections. The argument was over. Marshall had lost. The strategy devised by the War Department had been repudiated.

Upon his return to Washington, Marshall assured Stimson that he would step in to block Torch "if it seemed clearly headed to a disaster." But the situation was beyond his control. Despite the high regard in which Roosevelt—and Churchill—still held him, he had suffered the most serious defeat of his career. Neither a vain man nor given to vindictiveness, he was not personally offended. He was extremely angry but he accepted that the president, as Commander in Chief of the armed forces, had the right and authority to make final decisions and that he, as Army Chief of Staff, was required to act in accordance with those decisions to the best of his ability. However, he remained convinced that the Allies would needlessly pay a stiff price for the decision that had been made.

* * *

Morocco, Algeria, and Tunisia all gained their independence after World War II. But prior to the war, they had been under French dominance and control for many decades. Algeria was considered as much a part of France as any of its mainland geographic departments. Tunisia and Morocco were French protectorates. French North Africa covered an area more than a thousand miles across and was populated by some 25 million people, most of them Muslim Arabs and Berbers. The comparatively small European minority was mostly of French origin, identity, and allegiance. (Spanish Morocco, a narrow enclave on the northwesternmost tip of Africa, also with a predominantly Muslim population, was a Spanish colony.)

In all three countries, the French ran the administration, the civil service, the police, and the military, though the Sultan of Morocco and the Bey of Tunis were titular national leaders of their respective countries and were treated with great deference. The French residents-general in Morocco and Tunisia were effectively their chief executive and administrative officers, though they were appointed by and responsible to the government of France. Non-French persons were systematically excluded from government positions and political power. All senior French officials and officers had personally pledged allegiance to Marshall Pétain in Vichy after France's capitulation to Germany. With few exceptions, they were pleased to honor that pledge.

The French deployed a military force of some 125,000 troops in North Africa. About five hundred French military aircraft were also based there, as was part of the French Navy. Those forces, and details of the terrain, were the facts that mattered most to the Torch planning teams. Any help Murphy, his Disciples, and OSS operatives could provide would be appreciated. But it could not be assumed that the invasion would meet little or no resistance. The troops would have to go ashore ready for a fight.

There was much to do. Three months at most were left to prepare and launch what was to be the greatest amphibious operation ever undertaken, but even basic plans were still to be decided. Since only American troops were expected to participate in the initial landings, in the hope of minimizing resistance from Anglophobic French officials and officers, the British agreed that an American should be overall Torch commander. Still bristling over the Torch decision, Marshall wanted to consult Roosevelt on whom to choose when he returned to Washington from London. But while he was still in London, Admiral King pointed out to him that since Eisenhower was already on the spot, he would make a good choice.

Marshall agreed. At that stage, the operation did not seem as momentous as it later became. Besides, he liked having a Torch commander who had been involved in formulating basic American strategy and who therefore could be expected to guard preparations for Operation Round-Up the following spring, no matter how hard the British might try to discourage it. The British, who had come to respect and like Eisenhower, agreed to his appointment despite his lack of combat-command experience, though they assumed he would be in charge only until Marshall himself could cross the Atlantic to take charge of Torch or send someone else more experienced.

The initial plan was to appoint a British officer as Torch deputy commander. But it was decided that this slot should be filled by an American as well, in case anything happened to prevent Eisenhower, or the American who took over from him, from performing his duties. As his deputy, Eisenhower, with Marshall's approval, chose Major General Mark Clark, who was already in Britain as commander of the U.S. II Corps. Clark was a forceful, assertive personality upon whose vigor and stamina Eisenhower believed he could rely. His personal adventures would unexpectedly add a peripheral measure of both excitement and farce to Torch planning.

★ 8 ★

THE SUPREME COMMANDER TAKES CHARGE

*I am awfully sorry for Eisenhower—he has been
buggered about.*

—BRIGADIER VIVIAN DYKES

Rarely in recent times has a senior officer taken command of an
operation of which he thought so little. Eisenhower would later
change his mind about the merits of Torch. But in his account of
the war, written much later, he quoted another unnamed American
general as dismissing any plans for an operation in the Mediterranean as "idiocy," clearly implying that, at least at that stage, he
himself did not think such a judgment completely out of order. He
was fully aware of the enormity of the task to which he had been
assigned.

The decision to invade North Africa necessitated a complete reversal in
our thinking and drastic revision in our planning and preparation.
Where we had been counting on many months of orderly build-up, we
now had only weeks. Instead of a massed attack across narrow waters,
the proposed expedition would require movement across open ocean
areas where enemy submarines would constitute a real menace. Our
target was no longer a restricted front where we knew accurately terrain, facilities, and people as they affected military operations, but the
rim of a continent where no major military campaign had been con-
ducted for centuries. We were not to have the air power we had planned
to use against Europe and what we did have would be largely concen-

trated at a single, highly vulnerable base—Gibraltar—and immediate substantial success would have to be achieved in the first engagements. A beachhead could be held in Normandy and expanded, however slowly; a beachhead on the African coast might be impossible even to maintain.

In Washington, the Operations Division had difficulty shaking itself free of the conviction that Torch was a digression from the real war. Some senior officers doubted whether the operation would really take place. Few if any believed that if it did, it would contribute meaningfully to winning the war.

Their persisting lack of enthusiasm worried British officers based in Washington. Field Marshall Dill expressed concern about it to Marshall. "From what our planners tell me," he said, "there are some of your people who feel that Torch is not a good operation. That, of course, must be a matter of opinion, but those who are playing a part in mounting the operation must be entirely whole-hearted about it, or they cannot give it all the help it should have and overcome all the difficulties that will arise."

Marshall had no intention of apologizing. He told Dill that the officers responsible for executing Torch would "enthusiastically and effectively support decisions made by the Commander in Chief." But he did not intend to put blinkers on them simply because a strategic decision had been made.

> Planners who are responsible for the formulation of plans for projected operations, the assessment of their relative value to our war effort, and the integration of those plans with our overall strategy, must retain their intellectual integrity and view all military questions objectively. They must foresee and make provision to meet all difficulties involved in the execution of those plans. It is my opinion that we should demand absolute candor from our Planners when they discuss projected operations.

No study of the forces or equipment available for the operation had yet been undertaken. Neither specific strategy nor tactics had been formally spelled out. Preoccupied with difficulties elsewhere, the British had done comparatively little preliminary planning for the operation Churchill had so diligently promoted. Not suspecting that anything like Torch would actually happen, the Americans had not done so either.

There was no agreement yet on where in French North Africa the troops would go ashore, only that they would do so. There was no study of the assortment of troopships and cargo vessels that would be needed for the operation. During the first week in July, 400,000 tons of shipping was lost to German U-boats in the Atlantic alone. If that rate of loss was maintained, Torch preparations were bound to be seriously affected.

Though construction of landing craft had been accelerated in the United States, not even a preliminary examination had yet been made of how many of what kind would be available for Torch. Nor was there any detailed study of the number and kind of escort vessels that could be provided for the Torch convoys. The U.S. Navy was not anxious to specify the commitment it would be able to make. Admiral King said that "unless ordered," he would send no ships from the Pacific at all. When American naval officers attended their first Torch planning session in London, it was clear they were not happy about being there. Their response to questions put to them was a dismissive "We are here only to listen." It seemed to Secretary of War Stimson that the Navy Department "frequently seemed to retire from the realm of logic into a dim religious world in which Neptune was God ... and the United States Navy [was] the only true church." But the fact was the bulk of the American fleet was on the offensive in the Pacific, was sustaining losses there, and the navy did not want to be caught short or distracted by whatever nonsense the army might be concocting in another part of the world.

The Royal Navy's problem was different. British losses on convoy runs to Malta and Russia had mounted sharply. Meantime, the Admiralty still had to concentrate heavily on guarding Britain's lifelines by fighting the Battle of the Atlantic against German U-boats while also attempting to maintain a naval blockade against Germany. When initial Torch calculations were made, most Allied warships were found to be engaged or otherwise committed elsewhere.

The provision of aerial cover for an amphibious operation to be undertaken far from any Allied airfield also had to be examined. According to U.S. Army Air Force commander General Harold "Hap" Arnold, "Torch offered as poor an air deal as could have been dreamed up."

Practically every one of our . . . principles for the use of air power in amphibious landing operations on a hostile mainland had to be violated. The factor of surprise, the political machinations, fancied solutions, uncertain notions about whether the French would fight or not, ruled out any softening-up operations with our bombers. Anyway, even if there had been any strategic bases other than the jammed-up way station at Gibraltar, with the guns of Hitler's friend Franco pointing down on it through the barbed wire a few yards away . . . making . . . Eisenhower [when he established his forward command post at Gibraltar] look for an all-out German attack right up to the night of the invasion, there were no strategic targets in French north-west Africa. There was no industry to speak of . . . no depots, oil stores, railway yards, supply dumps other than a few installations we hoped to find intact for our own use if we got ashore. . . . There could be no land-based air support for the men hitting the beaches. . . .

Could aircraft carriers do the job? Could French airfields in North Africa be seized for use in covering the landings? These matters had to be assessed and decisions had to be made about them. And it had to be done in a way that would permit the various aspects of this elaborate endeavor to mesh together—and D-Day was at most three months away.

Troubled as well by nagging neuritis in his shoulder, Eisenhower found the difficulties he faced "nerve-wracking. Ordinarily," he later observed, "a commander is given, along with a general objective, a definite allocation of forces upon which to construct his strategical plan, supported by detailed tactical, organizational, and logistical programs. In this case the situation was vague, the amount of resources unknown, the final object indeterminate, and the only firm factor in the whole business our instructions to attack."

Not until August 13, three weeks after the Torch decision had been made, was Eisenhower issued a directive on his mission. It was an ambitious one. In conjunction with Allied forces in the Middle East—essentially the British Eighth Army that Rommel had driven back into Egypt—he was to take control of North Africa from the Atlantic Ocean to the Red Sea. The first two stages of Torch would be 1) to achieve and secure landings in French North Africa and 2) to take unchallenged control of Morocco, Algeria, and Tunisia.

The planners, both American and British, plunged into the task of preparing an exploit for which there was neither experience nor useful precedents to draw upon. Only once before in recent times had a government contemplated a major, complex amphibious military operation great distances from the points of embarkation of the task forces involved. That was for the Gallipoli campaign in World War I. That operation had also been promoted by Winston Churchill, who had been First Lord of the Admiralty at the time. And not only had the Gallipoli operation failed; it had been an unqualified disaster.*

Now, with everything from ships to trained troops in short supply, and with other urgent demands being made on resources, task forces had to be organized, assembled, equipped, trained, and rehearsed for amphibious landings on remote, unfamiliar shores—all in short order. Diplomatic and clandestine intelligence aspects had to be coordinated and properly timed. Extensive arrangements had to be made for massive follow-up logistics because, though essential to the operation, successful landings would serve only to make Torch flicker. To make it blaze, a lot of ground would then have to be covered.

To complicate matters still further, a multitude of personnel was concocting this broth—the British, the Americans in London, the Americans in Washington, and the American-British Combined Chiefs of Staff in Washington. Above all of these were Roosevelt and Churchill, who had no doubt that the war was too important to be left to their generals and who were in regular, direct communication, the results of which sometimes were transmitted to the American planners only through the generosity of their British colleagues, who were better briefed by their Commander in Chief than they were.

The original, tentative plan was for two landing sites, one near Casablanca on the Atlantic coast of French Morocco and the other near Oran on the Mediterranean coast of French Algeria. To command American ground forces in the operation, Eisenhower chose Major General George S. Patton, Jr., an experienced armored officer and an old friend. To command the British ground

---

*Suggestions were made that by promoting Operation Torch, Churchill was trying to prove that it need not have been.

forces that would be involved, the British Chiefs of Staff named Lieutenant General Sir Harold Alexander, who had already established a reputation for combat-command skills in France and Burma.

However, within days of being appointed to Torch, Alexander was moved instead to Cairo to command the faltering British and Commonwealth forces in the Middle East and inject some offensive spirit there. Rommel's drive into Egypt from Libya had been halted but by the end of July both sides were exhausted, having battered each other into a stalemate. Alexander was immediately replaced at Torch by Lieutenant General Bernard Montgomery. Montgomery was another tough officer, battle-hardened in France. Though Eisenhower later would have problems with him, he was pleased with that appointment as well.

But two days later, Montgomery was also removed from Torch by the British High Command and dispatched to the Middle East to succeed Lieutenant General W. H. E. Gott, the commander of the British Eighth Army who had been killed in an attack by enemy aircraft. To Eisenhower, it seemed that he and the operation he commanded were being trifled with by the people who had fought so hard to bring it into being. He was moved to wonder whether the British were really serious about Torch.

Lieutenant General Kenneth Anderson was named to replace Montgomery as commander of the British component of Torch ground forces. But Eisenhower soon had further reason to question attitudes toward Torch in London. Anderson was instructed by the British Chiefs of Staff to obey all orders issued by Eisenhower but he was to feel free to appeal to the War Office in London before executing an order that appeared to him "to imperil any British troops in the Allied Force." That directive was based on precedents established in World War I and used to crucial advantage during the retreat of the British Expeditionary Force through France to Dunkirk two years earlier.

Though employing the discretion that characterized all of his dealings with the British, Eisenhower made it clear he would not stand for it. If he was to be effective as Supreme Commander of the operation, under no circumstances would a subordinate be permitted to treat him as if he didn't exist. He conceded the right of the senior British officer in Torch to appeal to his own government against an order if he saw fit to do so, but only after informing him and giving his reasons. The British conceded the point and revised Anderson's instructions accordingly, but now it was the turn of some at the British War Office to grumble about concessions being made and the Americans too easily having their way.

Once agreement had been reached on Torch and a directive had been issued as to its mission, the British showed themselves eager for the operation to be implemented without delay. They urged that the Allies aim at launching the invasion by October 7. It would mean loading equipment and embarking troops toward the end of September. Though that would give Eisenhower less than two months to prepare, they warned it was important for the post-landing seizure of all of French northwest Africa to be well in hand before the onset of winter weather.

But the U.S. Joint Chiefs of Staff refused to be rushed. This was to be primarily an American operation. The British may have been anxious to begin closing the ring around Hitler, but starting from scratch in amphibious warfare, the Americans wanted extra time to train and rehearse assault forces and boat crews. Some of the American units that were to participate in the operation were not scheduled to take delivery of essential heavy equipment until mid-September. They would need time to grow accustomed to using it. Not without a touch of venom, the War Department warned against undue haste that might lead to another reverse like those already suffered by the British in France, Norway, and Crete. It preferred the landings to take place early in November, with the troops embarked and equipment loaded at departure points late in October.

The British were dismayed by the prospect of delay and the dangers it entailed because of worsening weather conditions in autumn and the increased possibility of security leaks. Through Field Marshal Dill in Washington, they urged the War Department to do everything they could, perhaps "departing from normal methods," to get the troops ready for early action. But Dill found that the Americans could not be budged on timing. He told London:

Possibly they are beginning to realize that they are not very highly trained. They also feel that as this is the first big venture of the American troops there must be no question of failure. This mentality makes for delay to ensure that last gaiter button is secure.

Differences on where the landings in French North Africa should take place had also immediately erupted between the Western Allies. These were even more pronounced and generated much exasperation on both sides. Although initial tentative plans were for two sites, four had by now come under consideration—Oran, Algiers, and Bône, all on the Mediterranean coast of Algeria, as well as Casablanca on the Atlantic coast of Morocco.

Soon after the Torch decision had been made, the British had begun downplaying the Morocco aspect of the operation while the Americans were less than enthusiastic about the proposed Algeria landings. Landings in Morocco had no immediate bearing on Britain's strategic objectives of trapping the Axis forces in North Africa, freeing the Mediterranean for Allied shipping, and securing the Middle East against the German threat. For Churchill's generals and admirals, the only sensible immediate purpose of the Torch landings was the seizure of the major Mediterranean ports of Bizerte and Tunis in Tunisia before the Germans got there in force, and that could be done only by landing as far east on the Algerian coast as circumstances permitted.

Those two Tunisian port cities were themselves ruled out as amphibious landing sites because they were within easy range of German airbases in Sicily less than one hundred miles away. But the British considered it essential for them to be taken "within a month" of the proposed landings on the Algerian coast. After Tunis and Bizerte were in Allied hands, Rommel's supply line could be severed, the German and Italian forces in North Africa would be doomed, and the southern shore of the Mediterranean would come under Allied control.

The British believed that Torch would "stand or fall on [the] question of early Allied occupation of Tunisia," and for that purpose, a landing in Morocco was irrelevant. Besides, British planners maintained that even if the Morocco component of the operation was included in the planning, it might have to be abandoned before the actual landings for reasons of weather and sea conditions. On four days out of every five, the Atlantic surf along the Moroccan coast was so high and rough that an amphibious operation could not even be attempted there. The Casablanca landings the Americans favored were too dependent on circumstances beyond human control and should, the British maintained, therefore be ruled out as too risky. They would in any case consume too large a proportion of the limited resources available for Torch. Once positions in Algeria had been secured, Morocco could be taken far more easily from landward.

The Joint Chiefs in Washington took strenuous exception to this British analysis of purposes and prospects. What little American tactical thinking had previously gone into planning a North Africa campaign had targeted Morocco rather than Algeria because of the threat a German takeover there might pose in the Atlantic and to South America. That was what had initially aroused Roosevelt's interest in a North Africa operation. Besides, the U.S. Navy had little experience of, or enthusiasm for, operating in inland seas like the Mediterranean.

There was also the Spanish factor to consider and the vulnerability of Gibraltar. A British crown colony, Gibraltar is a two-and-a-half-square-mile rocky headland attached to Spain and poking southward into the sea. The "Rock" is one of the two Pillars of Hercules that guard the Strait of Gibraltar, the narrow entrance to the Mediterranean from the Atlantic. The other Pillar of Hercules overlooks the sea at Jebel Musa, a mountain outcropping in Spanish Morocco.

At its narrowest point, the Gibraltar Strait is a mere eleven miles wide. If the Germans, with or without Spanish collusion, seized control of that channel, they would sever the line of communications for Operation Torch forces landed in Algeria. The operation then was likely to miscarry totally.

Gibraltar is honeycombed with tunnels. At the time, these formed the Rock's basic military fortifications. Gibraltar had a deep-water port and an airfield, but because of its diminutive size, the facilities at both were limited. Nevertheless, there would have been far less concern about its limitations had the Allies not looked upon Spain as a possible threat.

Spain was ruled by Generalissimo Francisco Franco, a fascist dictator who was under pressure from Germany and Italy to ally his country with the Axis powers. There was little doubt that with Spanish collusion, the Germans could close the Strait of Gibraltar to Allied shipping. German planes flying from air bases in nearby

Andalusia, Majorca, Minorca, or Ibiza could easily do that job, turning Operation Torch into a rout.

A natural fortress, Gibraltar might itself be able to hold out for a time against a land assault from Spain, but to little purpose if the Gibraltar Strait was closed. Its value as a forward command post for Eisenhower while the operation was being launched and as a safe harbor for troop and cargo ships en route to the Mediterranean could easily be lost, as Eisenhower well knew.

> Every movement at Gib is seen by the enemy. There is danger of the Spaniards making the airdrome unusable immediately [after] activity starts. The airfield is small; there will be 180–200 Spitfires closely assembled on the field when and if Torch gets under way—an easy target for bombing by the Germans and Italians; also for the Spanish machine-guns set up along the barbed-wire entanglement, some only twenty feet from the edge of the field. MacFarlane [Lieutenant General Sir Frank Mason-MacFarlane, Gibraltar's governor-general] says a million gallons of petrol in four-gallon tins have been cached on, about, in, over, and through the crevices of Gibraltar . . . a good target for incendiaries. Feared the whole damn Rock would blaze if the petrol is ignited.

Eisenhower knew that even if the initial Torch landings were not jeopardized by Spanish intercession because they came as a surprise, essential follow-up activity could be imperiled. The operation would have to be considerably widened. In addition to French North Africa, it would also have to target Spanish Morocco, from which the enemy could threaten the Allied invaders, and Spain's Canary Islands as well. Portugal's mid-Atlantic Azores would probably have to be taken too, since it was unlikely that the Portuguese would be permitted by the Germans to retain their neutrality if Spain was drawn into the war on the Axis side. If all those tasks had to be included in the operation, quick success for it was unlikely and failure had to be considered a distinct possibility.

Sir Samuel Hoare, the British ambassador in Madrid, warned London about the potential threat to Torch's lifeline through the Strait of Gibraltar.

> We shall appear to have put our neck between two Spanish knives, and Spanish knives are traditionally treacherous. The Germans will be on

General Franco's back, dinning into his ears, "Now is your time. You can cut the Allied throat, destroy the naval and air bases at Gibraltar and win a dazzling reward for your country in North Africa." Let no one underrate the power of this temptation, or think that because nine Spaniards out of ten do not want war General Franco might not risk it for the big stakes that it might offer him.

Similar messages received in Washington from the U.S. embassy in Madrid reinforced the argument of America's Torch planners that not too much should be gambled in the Mediterranean and that a landing on Morocco's Atlantic coast was essential. Only that way could it be guaranteed that the troops put ashore in Algeria would not to be stranded in French North Africa without a lifeline.

But weighing everything in the balance, the British High Command concluded that the danger of Spanish involvement was overstated. Its Joint Intelligence Committee forecast that the consequences of involvement for Spain, still struggling to recover from a bloody civil war, would be so momentous that Franco was certain to resist German efforts to draw him in.

Nevertheless, the Americans adamantly refused to risk all in the Mediterranean and continued to insist on an Atlantic-coast component to Torch. The summer was slipping by but Supreme Commander Eisenhower still did not know where in North Africa his troops would go ashore.

As Washington and London debated fundamental strategy and Torch details during the summer of 1942, the Soviet situation continued to deteriorate. The Germans were advancing ever deeper into the Soviet Union along a two-thousand-mile front. The U.S. War Department feared the Red Army might be on the verge of total collapse. Stalin complained bitterly that the Western Allies were not treating the issue of creating a second front in Europe "with the seriousness it deserves." Churchill realized that the Soviet dictator would be doubly furious when he learned that they had chosen instead to invade North Africa in the autumn.

He thought it advisable to go to Moscow to inform Stalin about it personally, explain to him why it was being done, and endeavor to calm his outrage. "It was," he said, "like carrying a large lump of ice to the North Pole." (Churchill did not know that, as revealed later by Nikita Khrushchev, Stalin, out of desperation, was trying to make a secret deal with Hitler, offering him large chunks of Soviet territory in return for an armistice.)

In Moscow, where he arrived August 13, Churchill explained in detail why he believed a second front in Europe would prove disastrously counterproductive. He told Stalin not only was it likely to fail but it was likely to result in such severe losses that the major cross-Channel invasion of France planned by the Western Allies for the spring of 1943 would be undermined. Stalin was not convinced. He said "a great many disagreeable things." He accused the Western Allies of acting in bad faith and the British of cowardice. However, he appeared to be impressed when Churchill got around to telling him about Torch.

> I unfolded a map of Southern Europe, the Mediterranean, and North Africa. What was a "Second Front"? Was it only a landing on a fortified coast opposite England? Or could it take the form of some other great enterprise which might be useful to the common cause? . . . As I told the whole story Stalin became intensely interested.

By the time Churchill left Moscow, en route to Cairo on his way home, he believed Stalin had been won over by his explanation of the benefits that would accrue to the Allies as a result of the Torch campaign. However, the fact was that Stalin was deeply disappointed. He was bitter that no second front in Europe would be opened before the end of the year, and that he had only a promise, which he had no reason to trust, that one would be opened the following spring. General Brooke, who was with the British party in Moscow, noted in his diary, "Stalin is a realist if ever there was one; facts only count with him. Plans, hypotheses, future possibility mean nothing to him. . . ."

While Churchill was in Moscow explaining to Stalin that no second front in Europe would be opened that year, a raid on Hitler's Atlantic Wall was in fact being readied in Britain. It was to be a comparatively small-scale operation.

Months before, Admiral Mountbatten's Combined Operations Headquarters had begun studying techniques that would have to be mastered for an eventual invasion of France. Reconnaissance

117

had provided a rough assessment of German strength on France's English Channel coast and an idea of how formidable German resistance would be. British amphibious training exercises were in progress in Scotland but it was believed that only by actually testing German defenses could there be any sort of firm understanding of what would be involved in trying to overwhelm them. The forces participating in the raid would land at Dieppe on the coast of northern France, raid enemy installations, and be quickly withdrawn.

As night fell on August 18, 1942, British minesweepers raced out into the English Channel to clear corridors for the assault ships setting off from southern England. The assault force included elements of three Canadian divisions that had been training in Britain plus a large contingent of British commandos. A small detachment of American Rangers was also taking part. Plans for a pre-assault softening-up bombing raid had been abandoned because it would alert the enemy, who might otherwise be caught by surprise by this daring exercise.

But surprise was lost well before the raiders reached the French shore, when ships carrying part of the assault force ran into a German freight convoy. The convoy's escort vessels opened fire, and though two of them were sunk by British gunboats, that section of the attack force's landing craft was scattered during the clash. Some were sunk and most of the rest limped back to England. Six that did reach the shore east of Dieppe did not do so until daylight. Watching them arrive, the Germans prepared their reception. Men storming ashore were mowed down by machinegun fire even before they could get off the beach.

Landings west of the city were more successful but the enemy had been alerted throughout the region. The attackers were met with murderous fire from guns positioned on the cliffs above the beaches and German reinforcements were rushed forward to repel them. Tanks that were successfully landed found their route obstructed by concrete barriers. They roared around in circles vainly seeking a way through. With communications and visibility poor, a misleading report of progress against the enemy induced the troop commander, Canadian Major General John H. Roberts, aboard a vessel offshore, to send in reserves. They too were slaughtered, some not even reaching dry land. Of 6,100 troops in the raid, more than 3,500 were killed, wounded, or captured. Three of the 50 Rangers participating were killed; 10 others were wounded.

Operation Sledgehammer, already canceled, had been planned as a much larger assault. It was to have included heavy preliminary air bombardment to soften up the enemy, greater aerial cover for the troops, and paratroops dropping behind enemy lines. But the slaughter at Dieppe was seen by those opposing an early cross-Channel invasion as grim justification of their forebodings.

☆ 9 ☆

TIME FOR DECISION

*In the whole of Torch . . . I consider myself your
lieutenant, asking only to put my viewpoint plainly
before you. . . . This is an American enterprise, in
which we are your helpmeets.*

—WINSTON S. CHURCHILL TO FRANKLIN D. ROOSEVELT

Being in England had considerable influence on Eisenhower as
he assembled a staff in London to plan the most audacious amphibious operation ever attempted. The British had already acquired extensive experience in fighting the war. They had not yet
won many battles and parts of their major cities had been reduced
to rubble. But their morale appeared to be high, their confidence
in ultimate victory appeared unshaken, and their staff work was
immaculate, with all sorts of details and expertise readily available.
The willingness of the three British services to work together without friction was in refreshing contrast to the traditional, persisting, and often petty rivalry between the U.S. Army and Navy.
And Eisenhower, together with the American forces that had
begun to arrive in England, were welcomed with affection and
gratitude.

True to his reputation for getting on with whatever job he was
given, Eisenhower spurned the temptation to wallow in regret
about the abandonment of his cherished Sledgehammer plan. He
quickly discarded his carefully forged perception of how the war
should be fought and committed himself fully to making Operation
Torch a success. Remote from Washington, he was spared exposure to festering resentments at the War Department about how

Churchill had expropriated the direction of Allied strategy. He was also fully exposed to the weight of British experience, concerns, perspectives, and it had its effect.

A British liaison officer in the United States accurately observed, "It is more difficult to convince Americans in Washington than their planning staffs in London." In the transatlantic debate on Torch operational details that had been in progress from the moment he had been named Supreme Commander, Eisenhower soon concluded that the position of the British on the key issue was the right one. He decided they were right about where the initial landings should take place. Despite the War Department's plans for a landing on Morocco's Atlantic coast, he was persuaded that such a move was not immediately essential and would overstretch the resources that were to be put at his disposal. He believed the invasion should be confined to the Mediterranean coast of Algeria. The Mediterranean, he decided, was the key to success for Torch.

Taking Oran, Algeria's second city, was important because it was a major Mediterranean port through which supplies for securing and expanding the initial bridgehead could flow for rapid advance along the coast. The early use of Oran's airfields would offer far greater aerial cover for ground forces than would otherwise be available. Taking Algiers, the capital of Algeria and French North Africa's main city, would have far-reaching political implications. Its Maison Blanche airfield and large port would also prove valuable in the fulfillment of Torch's wider objectives. Landing troops still farther east in Algeria, at Bône, would make it much easier to race on into Tunisia and seize Tunis and Bizerte before the Germans could rush enough forces there to block their advance.

Morocco, on the other hand, was likely to fall by itself once the Allies had succeeded in Algeria, or it could be seized from the rear by troops moving west after landing at Oran. There was no pressing need to risk and expend resources landing on the usually turbulent Atlantic coast when they could be far better deployed in the Mediterranean. Though nervous about possible Spanish intercession, Eisenhower was also persuaded that the threat to the Allied lifeline that was to be established through the Strait of Gibraltar was not as serious as the War Department people back home believed. After all, the Royal Navy had been cavorting in those waters for centuries.

His view was, however, quickly challenged in Washington. The

U.S. Chiefs of Staff made it clear they would insist on an Atlantic coast component to Torch, with landings at Casablanca to be synchronized with those on the Mediterranean shore. No matter what Eisenhower had come to believe and despite British assurances that such concern was unnecessary, General Marshall did not intend to risk stranding troops inside the Mediterranean without backup nearby. Besides, a landing at Bône would be particularly dangerous. What little air cover would be available at the launch of the operation could not safely be stretched to assist a landing so close to German air bases in Sicily.

Having no alternative but to acquiesce to this "intervention of higher authority," Eisenhower reverted to the idea of simultaneous landings on the Atlantic and Mediterranean shores—at Casablanca, Oran, and Algiers—though excluding Bône would mean the advance into Tunisia would require a longer overland trek. That compromise also immediately ran into trouble. Both the U.S. and Royal navies maintained that resources available to them would make it impossible to provide adequate escort for landings on both the Atlantic and Mediterranean coasts.

The seemingly interminable wrangle over place and time fueled existing disquiet about the operation. As the debate continued, some at the War Department came to believe with much satisfaction that Torch would be canceled before the troops were dispatched. Nor were the Americans alone in entertaining such suspicions. Still hard-pressed dealing with difficulties on other fronts, senior British planners raised questions about whether the operation could be adequately supported logistically. The governor of Gibraltar warned that if, as was planned, the Rock was too conspicuously prepared to service the operation as forward command post and supply depot, it would be difficult to conceal the fact "that some form of operation is being mounted." The Germans might deduce what the Allies were up to and take steps to thwart them.

Marshall asked Eisenhower for his frank assessment of Torch's prospects. Eisenhower's cabled reply, detailing many of the problems that would have to be overcome, hardly increased the War Department's confidence in the operation. He said, "[T]he chances of effecting initial landings are better than even but . . . the chances of overall success . . . including the capture of Tunis before it can be reinforced by the Axis, are considerably less than 50 per cent."

That judgment by the Supreme Commander, though shared by the War Department, had a jolting effect in Washington. If Tunisia was not quickly captured, the troops would bog down fighting in rough terrain for which the enemy was better equipped and better trained and would have greater aerial cover. Eisenhower told his aide, Captain Harry Butcher, that he thought it possible Marshall might recommend to the White House that the operation be called off in view of its dim prospects.

Marshall had earlier assured Secretary Stimson that he would block Torch if it seemed headed for disaster. That stage had not been reached but he clung to the belief that the implementation of Torch was "still subject to the vicissitudes of war." To underscore his position on that, he refused to release Brigadier General Walter Bedell Smith from duty in Washington to be Eisenhower's chief of staff in London until early September, when it was clear that there was no way short of prior catastrophe that the operation would be called off.

Whatever qualms were raised about the operation, Eisenhower had to proceed on the assumption that Torch would not be canceled and that it required his unwavering confidence and unstinting efforts to make it succeed. He sternly warned his subordinates that "the time for analyzing the wisdom of the original decision" had passed. His deputy, General Clark, also recognized morale problems arising from persisting doubts. He instructed his staff "that the operation was definitely on and that ways and means to make it successful would have to be found." However, it seemed to Clark during this period that only Churchill was "completely convinced" that Torch would be a triumph.

Despite Eisenhower's determination to get on with his assignment regardless of the difficulties and uncertainties, he was much troubled by the conflict of views between himself and officers at the War Department with whom he had been working intimately only a few weeks earlier. When Major General Thomas Handy, his friend and successor as head of the Operations Division, visited London in mid-August, Handy's presence graphically revealed to him how far he had distanced himself from their thinking.

Seeking a plan that would take account of limitations in naval cover available for the operation, Eisenhower again sketched out a proposal for landings confined only to the Mediterranean. Handy, whom Eisenhower greatly respected, declined to give the idea serious consideration. Not only did he repeat the War Department's firm rejection of the proposal but he wondered whether Torch was trying to take on too much at that stage of the war. The new chief of operations suggested that maybe some of the American troops who were being earmarked for the operation—not enough as far as Eisenhower was concerned—could be better employed elsewhere. When he returned to Washington, Handy reported his view that Torch as it was then shaping up involved an "unjustifiable hazard" and should be abandoned or significantly revised.

The transatlantic debate continued. The British softened their position and allowed that maybe an Atlantic landing should be included if the U.S. Navy would commit some extra warships. Marshall conceded in turn that landings at Oran, in addition to those at Casablanca, would not overly strain available resources. The British insisted, however, that if Algiers was excluded, the point of the operation—getting to Tunisia as well in a hurry— would be nullified.

Churchill returned from his trip to Moscow (and Cairo) on August 24 and in characteristic fashion quickly took charge of the situation. It was now a full month since the decision to invade French North Africa had been taken, though little planning progress had been made. The prime minister immediately called for up-to-date answers and assessments from his Chiefs of Staff and he conferred with Eisenhower. Eisenhower found himself in an awkward position. He knew that the prime minister had a direct line to Roosevelt which he himself did not enjoy and that points were being raised, and decisions possibly taken, about which he knew nothing. Already feeling alienated from many of his former colleagues at the War Department, he feared that answers he gave to the prime minister's questions might be used by Churchill out of context when the prime minister tried to persuade Roosevelt to see things his way.

Having assessed the situation, Churchill dispatched a long message to the president on August 28, urging that they act together to break the stalemate so that the necessary decisions could be made.

It would be an immense help if you and I were to give Eisenhower a directive something like this: "You will start Torch on October 14, attacking with such troops as are available and at such places as you deem fit." This will alter the whole character of the preparations. Eisenhower will really have the power he should have as the Allied Commander in Chief. Endless objections, misgivings, and well-meant improvements will fall back into their proper places, and action will emerge from what will otherwise be almost unending hemmings and hawings.

Churchill's intercession earned a quick response but not the one he wanted. The following day, after being consulted by Roosevelt, Marshall cabled Eisenhower that the president had ruled that, contrary to British wishes, the landings would be only at Oran and Casablanca. Only American troops would be initially employed in the operation. This was to enhance prospects for minimum French resistance. The British would follow afterward.

The message reached Eisenhower while he and Clark were spending a working weekend at Chequers with Churchill and his senior military men. It contained an instruction that the British were not to be informed yet; Roosevelt would be communicating directly with the prime minister on Monday. But everyone at Chequers knew that Eisenhower had received a confidential message from Washington, that it was bound to have concerned Torch, and that he was revealing none of its contents. The weekend's talks were therefore shrouded in an atmosphere of intrigue that compounded everyone's impatience and vexation.

Though previously known for his uncomplaining nature, Eisenhower grew increasingly somber. He knew that the differences had still not been resolved and that he still could not begin detailed Torch planning. He wearily informed Captain Butcher, "It would be quite impossible to give an account of—even in outline form—the numerous arguments and discussions that have taken place. . . . We have been living . . . under conditions of strain, uncertainty and tension that we can only hope will soon be terminated by a definite decision." Clark, more highstrung than the Torch Supreme Commander, was exasperated and apprehensive.

During this period of indecision [he noted in his diary] we have had at least half a dozen plans, but before we could even start laying a foundation for one we got another. Those who delay us keep reminding us that "Torch" must be carried out at the earliest possible moment. However,

125

we're still waiting for the mission directive. And there is an urgent need for time to plan, time to train, time to assemble for the assault. The longer we wait the less chance we have of security, and without security we can't get full success.

But the waiting was just about over. Informed of Roosevelt's decision that the landings would be confined to Casablanca and Oran and that only American troops would be initially involved, Churchill cabled back accepting the latter but maintaining that it would be a grievous mistake to exclude Algiers from the operation. Anxious now to reach accord and accepting that the British view was not without merit, Roosevelt gave in on that point. Algiers would be included by trimming the forces earmarked for Casablanca and Oran. What was more, British troops would participate in the Algiers landings, but only after the initial American assault.

At the president's instructions, the War Department drew up appropriate plans. As outlined to Churchill by the president, they were for 58,000 U.S. troops—the Western Task Force—to go ashore at Casablanca; 45,000 troops—the Center Task Force—at Oran; and 10,000 at Algiers, where they would be followed "within an hour" by an as yet unspecified number of British troops who, together with the Algiers-bound Americans, would constitute the Eastern Task Force. The Royal Navy would provide the warship escort and almost all of the shipping for the Mediterranean component of the operation. The U.S. Navy would be responsible for getting the Western Task Force to Morocco.

Churchill responded with enthusiasm. On September 5, a full six weeks after French North Africa had been targeted for the first major combined offensive operation by the western Allies, and only two months before the invasion was to be launched, agreement on basic operational plans was finally reached. "We agree to the military layout as you propose it," the prime minister cabled Roosevelt. "We have plenty of troops highly trained for landing. If convenient, they can wear your uniform. They will be proud to do so."

The involvement of British troops remained a delicate matter. Keenly aware of the feelings of the Vichy French officers from whom acquiescence or assistance was hoped, Colonel William Eddy, OSS station chief in North Africa, warned, "The highest military, diplomatic and political influences should be brought to bear to exclude British as well as Free French from landing on French territory in North Africa. If this proves impossible, there must at least be a promise by the highest American authority that the British troops included in the campaign are there only for the purpose of fighting the Germans and Italians, and are really in transit."

Barring the Free French from the operation was less of a problem. The Americans had already insisted that de Gaulle be kept in the dark about Torch. They believed he could contribute little and would only cause problems. They feared that if Free French forces were involved, it might lead to fighting between them and the Vichy French, a clash that would hoplessly complicate this already complicated undertaking.

De Gaulle had already concluded that the much discussed second front in Europe would not take place and accurately suspected that French North Africa would instead be the target of the first offensive of the Western Allies. He probably had received hints about Torch from sympathizers in British intelligence and the Foreign Office. He was bitter about being excluded from all planning and involvement. During the July visit by General Marshall and Admiral King to London, the normally haughty Free French leader had stooped to ask to meet with them to discuss war plans.

The Americans had felt obliged to receive him at their hotel. But they revealed nothing of substance to him and his dignity had not permitted him to pretend anything beyond stiff cordiality. He had offered Marshall and King an exaggerated assessment of the forces the Free French could contribute to Allied operations. But the session had been marked mostly by awkward exchanges and embarrassing silences and had been briskly concluded by the general when it had become apparent that the Americans were prepared to tell him nothing of significance. The only significant results of that meeting had been to confirm the opinion of the Americans that the man who was later to be the president of France was someone with whom they would rather not deal and to intensify his resentment of the United States.

Agreement on Torch landing sites having at last been reached, Eisenhower could proceed with stitching the operation together and appointing commanders for its constituent task forces. The

Casablanca-bound Western Task Force would remain under General Patton's command and would sail from Virginia. It would be transported and escorted by the U.S. Navy under the command of Rear Admiral Henry Kent Hewitt. Major General Lloyd R. Fredendall would command the Center Task Force making for Oran from Britain, transported and escorted by the Royal Navy under the command of Commodore Thomas Troubridge. The Eastern Task Force that was to go ashore near Algiers was to be under the overall command of Lieutenant General Anderson, whose British First Army was to spurt along the coast toward Tunisia to seize Bizerte and Tunis. The Task Force was to be transported and escorted by the Royal Navy under the command of Rear Admiral Sir H. M. Burrough and was to include American assault forces commanded by Major General Charles Ryder. These were to go ashore first, secure the beachhead, and then go on to capture the Algerian capital. Later in the planning stage, British troops were included in those assault forces.

Eisenhower's position as Commander in Chief, Allied Expeditionary Force, was unique. Never had an officer been given supreme authority over the armed forces of two nations, neither of which was subordinate to the other.

> I was determined from the first to do all in my power to make this a truly Allied force, with real unity of command and centralization of administrative responsibility. Alliances in the past have done no more than to name the common foe and "unity of command" had been a pious aspiration thinly disguising the national prejudices, ambitions and recriminations of high ranking officers, unwilling to subordinate themselves or their forces to a commander of different nationality or different service.

There were, of course, problems of communication at first. Language nuances caused some perplexity, as one British general soon discovered.

> I received a weighty document from General Eisenhower's Headquarters which I read and re-read and studied until it dawned on me that I did not understand one single word of it. Here was a vast assemblage of words each of which was undoubtedly English, but which in conjunction conveyed to me not one single thing, and I was eventually forced to

call for skilled interpretation to have the order put out of the American military language into the British military language.

Eisenhower was sensitive to the fact that he and the Americans under him were guests in Britain. He could issue military orders but could not tell the British how to comport themselves personally. However, he did issue strict instructions that all Americans under his command who failed to extend proper respect to and consideration for their British hosts should be disciplined at once. Soon after his arrival in Britain, he was informed that an American officer at Allied Forces Headquarters had called someone a British son of a bitch. He ordered that the officer be reduced in rank and shipped home despite the protest of the Englishman involved that no real insult had been intended and that the offending words could be interpreted as a term of endearment.

Eisenhower was anxious that there should be as little interference as possible on military details of the operation from on high—from either the War Department in Washington or the War Office in London. What was more, he confined himself and his headquarters staff to the fundamentals of Torch planning, including the assignment of the specific Task Force missions. Detailed operational planning was to be left to the commanders of the three Task Forces and their staffs.

In addition to securing the port of Casablanca and nearby airfields as quickly as possible, the Western Task Force was to prepare to move against and neutralize any danger to the overall operation from Spanish Morocco, if that proved necessary. Despite reports now coming in from the American and British embassies in Madrid and the intelligence services of both nations that Spain was unlikely to risk getting involved, the possibility that it might could not be ignored.

However, the Western Task Force's immediate and primary concern was to overcome possible resistance from the estimated 60,000 French and colonial troops in French Morocco, as well as from the French Navy and aircraft. The construction of France's mighty battleship *Jean Bart,* in Casablanca harbor, was still to be completed but its four 15-inch guns posed a threat to the invaders, as did French submarines based there. And intelligence reports

129

said that French military aircraft in Morocco included eighty-one bombers and seventy-four fighters.

During the early planning stage, Rabat on the coast to the south, the capital of French Morocco, was considered an easier and just as useful prize for the invaders as Casablanca. It was far less well defended and resistance there, if it materialized, was likely to be overcome with less difficulty. But it was also the seat of the Sultan of Morocco, official ruler of the French-dominated protectorate and a Muslim spiritual leader. Western Task Force commander Patton was advised that if damage was done to the city during the invasion, problems might arise for the Allies from the Muslim population.

That was less of a concern for the Center Task Force. But it was also to prepare for the possibility of strong French resistance when it proceeded with its mission of capturing Oran on the Mediteranean and securing the port and the region around it. French warships were usually moored in Oran harbor and shore batteries were positioned in the heights above it. The Oran Division of the French Army consisted of some 17,000 troops. If resistance was not quickly crushed, other troops could be rushed in to reinforce them. Some one hundred French combat aircraft were normally based at the airfield at Tafaraoui fifteen miles southeast of Oran. That airfield was a key installation and was to be quickly secured both to prevent air attacks on the invaders and for use by Allied aircraft in consolidating invasion gains.

The landings at Algiers might also run into trouble. Coastal batteries there would present a threat to the Eastern Task Force invaders. So would French combat aircraft based at Maison Blanche airfield near the Algerian capital, estimated at thirty-nine bombers and fifty-two fighters. It was also possible that German bombers might be dispatched from bases in Sicily and Sardinia to attack the Eastern Task Force's ships and troops. The threat on land at Algiers was from 35,000 French and colonial troops, equipped with tanks and motorized artillery, who might put up a stiff fight.

The Western and Center Task Forces were to share the job of establishing and maintaining communications between Oran and Casablanca. Only a single-gauge railway through the Rif Mountains linked the two cities. But it was believed that control of that rickety line could prove crucial for supplying the troops landing on the Mediterranean shore if the enemy was able to slam shut the Strait of Gibraltar.

Eisenhower was pleased to have Admiral Sir Andrew Cunningham, whom he admired and with whom he got along well, appointed to serve under him as naval commander for the operation. But he was not able to have his way when it came to naming a commander for Torch air operations. In accordance with his belief in unity of command, he preferred a single air commander. But because of the complexities of planned post-invasion operations and pressure from above, he had to agree to two—Brigadier General James H. Doolittle, who was already famous for having led the first American air raid on Tokyo earlier in the year, and Air Marshal Sir William Welsh.

Welsh would direct Torch's Eastern Air Command, which would provide cover for the ground operations when the campaign extended into Tunisia. Doolittle would head Torch's Western Air Command. It was much larger than the Eastern Air Command and was supposed to deal with problems that might arise if Torch was threatened by the Spaniards or the Germans through Spain or Spanish Morocco.

Contrary to conventional wisdom in dealing with forces that might resist an invasion, neither air command was to engage in preliminary softening-up raids on the landing sites. It was thought such raids would destroy the hope that the invasion would meet limited resistance at worst from the French. Preliminary air attacks might also eliminate the possibility that French North Africa would quickly come over to the Allied side in the war. Carrier-based aircraft would provide air cover if necessary after daybreak on D-Day. But land-based planes were to be quickly flown in from Gibraltar to air bases expected to be captured near Algiers, Oran, and Casablanca and to operate from them.

The Algiers and Oran Task Forces that were to set out from Britain were British-American combined operations. But the all-American Casablanca-bound Western Task Force being pieced together in the United States had to overcome greater command problems in its formative stage. That was largely because of the irascibility of Task Force commander Patton, a pugnacious hothead, and because Eisenhower's moderating influence was three thousand miles away in London. Soon after taking on the job,

Patton grew openly and abusively at odds with navy personnel who would be responsible for transporting his troops to the beaches of Morocco. He clashed so bitterly with them that the navy urged that the general be replaced by someone with whom it would be easier to cooperate. But Eisenhower was convinced that Patton was a uniquely hard-driving, high-achieving troop commander, which indeed he was. He stood by him, convinced Marshall to do the same, and the personalities row blew over in due course.

The fact that Patton's headquarters and that of Admiral Hewitt, who was commanding the naval elements of the Casablanca Task Force, were geographically some distance apart limited the friction between them. But it added to communications problems between the two services. Patton established his headquarters at the War Department's Old Munitions Building on Constitution Avenue in Washington, though Norfolk, Virginia, where Hewitt was based, was the installation where most of the Task Force would be organized and from which most of it would set sail. Though not eager to have much to do personally with Patton, Hewitt regretted that their headquarters personnel were stationed so far apart.

> We tried to convince [Patton] that daily personal contact between opposite numbers of the staff and the commanders was very important, but we couldn't convince him of it. Consequently, planning [staff members] had to do a lot of travelling between Washington and Ocean View [adjoining Norfolk]. They didn't get down there until the last week or so before the departure.

The complexities of preparing the stateside end of the operation were thereby compounded. Without the coordinating services of a Combined Operations staff such as the British had established, those complexities grew ever more troublesome. The army and navy had different administrative structures, communications systems, and supply procedures. They also had fundamentally different procedures for amphibious operations.

Among other things, their textbooks prescribed different ways for disembarking and unloading under combat conditions. Trusting only itself, the army wanted to get as much equipment and supplies ashore as possible as quickly as possible during an operation, a lot of it on the backs of the troops or along with them. The navy wanted the men disembarked as quickly as possible, and therefore as lightly equipped as possible, with the supplies and equipment to follow. Their differences reinforced the conviction of each that the other was incapable of understanding the intricacies of amphibious operations. An army officer was confirmed in his doubts about the navy's lack of comprehension of what was involved after observing one of the first combined training exercises in Chesapeake Bay.

I am of the opinion that the average Naval officer has no conception of amphibious warfare, his idea being to lay offshore, slap a brigade of Marines on the beach, and impatiently await their return aboard ship.

The navy was, in turn, appalled at having to nursemaid a horde of troops who, along with their officers, did not seem to know what they were doing, who untidily cluttered up transport vessels during rehearsals, who clambered clumsily down cargo nets, and as often as not, floundered about in the water before scrambling finally ashore. Being assigned to amphibious Torch rehearsals came quickly to be seen by navy personnel as a form of punishment. Inevitably, the navy as well as the army contended that it should command amphibious training exercises, with the other service merely providing staff assistance.

An early joint training exercise proved a total shambles with virtually no cooperation between the army and navy personnel involved and little understanding by each of what the other was up to. A navy officer reported afterward that "actual friction . . . was avoided only by the consummate tact of the Battalion Commander."

Nevertheless, training schedules had to be followed. Arrangements had to be made for pre-embarkation amphibious rehearsals. Specialist personnel in training, communications, administration, and intelligence had to be recruited from units scattered across the country and suitably assigned. The Marine Corps, the branch of service most trained and equipped for amphibious landing, was almost totally committed in the South Pacific and its specialists could not be extracted at short notice for Torch purposes. Admiral Hewitt was greatly distressed when the 1st Marine Division was removed from training for the operation. It had established a harmonious working relationship with navy personnel but was shipped to the Pacific to participate in the assault on Guadalcanal and was replaced in Torch by less well trained army infantrymen.

Troops of the 3rd Infantry Division who would take part in the Morocco landings had some amphibious training on the West Coast before being shipped east to be dispatched across the Atlantic. Men of the 1st Infantry Division did some amphibious landing practice on the East Coast. "That gave them some of the rudiments," Admiral Hewitt conceded, "but it was unfortunate in some respects because they knew just enough to think they knew it all, and they didn't." Many of the troops had their brief exposure to amphibious training in the comparatively smooth waters of Chesapeake Bay. Training on nearby open-sea beaches was ruled out because of enemy submarines operating off the coast and the limited availability of suitable escort vessels.

Bases were set up near Norfolk for training the officers and men, both army and navy, who would command and operate landing craft, direct landing traffic, serve in beach-command parties, constitute shore fire-control units, and maintain a steady flow of the appropriate supplies from the ships to the troops ashore. They started from scratch. U.S. forces had never engaged in anything like such an operation before.

Additional snags arose when some of the operation's training officers, though inexperienced themselves, were reassigned elsewhere. They were sent to units being newly formed as the huge U.S. Army that would be needed to fight the war gradually took shape and the process of whipping its great number of recruits into fighting trim was accelerated. Some of the troops who would land on the beaches of Morocco were to have virtually no training at all. Four hundred and fifty newly conscripted men would join the 47th Infantry Regiment only two days before it left for embarkation at Virginia and the trip across the Atlantic to Morocco where they would hit the beaches immediately upon arrival.

The condition of transport and cargo ships to be used by the Casablanca Task Force was also a worry. More than half were not in satisfactory operating shape when assigned to the mission. Some of them were still being fitted out at shipyards. There was no certainty that they would be ready when needed. Many were still making their way back from duty in the Pacific. The civilian crew of a Honduran merchant freighter jumped ship when the men learned that their vessel was assigned the job of transporting a cargo of bombs and gasoline for Torch aircraft. They had to be replaced by volunteers from the naval stockade at Norfolk.

The task of determining the supply, equipment, and troop storage capacity of each ship in the Task Force fell to the transport quartermaster assigned to each vessel. That officer was also to supervise the loading when the time came. Few of the officers available—also mostly newly recruited—were familiar either with ships or with the wide range of military equipment that would have to be loaded. There could be no practice sessions for them; neither the ships nor the equipment were yet available for dry runs. It would have to be on-the-job training, which was worrying in view of how important it was for equipment to be properly loaded so that it could be brought ashore for the troops in the right order as soon as possible.

The only air cover available at first for the Casablanca landings would be from the USS *Ranger,* the only large aircraft carrier in the U.S. Atlantic fleet, and from four escort carriers recently converted from tankers. But the navy pilots were so inexperienced that fear of accidents and of damage that might be done to the *Ranger,* and the effect that might have on the operation, was to rule out practice flights for them while crossing the Atlantic to Morocco. Of the pilots aboard the escort carrier *Santee,* only five were experienced. Twenty-one of the *Santee*'s thirty-one planes would be lost during the landing operations in Morocco. Of them, only one would fall "possibly" to enemy action.

Torch preparations in Britain for the Algiers and Oran Task Forces also faced serious problems. Most of those troops would be American, and training for them had to be suspended during their journey across the Atlantic to Britain. It was then further interrupted by procedures for settling them in at their new bases there, by waiting for their equipment to arrive from the United States, and by the process of transporting them to Scottish amphibious landing practice areas. For some, final training did not begin until a mere ten days before they boarded the transports that were to carry them from Britain more than two thousand miles into combat.

Amphibious landing practice was undertaken near Inveraray and elsewhere on the west coast of Scotland where strong southwesterly winds sometimes forced suspension of practice exercises.

Those sites bore little resemblance to the Mediterranean beaches the troops were to storm. The waters off some of the training beaches were studded with rocks, which meant the landing craft had to approach slowly and with great caution, not quite what was likely to be an option on D-Day when, possibly targeted by shore artillery, they would have to scoot in to unload quickly and scoot out again. As a consequence, those landing-craft crews had just as little prior understanding of the kind of conditions they could expect in action as those training in the United States.

To make matters worse, landing craft for the operation arrived in England with few spare parts. Some had to be cannibalized to replace parts that wore out or proved defective during training. For some landing-craft crews, the training was worse than useless because they were put through their paces in craft different from the ones they were to use in action. As a consequence, when the landings actually began, the ramps of some of the landing craft were lowered too soon and they sank offshore despite more favorable weather and water conditions.

Admiral Cunningham, Torch's British naval commander, was keenly aware of the shortcomings in training.

> It was only possible [he later reported] to give very brief training to officers and men from general service who were required to make up the numbers required for the landing craft crews and beach parties. Some of the latter landed on the North African coast without ever having fired even one practice round from their rifles or revolvers.

British troops to take part in the landings benefited from more protracted amphibious training than the Americans and from not having it interrupted by a journey across the Atlantic. In addition, they had the advantage of greater experience as a result of the participation of some of their officers and men in the Dieppe attack and in lesser raids on the French coast. But they too suffered from having to confine their practice operations to bleak Scottish shores nothing like those on the Mediterranean coast and from the shortage of landing craft and experienced crews with which to train. A British naval officer maintained that some of the British crews sent to North Africa for the operation "had in fact never seen a landing craft until they embarked in their ships for the expedition."

* * *

From the moment he had been appointed Torch Supreme Commander, Eisenhower realized he could not await full agreement on details between Washington and London to begin gathering the resources he would need for the operation. There was little enough time to prepare as it was. Equipment and supplies that might have been reserved for Torch had been and still were being diverted to the Pacific, where the demand was insatiable. Early on, Eisenhower was "torn between desire to go ahead and do the job with the tools available and the necessity of stating his belief that the assignment was ultra-risky without the ships and planes and other equipment which they [the Combined Chiefs of Staff] seem to expect him to have but which actually have not been made available."

Reluctant to be seen as cravenly preparing an excuse for the failure of Torch, but recognizing the critical importance of being adequately supplied, Eisenhower had quickly embarked on a campaign to accumulate all sorts of supplies and equipment that might be needed by his troops. Inevitably, howls of dismay rose from the U.S. Army's Service of Supply (SOS) organization. SOS officers grew even more anguished when a stream of subsequent requisitions, based on belated understandings of requirements, came in. Those updates invalidated detailed calculations they had made in the hope of anticipating the operation's needs on the basis of the initial requests.

In addition to standard ordnance, a wide range of special items was requested, such as a bulletproof seven-passenger car "of normal appearance" for Eisenhower's use, mechanical smoke generators for use in combat, 25 locomotives and 288 railway cars, two 1,000-bed hospitals, one 500-bed hospital, three 250-bed hospitals, insect repellent for the troops, mosquito head nets, fumigation substances, dust respirators, and goggles with supplementary colored lenses.

As was traditional in the army, some of the demands were irresponsible, considering the needs of the forces fighting in the Pacific. General Patton's staff in Washington issued requisitions before they had made a study of what might be needed and with little regard to port or ship capacities. It was a case of its being better to have too much than too little and of letting others worry about difficulties that might arise elsewhere as a result. So many requisition changes were subsequently made by Patton's team that SOS soon insisted that its further requests be accompanied by lists of previously requisitioned items that would not be needed after all.

Nevertheless, such great quantities of standard and specialized equipment were delivered for loading in Virginia that much of it would have to be left behind when the troops finally embarked for Morocco.* The problem of excessive requisitioning was compounded by last-minute equipment substitutions, as when quarter-ton trucks were replaced by amphibious vehicles, each of which required four additional feet of cargo space for which no account had been taken in loading calculations.

Much of the requisitioned equipment arrived later than scheduled on the docks and much could be tracked down only after exhaustive search of the vast amount of material piling up in the port. As a result of the get-what-you-can approach and the haste with which the operation was patched together, when the ships finally set off for Morocco from Virginia, half the TBA (Table of Basic Allowance) supplies and much special equipment had to be left behind.

Gathering essential equipment and supplies could not be expected to be easy or trouble-free for an undertaking as massive as Torch. Misjudgment was inevitable and rampant. The supply situation was most out of control at the British end, where a lot of the material sent from the United States was found simply to have gone astray. On September 8, Eisenhower cabled SOS that a prodigious assortment of supplies and maintenance items for his forces, things big and small, could not be found and would have to be replaced. German U-boats had sunk many of the cargo vessels as they made their way to Britain. But various consignments, listed as being on vessels that survived the crossing, also turned out not to be there.

General Clark complained that a cargo of equipment for the 1st Division, in training in Britain to go ashore near Oran, started out three times from New York and each time was lost or mysteriously diverted. Included were spare parts for weapons and vehicles of various descriptions needed both for training and for combat. As

*Patton told Air Force General James Doolittle he was being given everything he asked for. Doolittle told him, "They always give the condemned man what he wants to eat for his last meal."

time passed with no sign of the required equipment arriving, Clark informed Washington that unless it showed up within two weeks, "the assault teams will have to attack with insufficient arms and ammunition. Something must be done, and done fast, or those men will be going in virtually with their bare hands."

Faulty communications between London and Washington were partly responsible. Without informing the Americans, and with the Americans failing to make suitable inquiries, the British authorities arranged to split up arriving convoys and direct them into different ports according to port capacity. The equipment was unloaded and then often either sat in those ports or was shipped to warehouses to await retrieval by officers who had no idea it had arrived.

That explanation did not satisfy Brigadier General LeRoy Lutes, assistant chief of staff for Service of Supply operations. Lutes had grown increasingly riled by the wastage and what seemed to him the cavalier attitude of Torch commanders. While appreciating that many of the U.S. troops in Britain were busily training for the invasion, he wanted to know why Eisenhower could not "hire labor, or utilize his other troops to sort out these supplies. . . ." U.S. quartermaster officers, newly arrived in Britain, were, however, too inexperienced to handle such an assignment with any hope of success. Besides, much of the loss was due to pilferage at British docks and warehouses, estimated at up to 20 percent of the supplies arriving from the United States. Under the circumstances, little could be done to deal with that problem.

☆ 10 ☆

SPIES, LIES, AND
CONSPIRACIES

*Eisenhower listened with a kind of horrified
intentness to my description of the possible
complications.*

—ROBERT MURPHY

The summer of 1942 had been a busy time for the State Department's Robert Murphy and the various other Allied agents operating in North Africa. They had been building intelligence networks and gathering information. The Americans had been, and still were, seeking a handle on an insurrection that was to coincide with the invasion. Coup plans had been developing independently and they were ambitious. The French conspirators intended to act decisively to assist the invaders and thereby quickly terminate Vichy rule in North Africa so that a new French government could be formed there.

When the moment came, they planned to destroy or put out of action coastal batteries and take command of airfields. Radio stations and telephone and telegraph exchanges were to be seized. Teams were to be provided to guide the invading troops from the beaches to the cities they were to capture so that officers or officials disinclined to throw in their lot with the Allies would quickly be shown the futility of resistance. Members of the Axis Armistice Commission were to be taken into custody. Much detail on the beaches and harbors that were to be stormed was gathered for delivery to Eisenhower's Norfolk House headquarters in London's St. James's Square.

At the end of August, as operational plans for the invasion were being finalized, Murphy was summoned back to Washington. Though Roosevelt was impressed by what he had to report, Murphy was not greatly pleased by some of the attitudes he encountered there. The War Department was operationally fully committed to making Torch a success but Secretary Stimson and General Marshall made no secret that they still had "misgivings" about the African venture. Furthermore, Murphy's report that significant French assistance would rally to the Allied cause on D-Day was received skeptically. The military planners in Washington seemed to believe that Murphy's efforts merely introduced an additional complication to an already complex endeavor.

His suggestion that he inform his resistance contacts of Torch details, including the date of the landings, was received with horror despite his protests that the conspirators had to know this in order to muster effective support ashore at the proper moment. He was told that it was likely that whatever French assistance might or might not be forthcoming, it had to be assumed that the success of the operation would depend on surprise and military superiority. It seemed to Murphy that the only one in Washington deeply interested in how Frenchmen in North Africa could be rallied to the Allied cause was the president. The projected coup appealed to Roosevelt's sense of adventure. He was of course also much attracted by the possibility that assistance by the insurgents might help produce a relatively bloodless, morale-boosting victory for American troops.

From Washington, Murphy went on to London to advise Eisenhower on the possibilities. Fearing the omnipresence of enemy agents, he traveled incognito, sporting a fake name and a U.S. Army lieutenant colonel's uniform—lieutenant colonels existing at the time in great profusion and being commonly held to be indistinguishable one from another. Despite these precautions, after Murphy's plane landed at Prestwick in Scotland on September 16, he was greeted at the airfield by a State Department colleague who was also in transit and who loudly cried, "Why, Bob! What are you doing here?" The man was quickly hushed up and bundled aside but the incident aroused much concern because no unauthorized person was supposed to know that this North Africa–based senior diplomat was in England at a time when some sort of major Allied operation was in the works.

Upon arriving in London, Murphy proceeded to Telegraph Cottage, Eisenhower's secluded retreat near Richmond Park on the southwest fringe of the British capital. There he briefed the Torch commander on the complexities of the French conspiracy brewing in Algeria and Morocco. He described the sometimes bitter political rivalries between the various factions involved. He assessed the likelihood of gaining the collaboration of individuals well enough placed to influence the course of events and the improbability of winning the support of others. He described the attitudes of the Arab and Berber majority populations who were likely to remain largely aloof from the proceedings but who had to be treated cautiously. According to Eisenhower's aide, Captain Butcher, Murphy "talked more like an American businessman canvassing the ins and outs of a perspective merger than either a diplomat or a soldier."

> Murphy impressed all of us as an honest reporter who delivered his story objectively. If all that he anticipates in the way of French cooperation comes to pass, many of our worries will have been needless. However, he couldn't answer the two big questions: 1. Would the Spaniards fight, especially in Spanish Morocco, and would they attempt to close the Strait of Gibraltar or attack Gib airdrome and harbor? 2. What would happen in France itself? . . . [But] on the whole, [he] was confident that he would be able to do a great deal to help the landing forces.

That was only partially reassuring. It was all too glib for Eisenhower, who was not always able to suppress his fears about the operation's prospects. His immediate reaction to Murphy's polished presentation was dismay at the can of worms that was being opened on his behalf.

> The General [Murphy later wrote] disliked almost everything about the expedition: its diversion from the central campaign in Europe; its obvious risks in a vast, untried territory; its dependence on local forces who were doubtful at best and perhaps treacherous; its bewildering complexities involving deadly quarrels among French factions, and Spanish, Italian, Arab, Berber, German and Russian politics. Eisenhower listened with a kind of horrified intentness to my description of the possible complications. Perhaps some of the things I said were as incomprehensible to him as military mappings and logistics would have

been to me. The General seemed to sense that this first campaign would present him with problems running the entire geopolitical gamut—as it certainly did.

Having alarmed Eisenhower with his rundown on the various elements and influences at play in North Africa, Murphy then tried to persuade him that things appeared to be more convoluted than they actually were. He assured him that arrangements could be made so that French military resistance to the landings would be minimal. He was so confident that, as in Washington, he suggested that he offer his main contacts in North Africa an inkling of when the landings would take place so that they could prepare to render the valuable assistance he expected of them. Eisenhower flatly rejected the idea. His fear that word would reach the Germans far outweighed the limited confidence he had that Murphy had the situation under control. It was decided that Murphy would tell French contacts he considered reliable that a half million U.S. troops would take part in the invasion, a gross exaggeration, and that it was scheduled for early 1943 rather than in less than two months. They could be more accurately informed of the timing later.

Eisenhower and his staff harbored doubts about whether a pre-arranged coup could succeed and contribute to the success of Operation Torch. They were also uneasy about the unorthodox activities of William Donovan's OSS agents. A proposal by Colonel Eddy, the OSS station chief for the region, that members of the German Armistice Commission in North Africa be assassinated on D-Day was rejected.

During and after the war, dramatic tales were told about the activities of Nazi spies. Enemy agents were believed to have been fielded in great numbers in Britain and the United States to pick up every possible bit of information about military planning and deployment for transmission back to Berlin. Those stories were great exaggerations. Postwar studies revealed that the German intelligence services had very limited success in their operations in the two countries. Counterspy activities proved far more effective than was imagined at the time.

However, it was justifiably assumed that the Germans would know that something was afoot once Torch preparations and train-

143

ing went into high gear and that they would try to determine what that something was. Accordingly, Allied intelligence services undertook a variety of campaigns to mislead the German High Command as to what was about to happen.

Reports were fabricated and circulated in Washington about a major British-American operation planned for the Middle East. At the War Department, fictitious plans were drawn up for an invasion of the Dodecanese Islands in the Aegean Sea. When an officer assigned to that operation came to consult with General Patton about it, Patton, who knew it was only part of the deception campaign, reviewed the planning with him with great seriousness. "I hated to do it," he confided to his diary.

Some hoaxes were even more elaborate. The U.S. minister in Haiti was instructed to approach the Haitian president for permission to undertake amphibious training exercises on his country's beaches. Enemy agents were expected to learn of that request and conclude the troops were preparing for warfare in a tropical region (Dakar?) rather than on the less steamy shores of North Africa. In a move thought to guarantee immediate leakage, it was stressed to the Haitians that absolute secrecy about the exercises was essential.

Once the Haitians gave permission for the fictitious exercises, a team of American experts—none of whom were told the exercises would never actually take place—flew to Haiti to choose suitable training beaches. In case word still had not been leaked to the enemy, the Haitian government was invited to send a representative to Washington to join in exercise planning and to confer on how Haitian forces might participate. A diligent State Department official who had not been informed that the operation was a scam was horrified when he learned about the invitation. He warned that the enemy might easily learn about the exercises and draw conclusions from them. He was instructed to mind his own business.

It is not known whether word of that mock exercise ever reached the Germans, but two days after the North Africa landings took place, the American inspection team, still in the dark, reported that the Haitian beaches they had examined were unsuitable for training.

Torch-related deception schemes were much more elaborate in Britain where it was assumed that German agents were far more active and where, because of the comparative smallness of the country, military preparations were much more difficult to conceal from prying eyes. With troops engaged in amphibious combat training, equipment being accumulated for their use, and vessels being gathered to carry them and their equipment to their target destinations, there could be no hope of preventing the enemy from learning that a major operation was being prepared. Instead, the British intended to take advantage of the presumed omnipresence of German agents.

> The enemy Intelligence receives, through a variety of channels, scraps of information regarding our strength, dispositions, organization and activities, from which it finally draws deductions regarding our intentions. It follows that if we want the enemy's General Staff (Intelligence) to draw false conclusions we must feed it with scraps of false information which, when built up, will produce the required picture.

The task of organizing this effort fell to the Joint Planning Staff's London Controlling Section, which had been created to deceive the enemy about Allied plans and intentions. The section was commanded by Colonel John Bevan, a World War I officer who had been a stockbroker until drawn back into uniform. Bevan decided on a double-faceted approach to Torch deception. Misleading reports and rumors would be disseminated by word of mouth. At the same time, false physical evidence would be planted about the objectives of the operation, from which enemy agents and enemy aerial surveillance were intended to draw mistaken conclusions.

For word-of-mouth deception, rumors were circulated in Lisbon, Madrid, Geneva, Buenos Aires, and other neutral capitals where German intelligence was known to be active that the Allies were planning landings in northern France or Norway; alternatively, that reinforcements were being readied for shipment to the Middle East. British counterintelligence had captured and turned a number of enemy spies and employed them as well to further this misinformation campaign.

The British could allot few resources to physical acts of deception, but a determined effort was made nevertheless. To make the Germans suspect that an attack on France was imminent, fake coverings were constructed at ports in southeastern England closest to France, as if concealing landing craft that would be employed in a cross-Channel invasion. Coastal shipping was staggered in such a way as to give the impression that an invasion fleet was being assembled. Aerial reconnaissance over northern France, across the Channel, was conspicuously stepped up. Quantities of English-French dictionaries and French currency were conspicuously acquired. A call was issued from London for marine pilots who knew the northern French coast. It was recognized that the Germans might suspect that such openly revealed emphasis pointed to deliberate deception. But they would have to weigh it against evidence of other Allied plans for which campaigns of deception had also been launched by the British, against Norway for example.

A call was issued for Norwegian speakers and specialists in mountain warfare. A course in mountain warfare for junior officers was begun and models of Norwegian targets were constructed. Norwegian officers and troops who had taken refuge in Britain when the Nazis had overrun their country were gathered together in Scotland, from which an assault on the Norwegian coast might be launched. Inquiries were made about the availability of large quantities of arctic clothing and boots, some of which were distributed to troops who, in addition, were subjected to lectures on the dangers of frostbite and how to survive subfreezing temperatures.

In October, when it was obvious to all that Allied landings in northern Europe had to be ruled out by adverse weather conditions, efforts were concentrated on deluding the enemy into believing the accelerating pace of Torch preparations in Britain was for an operation in the Middle East or the tropics. Word was put about that troops would be inoculated against tropical diseases on board ship en route to their destinations. Men were warned against buying unwashed fruit at ports of call on their way around the Cape of Good Hope toward Port Said. The troops also had to endure lectures about the dangers of malaria-carrying mosquitoes and other tropical hazards.

As stores of supplies and equipment, including unconcealable aircraft, began to be accumulated at Gibraltar for use in Torch, the emphasis shifted once more. Suggestions were spread in rumor mills around Europe, the Middle East, and elsewhere that a major relief of Malta, the primary British base in the Mediterranean, a mere fifty miles from Sicily, was being readied and that Gibraltar was a staging post for it. The last convoy to the beleaguered island colony had not been able to get through a German aerial blockade. The supply situation there had grown desperate; ammunition and even food were running out. No effort was being made to conceal the fact that Malta might fall to the Germans unless help soon came. The dispatch of another large convoy to rescue it was entirely credible; so were the planted rumors attributing the Gibraltar buildup to preparations for that rescue attempt rather than to an impending operation against French North Africa.

In the weeks before D-Day, a number of potentially dangerous security breaches caused much concern. Early in the planning stage for the operation, General Truscott, who had been attached to Mountbatten's Combined Operations Headquarters, was almost court-martialed because of security negligence. He had made notes during a planning session one day and thought that he had locked them up in his desk that night, along with other classified papers. The next morning, some of those notes were found lying about on the ground outside the building. No one knew how they got there and it appeared that no damage had been done, but Truscott was sharply rebuked and might well have been sent home had Eisenhower not thought so highly of him.

There could not be total security. Accidents happened, as when a page of the war diary Eisenhower had instructed his aide to keep went missing. The lost page made reference to instructions to the Torch commander from the Combined Chiefs of Staff "to clean up the North African coast." Its loss was discovered while diary pages were being microfilmed. In view of the tight security in which the diary was kept and with which its pages were escorted to and from the film laboratory, the loss was inexplicable and therefore even more worrying. The missing page was never found.

In October, Ivan Maisky, the Soviet ambassador to Britain, aroused much worry when he indiscreetly dropped hints about Torch's objective to reporters in London. It led to suggestions that the Russians, still pressing for a second front in Europe, were not overly anxious for Torch to succeed. Even greater concern was triggered when a British flying boat crashed off the Spanish coast and the body of a British officer carrying a letter with some of the details of the invasion plans was washed ashore near Cádiz. The sealed letter was retrieved along with the body and handed over to the British. But there was no certainty that it had not been opened by the Spanish and its contents revealed to the Germans.

One Englishwoman went to great lengths to keep from unwittingly revealing secret Torch information to which she had fallen privy. Two days before D-Day, Colonel Ian Jacob, deputy military secretary to the War Cabinet, invited Eisenhower's chief of staff, General Walter Bedell Smith, to meet his parents. Delighted to be warmly received by a British family at their home and aware that Jacob's father was a retired field marshal in the British army, Smith indiscreetly told them about Torch, details of which had been kept from them by their well-informed, security-conscious son. Jacob's mother was so worried at having been entrusted with such highly classified information that she remained in bed all of the next day, fearing that if she went out she might inadvertently reveal what she knew.

Anxiety about security leaks persisted till the last moment. Through Ultra, the system through which the British intercepted and deciphered German military coded messages, British intelligence was able to learn much of what the enemy knew and did not know. It knew that the Germans had received reports that the return of transport and cargo vessels that had arrived in Britain from the United States had been suspended from mid-September on, which indicated that high-priority alternative use for them was impending. As the date for loading the troop transports approached, it was learned that the enemy knew that leave had been canceled for many troops in Britain, both American and British. But though not yet fully trusted, Ultra intercepts indicated that the Germans were unaware of the objective and purpose of the Allied operation that was so evidently imminent.

Whether the disinformation campaigns served the purpose for which they were intended would later be a matter of debate. It may have been that the rumors and red herrings were not as effective as secrecy in keeping the enemy from knowing what was truly happening, despite the smattering of security mishaps. According to Sir John Masterman, who was a central figure in Britain's intensive counterespionage campaign, "The real triumph of Torch from our angle was *not* that the cover plans were successfully planted on the Germans but that the real plan was not disclosed or guessed. In other words, it was a triumph of security."

* * *

To a team of British officers sent to the United States to observe Torch preparations there, secrecy appeared to be carried to such great lengths that it hampered operational planning and preparations. They reported back to London, "The lack of coordination between departments of the respective staffs [engaged in Torch planning] is almost as marked as the lack of inter-service coordination."

> The wisecrack "Nobody tells me anything—I only work around here" is constantly heard and unfortunately extremely true. There appears to be a tradition of secrecy whereby each officer likes to withhold from his neighbour in the same department, let alone the next door department, exactly what he is doing. . . . Major decisions are disseminated throughout the staff in a most haphazard way, and departments are often left working out problems which are long out of date.

However, the British officers generously concluded their report by observing, "In spite of all difficulties, this operation [is being] mounted in a way which would certainly have not been possible in England after we had been at war for less than a year." For all the confusion and haste, the various elements of Torch were falling into place.

Departure date for the troops of the Western Task Force, who would sail directly from Hampton Roads, Virginia, to Morocco, was set for October 23. The men—from the 3rd and 9th Infantry Divisions and elements of the 2nd Armored Division—had been training for the operation at their respective bases. As embarkation date approached, some had still to be supplied with all of their necessary equipment. Nevertheless, they converged on Chesapeake Bay in mid-September for invasion rehearsals, going ashore on Solomons Island in the bay from the ships that were to carry them into battle. Some of those vessels had already been partially loaded.

The rehearsals proved largely haphazard. The surf was calm in the sheltered waters of the bay, severely limiting the value of the practice runs for men who would be struggling ashore through what was certain to be rougher water on the Atlantic coast of Morocco. Underwater obstructions that could have damaged the propellers of the landing craft confined practice to a small beach area. But even there, vessels could not move in close enough for vehicles to be landed, though they would have to be put ashore for use by the troops on the beaches of Morocco.

Practice was held in lowering landing craft from ships and handling them. Some navy officers were less easy to convince of the need to risk their limited supply of landing craft in night exercises. It seemed to General Truscott, who had managed to turn his back on desk duty in London to take an operational command with the Western Task Force, that those officers simply did not understand the importance of rehearsals for the men who were scheduled to storm ashore in North Africa before dawn one morning in a few weeks' time. He complained to General Patton about it. But Patton had difficulty enough controlling his fiery temper when up against the snags and hitches he had encountered. Having come to terms with the requirement that he get along amicably with Admiral Hewitt, he was unsympathetic:

> Dammit, Lucian, I've already had enough trouble getting the Navy to agree to undertake this operation. All I want is to get them to sea to take us to Africa. Don't you do a damn thing that will upset them in any way.

Nevertheless, Truscott took his grievance to Hewitt, who fully appreciated the need for the nighttime rehearsals. The admiral sent word down the line that the navy was to cooperate fully. But more than cooperation was needed. In one night-training exercise, only a single landing craft reached the shore at the designated spot. The others "were scattered up and down Maryland's coast and it took until noon the next day to get the erring lambs back to the fold." General Ernest Harmon, commander of the 2nd Armored Division, wondered, "If they can't find an objective in peaceful Chesapeake Bay, with a lighthouse beacon for help, how are they going to find an objective on a foreign shore and under conditions of war?"

It was apparent as time ran out that the troops needed a lot more practice disembarking from the transports. They were prone to accidents while scrambling down cargo nets with heavy packs on their backs into waiting landing craft. They grew cautious in their descents and the disembarkation process seemed to take forever. They also needed more practice in what to do after being deposited on a beach, if their performance was to be anywhere near adequate to meet any resistance that might materialize once they were there. Despite crash programs, naval crews also remained appallingly undertrained in everything from naval gunfire through mine disposal to landing-craft procedures. The experienced men were off in the Pacific fighting the war against the Japanese and Admiral King jealously guarded their continuing presence there. Few adequately trained personnel were available to instruct the ones assigned to Torch, but instruction had to be given. One officer later complained, "Having to use the incompetent to train the ignorant was not a method calculated to produce the best condition of readiness."

Final rehearsals proved farcical at times. During one supposedly secret exercise, when the men stormed ashore on an island in Chesapeake Bay, they found a refrigerated ice-cream wagon waiting for them and were distracted from their training mission by the selection of cones and ice-cream Popsicles it had to offer.

A zealot on training, Patton was dismayed at how unready his men were to seize control of a beach that might be strongly defended. But he assured Roosevelt, and Marshall as well, that he would "leave the beaches either a conqueror or a corpse." To Admiral Hewitt, he said, "Never in history has the Navy landed an Army at the planned time and place. If you land us anywhere within fifty miles of Fedhala [near Casablanca] and within one week of D-Day, I'll go ahead and win."

Bravado came naturally to Patton. However, he recognized a hastily cobbled together, politically determined operation when he saw one and had no wish to carry the blame if his part of it ended badly. He indicated as much to the Combined Chiefs of Staff. A memo issued by them the day before his troops set sail noted: "It is General Patton's view, with which we concur, that this is primarily a political operation, since it is based on the conception that the enemy will not offer severe or sustained opposition. . . . This [the Morocco invasion] cannot be considered a militarily sound operation of war. (Note: This is not intended to suggest that the operation is doomed before it starts, but rather to record the obstacles which it will have to overcome and the conditions under which it has been planned.)"

Similar thoughts were entertained by commanders of the U.S. troops concluding their training in Britain for the Mediterranean end of the operation. Some of the troops assigned to the Algiers and Oran Task Forces had been there since early August and had been training extensively in Northern Ireland and Scotland. But troops of the 39th Regimental Combat Team, who were to take Algiers, had set out to cross the Atlantic as late as September 19. They had arrived in Belfast on October 6, to be shifted a week later to Inveraray in Scotland for training and then shifted again barely ten days later to prepare for embarkation October 23. None of the Torch troops had trained in conditions anything like those they would meet on the Mediterranean shore. But for the men of the 39th, amphibious rehearsals had been little more than a gesture.

After his consultations in Washington and London, Robert Murphy returned to North Africa at the beginning of October, one month before the Allies were due to invade, to put the finishing touches to his efforts to deter or minimize armed resistance to the Torch landings. By that time, the Vichy regime and the officers it had entrusted with the defense of French North Africa had become jittery. Everyone knew the Allies were preparing a major offensive operation and it was apparent that France's African territories were a possible target.

Murphy realized that if the Allies were to have any hope of gaining the support of French officers in North Africa, it would be necessary to satisfy their sense of honor and at the same time assure them about their personal prospects. Torch was not to be seen by them as an attempt by a foreign power to seize French territory and unceremoniously thrust them aside in the process. Accordingly, a suitable declaration was drawn up in Washington to be presented to trusted officers in North Africa at the appropriate time prior to the landings:

> Information having been received from a reliable source that the Germans and Italians are planning an intervention in French North Africa, the United States contemplates sending at an early date a sufficient number of American troops to land in that area for the purpose of preventing occupation by the Axis, and of preserving the French sovereignty in Algeria, and the French administrations in Morocco and Tunisia. No change in the existing French civil administrations is contemplated by the United States. Any resistance to the American landing will of course be put down by force of arms. The American forces will

hope for and will welcome French assistance. The American forces will provide equipment as rapidly as possible for those French troops who join in denying access to French North Africa to our common enemies. . . . The American Government will guarantee salaries and allowances, death benefits and pensions of those French and other military, naval and civilian officials who join with the American expeditionary forces. The proposed expedition will be American, under American command, and it will not include any of the forces of General de Gaulle.

Murphy had much to do upon his return to North Africa to win confidence and ease the way for the Torch invaders. Admiral Darlan, still commanding Vichy France's military forces, and General Giraud, the elderly escape artist ostensibly in retirement in Lyons, wanted badly to know what the Allies were up to. Nazi collaborator and Anglophobe Darlan was beginning to think that Hitler might lose the war after all. Though not yet prepared to risk distancing himself from the Germans, he had authorized intermediaries to indicate to the Americans that he might be prepared to collaborate with them instead, given the right circumstances.

Giraud meanwhile had never ceased fantasizing about leading the liberation of France and the rest of Europe from German occupation. Anxious to sustain his enthusiasm and zeal, Murphy had no intention of prematurely disabusing him of his belief that the forthcoming invasion would be of southern France, as he wished, rather than of North Africa. And Torch command failed to appreciate that Giraud was profoundly serious in expecting to be named supreme Allied commander when the Allies launched their invasion of French territory, wherever it took place.

Vichy France was teeming with German and pro-German agents, so Murphy could not very well approach either Darlan or Giraud directly. He had to confine his conspiratorial activities to North Africa. Upon his return there from the Allied capitals, he went first to Rabat to see the senior Vichy figure there, General Auguste Noguès, resident-general of Morocco. Authoritarian by belief and inclination, Noguès had served the Vichy regime without qualm or question. Like virtually all other senior French officers in North Africa, he appeared unlikely to act except on orders from Marshal Pétain.

Murphy tried nevertheless to win him over. He described to him the formidable military power America was rapidly becoming and asked what his position would be if half a million heavily armed U.S. troops were sent to French North Africa, escorted by powerful warships and an armada of war planes. Noguès was outraged by the suggestion. "Do not try that!" he snapped. "If you do, I will meet you with all the firepower I possess. It is too late for France to participate in this war now. We will do better to stay out. If Morocco becomes a battleground, it will be lost to France!"

Another senior figure whose support Murphy would have liked to enroll in the Allied cause was Admiral François Michelier who commanded French naval forces in Morocco. But Michelier was as adamantly opposed as Noguès to the prospect of an American invasion unless it had Pétain's blessings. Denied top-echelon support in Morocco, Murphy decided that he would have to rely on a less senior officer, General Emile Béthouart, and hope for the best. In addition to being devoutly anti-German, Béthouart, commander of the Casablanca Division, was one of the very few high-ranking French officers in North Africa known to the Americans to hold the Vichy regime in low regard. Approached by Murphy, he readily agreed to do what he could to preempt French resistance to the Morocco landings when they took place, even if it meant taking action to keep Noguès, his superior officer, from obstructing them. For a veteran soldier, that was indeed a dangerous commitment.

Having done what he could in Casablanca, Murphy flew on to Algiers. The prospects for him in French North Africa's main city were both better and more complicated. His was a journey back into the atmosphere of intrigue to which he had grown accustomed during the previous sixteen months but in which, at that stage of the proceedings, matters had to be left frustratingly inconclusive.

Murphy had been away from Algiers for eight weeks and found the situation there much changed. Conspiracies had blossomed. Positions had hardened. The imminence of a major American military operation in North Africa appeared to have become a secret shared by many, if only through rumor and speculation that contended with rumor and speculation that the Germans were likely to strike first.

Reestablishing contact with conspirators, Murphy found himself facing renewed demands for arms. They were far from content with the vague, insubstantial promises he could make. Meantime, French factions involved were maneuvering for position. The focus of the individuals involved was on who would lead a resurgent France and where their place would be in it. But for the Allies, the only serious question remained the amount of assistance, active or passive, the French would offer the invading task forces.

The tentative approach from Darlan was particularly tempting. Enormous benefits might accrue if he could be won over to the Allied side. Aside from Pétain himself, Darlan was the only person who could order the French forces in North Africa not to resist the Allied landings. As Commander in Chief of France's armed forces, he was also in a position to bring the French fleet, the bulk of which was at anchor at Toulon, over to the Allies. Churchill had told Eisenhower, ". . . much as I hate [Darlan], I would cheerfully crawl on my hands and knees for a mile if by doing so I could get him to bring that fleet of his into the circle of Allied forces."

A year earlier, Darlan had indicated to Admiral Leahy, then ambassador in Vichy, that if the Americans appeared with sufficient force in the Mediterranean to rule out any successful German countermoves, he would take no action to oppose them. Now, regardless of how unsavory Darlan was considered, an opportunity had arisen that an opportunist of his caliber might find difficult to resist. Roosevelt himself authorized Murphy to enter into dealings with Darlan if he thought they could serve a useful purpose.

However, by making any sort of arrangement with the admiral, whose reliability was questionable, the Allies risked alienating General Giraud, whose pro-Allied credentials were beyond question, as well as Giraud's intermediaries in North Africa, particularly General Charles Emmanuel Mast. Chief of staff of the French XIX Army Corps in Algeria, Mast was prepared to render practical assistance to the invading forces regardless of orders to the contrary he might receive from his superiors. He was aware of Darlan's overtures to Murphy and urged him to reject them. Darlan, he said, could not be trusted. He said that the French Army was loyal to and would follow Giraud and that once that had happened, the French Navy would quickly follow suit.

Churchill, Eisenhower, and the British Chiefs of Staff assessed the possibilities and concluded that the Allies should consider Giraud "our principal collaborator on the French side." He would be rewarded with the position of governor-general of North Africa. But if Darlan could be won over as well, all to the good. With D-Day fast approaching but with invasion prospects still uncertain, Eisenhower toyed with the idea of shifting Clark to the command of the U.S. Fifth Army, which was about to be activated, so that if Darlan rallied to the Allied cause and circumstances made it advisable, he might succeed the general as deputy Torch commander.

Eisenhower urged Murphy to try to get Darlan and Giraud to work as a team, assisting the Allies and perhaps dividing the French command between them. But the invasion troops were about to board the transports that would carry them to North Africa. It was naïve to believe that harmony might be quickly achieved between stubborn luminaries whose loyalties and aspirations diverged sharply, and between their adherents and others in key positions who had motives and aspirations of their own.

In Murphy's view, whatever contribution Darlan might conceivably make, it was Giraud and his supporters in Algiers who were anxious to lend assistance, and they appeared able to do so. General Mast was, for example, not only prepared to work with the Allies but he proposed secret talks with a high-ranking American military delegation to work out details of how he and other insurgents could help once the invasion was launched. Thus, with D-Day only three weeks away, came the most promising indication from Mast that arrangements could be made for it to succeed "practically without firing a shot."

The secret consultations with American officers proposed by Mast had to take place near Algiers. The general could not leave his post there for any length of time without arousing suspicion. Arrangements would have to be made for the participating Americans to make a clandestine visit to North Africa. The Combined Chiefs of Staff readily gave their approval. It had been suggested that General Giraud might be able to slip away from France to attend personally. If Giraud could be brought into direct involvement from the very start, it would be an important development, very much worth exploring, important enough for an officer as senior as Torch Deputy Supreme Commander General Clark to make the dangerous journey. The escapade might have been considered reckless in view of the possibility that Torch's second in command was being lured into a trap set by German intelligence. If as a result, the enemy discovered the purpose of his mission, the invasion would have to be called off.

* * *

Before setting off for Algeria, Clark was closely briefed on matters to be discussed when he got there. In his talks with Mast, he was to avoid the subject of Darlan if possible. Whatever happened, he was to reach no agreement concerning the admiral, nor otherwise get enmeshed in French rivalries and maneuverings for power. However, the dispatch of the operation's deputy commander to confer with supporters of General Giraud, and perhaps even Giraud himself, was in itself a high-level commitment of sorts. It implied a far greater measure of official recognition for one of the rival French protagonists than had previously been authorized—aside from de Gaulle, who had de facto recognition from the British but who still was told nothing officially of what was going on. This remained tricky terrain in view of the desire not to get ensnarled in the morass of French politics while there was a war to win.

Traveling with Clark would be a high-powered team of American military experts to extract as much information as possible for use during the invasion and to further convince the French of the seriousness of Allied intentions. They included Brigadier General Lyman Lemnitzer, who was in charge of the Allied Forces Plans Section; Captain Jerauld Wright, Torch's U.S. Navy liaison man; Colonel Archelaus Hamblin, Torch's supply and shipping specialist; and Colonel Julius Holmes, who headed the Civil Affairs Branch of Torch and who was fluent in French. They would carry $1,000 in five- and ten-dollar Canadian gold coins in case it became necessary, and possible, to bribe their way out of trouble.

Churchill regretted that British personnel were excluded from this escapade, except for the crew of the submarine that was to carry the Americans to and from Algeria and three officers of the elite Special Boat Squadron—Captains G. B. Courtney and R. P. Livingstone and Lieutenant James Foot—commandos trained in secret coastal landing procedures. But the episode, and its adventure-story aspects, excited the prime minister enormously. "This is great," he kept intoning, as the details were spelled out. He suggested that Clark take along civilian clothes in case he needed to disguise himself while ashore. Clark did so but left them in the submarine, believing he would have greater problems if he was taken into custody by hostile forces on the shore while out of uniform.

The Clark party was to divide at takeoff for Gibraltar from the U.S. Army Air Force base that had been established at Polebrook, seventy miles northwest of London. They would fly in two heavily armed and heavily armored B-17 Flying Fortresses. If Clark was lost en route, Lemnitzer, in the second plane, was to assume leadership of the delegation. At Gibraltar, the waiting British submarine was to carry them across the Mediterranean to a point about fifteen miles west of the small port of Cherchell on the Algerian coast. The submarine was to reach the assigned position and surface on the night of October 20-21. A steady white light shining from the window of a large house above the beach would signal that the coast was clear. The delegation would then go ashore.

To the frustration of Eisenhower, Clark, and everyone else involved, arrangements had not made allowances for travel being delayed by inclement weather. Washington, through whom contact with Murphy was maintained, was asked to signal him to make alternative arrangements in case everything did not work out as planned. But no notification of alternatives had come through by the evening of October 18 when Clark and his team arrived at Polebrook to learn that the weather would in fact delay takeoff at least until the following morning. That meant they might not make the rendezvous near Cherchell on time and that the French might be led to doubt their good faith. Suddenly, the excitement of the adventure gave way to a sense that everything had been organized in too slipshod a fashion for an exercise upon which a great deal might depend.

They were able to take off shortly after dawn, Lemnitzer carrying secret documents in a weighted tube that could be jettisoned in the sea if necessary. Clark had instructed the pilots of the two Flying Fortresses—one of whom was Major Paul Tibbets, who would later pilot the B-29 *Enola Gay* from which the atom bomb was dropped on Hiroshima—that under no circumstances were they to land in Spain or Portugal. That meant that if they did run into trouble en route, they might have little chance of surviving. To avoid being conspicuous, they were given no fighter escort, even for the start of their journey, despite reports of German fighter aircraft active off the English coast.

They reached Gibraltar after an uneventful flight, though there was some concern as they came in to land about whether the runaway at Gibraltar was long enough. No aircraft requiring as much landing space as the Flying Fortress had ever touched down there before. To the relief of all on board, the giant bombers landed without difficulty. But before they could leave the aircraft, British personnel rushed up and told them to wait until cars with drawn curtains could drive up close and they could quickly scramble into them to be driven off. The airfield was only three hundred yards from the Spanish border town of La Línea, from which German agents with binoculars were known to be monitoring everything that happened. It was bad enough that the unprecedented arrival in Gibraltar of the two giant American bombers would get the telegraph lines to Berlin humming. The sight of senior American officers clambering out of those aircraft would concentrate German attention even more.

Uneasy about the arrangements that had been made for his mission, Clark found that British officers with whom he conferred in Gibraltar provided little encouragement.

> They talked of thick shore patrols [on the Mediteranean coast], plenty of spotting planes, and a French Navy and Air Force bolder than it had been before. What I needed was someone to say, "Okay; we'll get you there, and get you out too." They talked on until I said, "Gentleman, there is no help for this. We are going. It has been decided by our two Governments, and I don't intend to call it off."

Clark later confessed that he too had "hardly ever been less certain of the success of an operational mission in my life." Not until he was introduced to the comparatively junior Lieutenant Norman Ambury Auchinleck Jewell, commander of the HMS *Seraph,* the submarine that was to take the Americans and the trio of commandos to Algiers, did he receive the reassurance he so badly wanted. Jewell had no doubt that he could get Clark and his team to their destination and bring them back. However, he could not guarantee that he would be able to reach the rendezvous point on time.

They would have to do most of the journey submerged, which limited the speed at which they would be able to travel to two to three knots, compared to five times that speed if they could risk crossing the Mediterranean on the surface. Clark rushed a message to Colonel Eddy, working under diplomatic cover in the International Zone of Tangier, instructing him to contact Murphy and ask that he and the French reception party he had organized wait from 9:00 P.M. on October 20 till the following dawn and if they did not appear to look for them again on the night of the twenty-first. No reply had come by the time he left Gibraltar.

The *Seraph* was still negotiating its slow passage across the Mediterranean at the initial appointed time when General Mast and a team of trusted officers and some civilian conspirators gathered at the villa picked for the rendezvous above the beach near Cherchell. The group dispersed when Clark's party did not show up at the designated time. But though the message on contingency timing had not been received, they agreed to stand by to gather again the following night if contact was made.

The *Seraph* reached the rendezvous point on the morning of October 21 and waited submerged offshore that day. It surfaced at night for Clark and his team to disembark into kayaklike foldboat canoes in which they paddled ashore. They landed without being challenged—discovering subsequently that the conspirators had made arrangements for coastal patrols in the area to be suspended—and found themselves on a completely deserted beach fronting a steep bluff. They were met just beneath the bluff by Murphy, who was covered immediately by the armed British commandos until his identity was established in the darkness. For him, the arrival of Clark's team seemed to herald the fulfillment of all he had been working toward for months.

They were led to the white-walled villa atop the bluff belonging to a local landowner, a Monsieur Teissier, the father-in-law of a member of the local underground resistance organization. Teissier had sent his Arab servants away, as he had the night before, so that they would not intrude on the secret gathering. Informed that Clark had finally shown up, Mast and five of his staff officers had slipped out of Algiers again and arrived by car at the Teissier villa at 5:00 A.M. Clark had instructed his commando escorts to stay out of sight in the villa to avoid complications if anti-British feeling among the French was as extreme as he had been led to believe.

The meeting was a difficult one for Clark, who had no experience in diplomacy, especially since his performance on this occasion required a strong measure of deception. Mast wanted to know details of the Torch operation but Clark had been instructed not to give much away. He was in no position to share Murphy's confidence in those with whom he was dealing. The following day, the Western Task Force was to begin setting off from Virginia and Center and Eastern Task Force ships were already leaving from Britain. He did not intend to reveal anything related to Operation Torch security that might be transmitted directly or indirectly to the enemy and endanger the convoys.

Mast was left with the impression that Torch was still in a late planning stage, that it would be at least a month before it was launched, and that he would be informed closer to D-Day so that he would be able to organize appropriate support in time. He was concerned that he was being drawn into an escapade that might turn sour. He sought assurances from Clark that the projected invasion would not be merely a smallish Dieppe-style raid that would serve no purpose other than to provoke the Germans into occupying Vichy France and perhaps sending their own invasion armada to French North Africa. He wanted to know how many troops the Americans were committing to the landings. Confirming suggestions Murphy had previously offered his contacts, Clark exaggerated by a factor of five ("I tried to keep a poker face.") and said 500,000 troops would be put ashore. They would be escorted by a strong naval contingent and have aerial support from two thousand aircraft.

Mast expressed doubts about whether the Americans could muster sufficient shipping for so vast an operation. Clark felt he could not avoid admitting that British naval and air units would participate. Mast warned that British participation had to be kept to a minimum and that de Gaulle's Free French forces definitely had to be excluded altogether; otherwise resistance to the landings might well be vigorous. But he was persuaded that the Americans did mean business and was clearly willing to render valuable assistance to the operation. He urged that an American submarine be sent to spirit Giraud, whose presence at this secret meeting had never even been contemplated by his supporters, out of France so that he could lead this great campaign against the Axis enemy with the full support of the French Army in North Africa.

Mast reiterated Giraud's earlier insistence that he should take command of all Allied military forces operating on French territory, American as well as French. Clark had difficulty responding on that point. The idea that a French officer, whose only claim to fame was to have escaped from prison after having been defeated in battle, might emerge at the last moment from retirement to take overall command of an intricate operation into which so much planning had gone was so outlandish that neither Washington nor London had ever seriously considered it. But Clark realized that to turn the demand down flatly would cause problems that could be avoided. He agreed to a draft formula that was ambiguous enough to satisfy both parties for the moment.

> ... the United States has no other thought or desire but that military command in the area be placed in French hands at the earliest possible date. However, during the initial phase of the operation ... it is considered essential that the command be not changed. ... During this period we shall lend every effort to provide French Forces with modern arms and equipment. While French Forces are being thus equipped and organized, the command machinery can be perfected so as to permit French assumption of the supreme command at the appropriate time.

Neither "supreme command" nor "appropriate time" was defined. But not for a moment did Roosevelt, Churchill, or Eisenhower accept that the supreme command of Torch could be handed over to Giraud at any time. Later Giraud and his partisans would come to realize they had been deceived, and not only about that. While conferring with Clark, Mast referred to Giraud's desire for an early Allied invasion of France itself, rather than of France's African territories. Clark told him the subject would be reviewed in London. He did not disclose that the idea had already been rejected in favor of Torch.

During the meeting, French sentries were posted to warn of any suspicious developments outside the Teissier villa. There were none but Mast was disinclined to risk that his absence from his duties would be noticed at a time when the atmosphere was heavy with rumor and speculation. Accordingly, he left at midday to return to Algiers. After he had gone, the Americans continued conferring on operational and technical details with the French officers who stayed behind. They discussed the early seizure of key airfields by the Allies, the suitability of certain landing beaches— though the Americans did not reveal which had already been chosen by Torch planners—and the position of shore batteries. The

French provided information on arms dumps, the deployment of troops, and details of key harbors and ports. Clark was greatly impressed.

> The French were ready with voluminous written information, which later turned out to be accurate in every respect. They gave us positions and strengths of troops and naval units; told us where supplies, including petrol and ammunition, were stored; supplied details about airports where resistance would be heaviest, and information as to where airborne troops could land safely.

Right through his brief stay at the Teissier villa, Clark remained aware that his mission was a perilous one and that it very likely would have been proved pointless at best if he did not return safely to the submarine waiting offshore to transport him back to Gibraltar. The clacking sound made by the rotating vanes of a nearby windmill became increasingly rapid during the afternoon, offering audible evidence of a rising wind. Through the window of the villa he saw the surf grow rougher. Clark feared that the departure planned for the evening might prove much more difficult than earlier expected.

He did not have to wait long for his fears to be confirmed, but not yet because of the elements. At 6:00 P.M., a phone call tipped off the French participants at the meeting that the local police were on their way and would be there in a few minutes. It was later learned that Teissier's Arab servants, annoyed and suspicious at having been sent away, had been muttering that something strange appeared to be going on at the villa. Those mutterings had reached the police, who offered standing rewards for information leading to the arrest of smugglers who were known to be active along the coast.

The police alarm sent everyone in the villa scrambling. The French officers switched into civilian clothes with a speed Clark had seen "exceeded only by professional quick-change artists." Some sped away in cars. Others fled through windows and into the brush along the shore. The British commando officers who had been sleeping in an upstairs room were awakened. One of them slipped out of the villa and down to the beach to warn the submarine by walkie-talkie of what was happening. Clark and the others hurried through a trapdoor in the patio and down a crumbling ladder to the wine cellar, where the general, tinkering with a carbine, prepared for the worst. "How does this thing work?" he muttered, scaring one of the British officers, who snapped at him to put the loaded rifle down "in a tone no-one should use to a general."

When the police arrived, Murphy, who had not gone into hiding, was identified to them by Teissier as the American consul in Vichy, temporarily visiting Algiers. He told them he had come to the villa, together with Vice-Consul Ridgeway Knight, who also remained unhidden, for a party and intimated that women who were partaking of the festivities were in a room above. While the police looked over the place, one of the commandos hiding in the wine cellar had a coughing fit which he tried to suppress by chomping on chewing gum Clark handed him. When he commented later that the gum had little taste, the general explained that before handing it to him, he had chewed all the taste out of it.

The police remained in and near the villa for the better part of two hours and finally left without discovering the visitors. But they remained suspicious and indicated they would return. As soon as they had gone, the visitors fled the villa. They recovered the fold-boat canoes, which villa owner Teissier had locked away, and carried them down to the shore. The breakers were now coming in so strong that departure seemed impossible. The canoes capsized in the first attempt. Alternatives were considered, including a possible escape through Spanish Morocco. But Clark thought that was too risky. A Frenchman who had stayed with them was dispatched to Cherchell to buy a fishing boat to carry them out to the submarine but was unable to do so.

Terrified that they would be discovered and he would be arrested, Teissier kept coming down to the beach to see whether they had been able to make their departure. The men were cold, wet, and hungry. They hadn't eaten since lunch. After midnight, Clark went back to the villa to find some food and dry clothes. The police returned while he was there. Clutching bread and bottles of wine, he escaped over a cement wall and scampered undetected back to the beach.

At 4:00 A.M., one of the commandos suggested that they try wading out past the worst of the breakers, carrying the canoes and climbing into them there. There was further capsizing and buffeting but eventually it worked. They managed finally to get out to the submarine to be taken aboard, though they lost a bag of papers containing some of the information they had acquired from the French with whom they had conferred. It apparently remained lost at sea, though the possibility that it might be found ashore and passed to the authorities aroused much anxiety. Picked up from the submarine by flying boat in the Mediterranean, Clark and his team were back that same day in Gibraltar, from which he cabled Eisenhower the results of his mission.

> All questions were settled satisfactorily, except for the time the French would assume supreme command. . . . Have obtained extremely valuable intelligence data. . . . Our operations plans appear to be sound considering discussions and information received. . . . Anticipate that the bulk of the French Army and Air Forces will offer little resistance. . . .

Clark flew on to England that night to report in detail to Eisenhower and Churchill and recount his hair-raising escape from Algeria to the general, the prime minister, King George, and various others. He had accomplished his mission; to what effect was still to be seen.

☆ 11 ☆

TORCH IS LIT

At last the hour has arrived for the stroke ... against the monstrous tyranny which has set the entire world in flames.

—The Washington Post

The Western Task Force that was to cross the Atlantic to Morocco was composed of three attack groups, as well as a covering escort and an air group. It consisted of more than one hundred warships, transports, freighters, and tankers. They were to set out from different ports on the East Coast of the United States at different times so as not to attract the attention of enemy agents who were believed active at key centers along the coast.

Starting as early as October 3, the Air Group, consisting of the carrier *Ranger,* three escort carriers, and a screen of nine destroyers and one light cruiser, set off from Casco Bay in Maine, heading for Bermuda for preoperational training. Five submarines that were to be the vanguard of the operation, reconnoitering the landing areas and helping to guide the transports to their target areas, set off for Africa from Montauk Point, Long Island, on October 19 and 20. Most of the troop transports and cargo vessels left Hampton Roads on October 23, on a course that indicated they were bound for the West Indies. Ostensibly bound for Britain, the remainder followed the next day, at around the time General Clark was making his dramatic departure from Algeria and heading back to London via Gibraltar to report on the chances of the invading forces meeting little resistance when they went ashore.

Some five hundred miles out at sea, the ships of the Western Task Force altered course to rendezvous on October 28 and form up in a massive convoy consisting of nine long sea columns. Each was led by a battleship or a cruiser, "like a file of Indian squaws trailing an Indian warrior." Destroyers screened their flanks and rear. Everything finally appeared to be as it should be. The confusion and difficulties that had marked the planning period seemed to have been overcome. Concern remained about the level of training of the troops and naval crews, but everything else appeared to be in order, though commanding officers could not help worrying about what might happen if a German U-boat slipped through the protective screen of warships and struck home with a torpedo. Each unit of troops had a specific mission once the landings began. The loss of one troop transport en route would complicate matters. It was believed that if two were lost, "the operation would not be practicable."

Deception continued to be practiced even after the convoy had formed up. It first set a course southeast, as if intending to head down the west coast of Africa toward Dakar, then turned northward to make for Morocco and the landing beaches. Navy prize crews were placed on neutral merchant ships encountered during the closing phase of the crossing to guarantee that the position of the convoy would not be communicated to the enemy.

The transports were jammed with troops. In what little spare space was available, training of the men continued. Instruction on what to expect was given to improve "individual and team techniques and skills and maintain physical condition and avoid boredom." Every available moment was to be devoted to intensive training so that "all men of the command would be conditioned mentally and physically to achieve victory regardless of hostile resistance or privation." Models of the Moroccan shore were studied. Lectures were given on what the men could expect. General Patton commanded his officers to instill in the troops the conviction "that we are better in all respects than our enemies. . . . It must be their absolute belief. WE MUST HAVE A SUPERIORITY COMPLEX!"

It was known that a pack of German U-boats was in operation near the Canary Islands. But the Task Force was spared its attention by the fortuitous passage through the area of a convoy of British merchant ships en route to England from Sierra Leone after having deposited its cargo of goods there. The U-boats spotted that convoy and concentrated its attention upon it. In a one-sided battle that lasted more than a week, twelve of its ships were lost, but by that time, the Western Task Force had slipped by unnoticed and was well clear, heading for the Atlantic coast assault areas. The commander of that convoy later observed that it was the only time in his career that he had ever been congratulated for losing ships.

For all the attendant confusions and shortcomings, final preparations for the Mediterranean coast landings turned out to be an even more remarkable feat of organization. Not only had the operations of the Royal Navy, British Army, and Royal Air Force been smoothly coordinated—they had already been acting in concert for three years—they had been coordinated with those of the U.S. Army and Navy in a way that had never been achieved before or even attempted. Differences over strategy and tactics had been resolved or laid aside by the time the first of the vessels set sail from British ports en route to Algiers and Oran.

Most of the supply vessels were loaded at various ports before assembling in the Firth of Clyde, starting on October 17. Troop transports made a brief excursion up the coast of Scotland to Loch Linnhe for the men to participate in a final rehearsal before their vessels joined the flotilla for the voyage through the Strait of Gibraltar. Slower support ships having already set off, the first large group of vessels set out from Scotland on October 22, to be followed by most of the rest of the participating ships over the next three days. Among the warships escorting the Algiers-bound Eastern Task Force were two aircraft carriers, three light cruisers, three antiaircraft cruisers, thirteen destroyers, seven mine sweepers, and seven corvettes. Warships escorting Oran-bound Center Task Force included a battleship and an aircraft carrier, two escort carriers, thirteen destroyers, eight minesweepers, and six corvettes. Included also were two former U.S. Coast Guard cutters, now under Royal Navy command, that were to play a tragic role in the Oran operation.

There was much concern at the Admiralty about the danger posed by the enemy, and particularly by German submarines, to "the most valuable convoys ever to leave these shores." In addition to the escort vessels for the convoys, a special Royal Navy force—Force H—consisting of two carriers, three battleships, four cruisers, and seventeen destroyers was placed on patrol in the Mediterranean.

It was confirmed that no attacks were to be made against French air bases prior to the landings. Such action might provoke a response when minimal resistance or none at all might otherwise be forthcoming. But once resistance was. met, no effort was to be spared to eliminate it quickly and conclusively.

Despite Clark's promising report on chances for French cooperation, no risks were to be taken with this first major combined Allied offensive in the war. Preparations were for all-out combat. It had to be assumed that unless far more reliable guarantees were forthcoming from French officers actually in positions of supreme authority, the troops would be met as enemies when they stormed ashore. And it was anybody's guess what the Germans and the Spanish would do.

The U.S. Navy introduced baseball terminology for its coded instructions on how its warships were to respond to whatever resistance the Western Task Force might encounter once the invasion of Morocco had begun. The instruction "Batter Up" would mean specific isolated targets, such as individual artillery or machine-gun positions on land, should be silenced. With the signal "Play Ball," greater firepower was to be unleashed to knock out coastal batteries and more generalized resistance. France was not an enemy nation but there was to be no shilly-shallying in guaranteeing the success of the landings and providing for the safety of the troops.

The Germans failed to anticipate the Torch landings largely because their High Command had what appeared to it to be more pressing problems. Among them was what was happening elsewhere in North Africa. When the decision to invade the French territories had been made in July 1942, there had been stalemate at El Alamein in the Egyptian desert. Rommel's Panzerarmee Afrika had lunged within sixty miles of Alexandria. But suffering extreme supply shortages, it had been stopped there. In an attack launched by the British on July 21, Rommel had been able to send only thirty tanks against the Eighth Army's four hundred. Nevertheless, his superior tactical skills had led to a standoff rather than a rout.

Bitterly disappointed, Churchill had reorganized his command structure in the Middle East. General Alexander, removed from the role he had been assigned in OperationTorch, had been put in overall charge in the region and General Montgomery had been sent to serve under him. Montgomery's assignment had been to whip the dispirited Eighth Army into shape and send Rommel's forces reeling back toward Tunisia before the end of October. Not only would that set Rommel up for a trap but such a victory on the eve of the Torch landings might help persuade the French in North Africa to cooperate with the Allies. It would also discourage the Spanish from getting involved.

Montgomery was not a man to be rushed. Repeatedly during the war he would be criticized for missing opportunities because of what his critics called excessive caution. Whenever pressed to act sooner than he intended, he would demand huffily, "Do you want a failure? Do you want a failure?" No matter what plans were being made for Torch, he did not intend to engage Rommel's forces at El Alamein until his reinforced troops were trained to his own exacting standards and until he had accumulated and deployed the necessary equipment to guarantee victory.

That moment came for him seven weeks after he had taken command, at ten o'clock on the night of October 23, 1942. The boom of more than a thousand British guns shattered the desert silence near El Alamein as hundreds of tanks moved forward to pummel the enemy. Montgomery had made certain of the outcome. Facing his 195,000 troops were 104,000 Axis troops, more than half of them Italians who were not as well armed as the Germans and whose fighting abilities the Germans, through experience, held in low regard. The Eighth Army could field more than 1,000 mostly superior tanks against fewer than 240 for the Germans and 280 obsolete models for the Italians.

The British had mastery in the air over the battlefield as well— some 1,500 attack aircraft to 350 for the Axis forces. "Air raid after air raid after air raid!" Rommel moaned. What was more, Montgomery knew through Ultra intercepts what the enemy could and could not do against his onslaught. Rommel had been recuperating from circulation problems back in Germany and had rushed back to Africa to resume command of his forces and try to salvage something of the situation.

Assessing prospects upon his return to the front, he reported that unless he executed a massive withdrawal back across the Libyan border, his forces would be destroyed. Outraged by such defeatism, Hitler instructed him to hold fast regardless. He told him, "In the situation in which you find yourself there can be no other thought but to stand fast, yield not a yard of ground and throw every gun and every man into the battle. . . . As to your

170

troops, you can show them no other road than that to victory or death." But when it became evident on November 4 that the Axis forces might be completely annihilated, Hitler grudgingly permitted Rommel to withdraw into Libya.

Hitler had not expected the Allies to invade French North Africa, but when they did, it did not come as a complete surprise to senior Axis figures. On October 9, a full month before D-Day, Italian Foreign Minister Count Ciano observed, "All the information and the conversations [with his intelligence services] lead one to conclude that the Anglo-Saxons are preparing to land in force in North Africa." That conclusion was conveyed to Berlin but, bombarded with rumors of all sorts and having little regard for Italian perspicacity, Hitler ignored it. Their remaining military resources fully stretched, the Italians were in no position to do anything about it themselves.

But they were not alone in their suspicions. The Operations Staff of the German Armed Forces High Command had been studying possible points where the Allies would launch the operation for which they were known to be preparing and for which increasing numbers of American troops had been pouring into Britain. The conclusion it reached was that French North Africa offered "the best jumping-off point" for an assault on Hitler's Fortress Europe and was therefore a likely Allied target.

In mid-October, General Alfred Jodl, the German chief of operations, noted "the increased number of reports of imminent Anglo-Saxon landings in West Africa," and suggested that the Vichy regime be permitted to dispatch additional army units to North Africa in case they were needed to cope with any Allied invasion attempt there. Fearing they might turn against the Axis, Hitler rejected the idea. General Walter Warlimont, deputy chief of the Operations Staff, later claimed to have repeatedly urged serious consideration be given to the defense of French North Africa but the proposal was just as repeatedly spurned by the German Führer.

Field Marshal Albert Kesselring, the German commander in southern Europe, knew just before D-Day that a major Allied operation was imminent but he did not know where it would take place. He thought it likely that it would be in North Africa, Sicily, or Sardinia. He requested precautionary reinforcements for his troops in southern Italy and Sicily. Hitler turned him down. He told those who suggested that an Allied assault on French North Africa was likely that they failed to appreciate that the Allies would refrain from such a move because they realized it would only drive Vichy France more tightly into the ranks of the Axis powers.

The inability of German intelligence to produce hard information about Torch in the weeks before the landings was one of its great failures in the war. During that period, Rommel's difficulties, and developments on the Russian Front where another fierce winter was setting in, effectively absorbed Hitler's full attention and the German command structure was such that no important move could be made without the Führer's express approval.

When it was reported to him on October 31 at his command post in East Prussia that a convoy of Allied merchant ships—slow-moving Torch cargo vessels making a head start from Scotland— had arrived at Gibraltar, he concluded it was another desperate attempt to bring supplies to Malta, another bid to run the gauntlet of U-boats and Luftwaffe bombers positioned to deal with it as ferociously as they had dealt with the previous one.

On November 5, his headquarters began receiving new streams of reports about great numbers of Allied ships, under strong Royal Navy escort, streaming through the Gibraltar Strait. German intelligence suggested a number of possible destinations for them, including Malta, Crete, Sardinia, Sicily, and the Middle East. French North Africa was low on that list. It was considered most probable that the ships were carrying troops to land in Libya, at Rommel's rear, to try to trap his forces. Orders were given for the Luftwaffe to prepare to deal with the convoys from its bases in Italy when they came within range. Luftwaffe commander Reichsmarschall Hermann Göring ordered that when that happened, the convoys were to be "attacked and destroyed by continuous action both by day and by night." Even when the Torch convoys in the Mediterranean began to position themselves to move against Algiers and Oran, Hitler persisted in rejecting the growing number of reports suggesting that French North Africa might well be their destination.

The Allies took comfort from their own intelligence reports that no signs could be detected that the Germans had any suspicion, even at that late date, that the Torch convoys in the Mediterranean were bound for Algeria or that the Morocco-bound Torch convoy in the Atlantic even existed. But Eisenhower remained apprehensive. If surprise was not maintained, German U-boats and aircraft

could still pounce on the convoys. What was more, if Hitler realized what was happening, even at the last moment he might apply
pressure on Vichy to order its forces in North Africa to resist the
landings with all the strength at their command. This first combined Allied offensive action against Nazi Germany could end as a
washout, with incalculable consequences for morale in both the
United States and Britain, for the unity of the British-American
alliance, and for the course of the war.

The British and American embassies in Madrid stepped up their
efforts to make certain that Spain would stay clear of the operation
and that it would not permit the Germans transit rights through
Spanish territory to challenge it. There was still no certainty that
Spain would comply. A Northern Task Force was standing by in
Britain to deal with a Spanish problem if it materialized—a plan
rather than a practicality since neither enough troops nor enough
shipping was available for such an additional operation. It was
decided finally that if Spain appeared about to involve itself in the
situation to the detriment of the Allied cause, it would merely be
warned off with the advice that it was creating serious complications for itself in its relations with the United States and Britain.

On October 29, with D-Day little more than a week away,
Robert Murphy was permitted to inform General Mast in Algiers
that the invasion was set for "early in November." General Giraud,
who still was not overly enthusiastic about an Allied attack on
North Africa rather than the French mainland, needed advance
notice to prepare to flee from France and make his way to Algeria
to publicly proclaim his endorsement of Torch at the time of the
landings. Key conspirators in Algeria and Morocco also had to be
alerted and made ready. It was to be understood that the information on timing could not be spread about indiscriminately. Only
those who absolutely needed to know could be told. The success of
the operation might depend on it.

Murphy refrained from informing General Mast that instructions he had received from London made it absolutely clear that
contrary to his expectations, Giraud would not be entrusted with
the command of all Allied troops under any circumstances. It
would only have intensified Mast's anger when, though still not
given the exact date, he was informed that the invasion was imminent. He protested that he needed, and had been promised, more

time to organize his end of the operation. There was much for Giraud, himself, and his co-conspirators to do to prepare to assist the invasion. He was furious at how little the Americans had trusted him when he had risked his career, and possibly his life, by trusting them.

Murphy managed to calm Mast down. Though still deeply offended, he agreed to proceed with his preparations for the planned pro-Allied coup in Algiers to coincide with the landings. But on November 1, Murphy sent word to Washington that a serious hitch had developed concerning Giraud. The general was to be picked up by submarine in the Gulf of Lions off the southern coast of France. Before making his way to North Africa, he was to be delivered to Gibraltar for final arrangements on the role he was to play in Torch. But Murphy had now been informed by Giraud's intermediaries in Algiers that the general needed more time to prepare for his flight from France.

The contribution the general was due to make to the success of Torch was expected by Murphy to be the crowning achievement of his many months of exhaustive, diligent espionage, intrigue, and clandestine negotiations. Giraud would rally France's armed forces in North Africa to the Allied cause and turn the operation into a bloodless romp. Murphy had come to believe that without Giraud, there would be slaughter on the beaches when the troops came ashore. When informed that Giraud was not ready, he dispatched an urgent message to Roosevelt urging that the invasion be delayed.

I am convinced that the invasion of North Africa without favorable French High Command will be a catastrophe. The delay of two weeks, unpleasant as it may be, involving technical considerations of which I am ignorant, is insignificant compared with the result involving serious opposition of the French Army to our landing.

The naïveté of the suggestion, when Murphy knew the convoys had already been at sea several days, astonished those in Washington and London who been anxiously involved in patching Torch together. They had finally come to hope that the worst of their confusions and muddles had been sorted out. Eisenhower was flabbergasted. "It is inconceivable," he cabled General Marshall, "that [Murphy] can recommend such a delay with his intimate knowledge of the operation and the present location of troops and

174

convoys afloat." Clark was anxious that the French conspirators in North Africa, who would surely be peeved not to be granted the requested delay, might use information made available to them against the Allies. He angrily drafted a memorandum to Washington saying that the invasion would go ahead with or without French support.

> Recommend Murphy be advised his suggested action is out of the question and impracticable; that we will proceed to execute this operation more determined than ever to blast our way ashore. He should be directed to tell Mast that we are coming as planned; that all hell and the North African Army can't stop us; that if he uses the information already furnished him on the operation as to the time of its execution to our disadvantage either by regrouping his troops to more effectively stop us, or otherwise betraying our cause, we'll hang him higher than a kite when we get ashore.

That message was much toned down before it was dispatched. Murphy was informed that the submarine that had been sent to whisk Giraud to Gibraltar would stay on station in the Mediterranean, fifty miles off the port of Toulon, until further notice. He was told, "[T]he operation will be carried out as now planned and . . . you will do your utmost to secure the understanding and cooperation of the French officials with whom you are now in contact." Meantime, reports came in that the Torch convoys, from both Britain and the United States, were on course and had encountered no obstructions or other difficulties.

On November 2, it was leaked to the press that Eisenhower was returning from London to Washington for consultations. In fact, Eisenhower was doing no such thing. It was a cover story issued to mask the imminent shift of the general's command headquarters to Gibraltar. The Rock was the Allied base closest to the invasion points from which communications could be maintained with all three task forces once the landings had begun, as well as with Washington and London.

The Supreme Commander's departure by Flying Fortress from Hurn Airdrome near Bournemouth in southern England was delayed by adverse weather conditions. The skies remained overcast for several days and Eisenhower finally, on the morning of November 5, had to order his pilot to discount his concerns about how the weather would affect safety and take off in pouring rain. As a precaution, Clark traveled on one of the other four Flying Fortresses carrying the command staff to Gibraltar. A sixth aircraft was delayed by engine trouble and followed the next day. It was attacked en route by two German fighter-bombers. The co-pilot was wounded, but the attacking aircraft, apparently low on fuel, broke off the attack.

It was a bumpy ride to Gibraltar even for those whose aircraft did not attract the attention of the Luftwaffe. To evade detection from German radar installations on the French coast and enemy aircraft, Eisenhower's plane wave-hopped over the sea under a low cloud ceiling much of the way. As the pilot prepared to land, he observed, "This is the first time I have ever had to climb to get into landing traffic at the end of a long trip!" But the end of the journey was still to come. The plane had to circle Gibraltar for an hour and a half because of aerial crosscurrents and congestion on the runway clogged with parked fighter aircraft, lined up to play their role in Torch.* It gave Eisenhower an unsettling graphic view of how tiny Gibraltar was and how exposed the narrow Gibraltar Strait was to enemy action that could turn the operation, and his first combat command, into a calamity.

Torch headquarters had been established in the subterranean tunnels of the Rock. It was an eerie setting. Dim light bulbs provided what little illumination there was in the passageways. Clattering electric fans did little to disperse the dank smell of stale, cold air. Water ran down the walls. The agony of waiting for whatever the Germans or Spanish might be up to was magnified by a constant drip, drip, drip from the arched tunnel ceilings to the stone floor. It was a far cry from the comforts of London. Eisenhower later described it as "the most dismal setting we occupied during the war."

Nevertheless, at ten o'clock on the night of November 5, London and Washington were informed that the Allied Forces Headquarters Gibraltar, overseeing Operation Torch, was open for business. By then, the Torch convoys heading for Algeria had begun slipping past the Rock into the Mediterranean en route to the landing

---

*At the Gibraltar airfield, "aircraft were stacked in closely-packed ranks as if for the flying deck of some gigantic carrier, leaving only a single narrow runway down the center; while solid walls of stores and supplies flanked the streets leading into town."

beaches. Eisenhower confided to his senior aides that at that moment he would much rather be leading an invasion of France.

On the morning of November 6, he conferred with General Clark, Admiral Cunningham, Air Marshal Welsh, General Doolittle, and other senior members of his staff so that all could take their bearings at the new command post. The convoys traversing the Strait apparently had attracted remarkably little enemy attention. Two German submarines had been spotted and destroyed by escorting British aircraft before the convoys reached Gibraltar and it was subsequently learned from German records that sightings were reported by other U-boats and by at least one German reconnaissance plane. But none hinted at the dimensions of what was happening and no measures were taken by the enemy to deal with the situation.

As far as was known at the Allied Forces Headquarters, the Western Task Force was also still encountering no problems on its Atlantic crossing. Nevertheless, it was difficult not to concentrate on the imponderables. Were packs of U-boats lying in wait? Would the Spanish pounce? Would the ambitious plans of the pro-Allied French conspirators amount to anything? How much resistance would the troops meet when they stormed their respective beaches?

Fearing that his carefully orchestrated conspiracy in Algiers was beginning to unravel, Murphy had shown signs of panicking. Not only had he called for postponement of the operation after the convoys had been well on their way to their destinations but, though the Allies had trouble mustering sufficient resources for Torch, he had suggested elaborate diversions to distract the enemy —a landing of 50,000 men in southern France and simultaneous attacks on western France and Norway. Eisenhower generously dismissed such farfetched urgings as "a case of the jitters." He allowed that the work Murphy had done was of the kind that might generate "a bit of hysteria as the critical hour approaches."

But as Murphy had warned, a message had come saying that Giraud's departure from France would be delayed. It was not known for certain when the general could get away. The operation might have to be launched without whatever assistance he might have been able to provide. However, word was subsequently received that having evaded police and Gestapo surveillance, the general was after all expected soon to board a British submarine off Le Lavandou to be brought to Gibraltar. It would be the HMS

Seraph, the same submarine that had carried Clark to and from Algiers on his secret mission two weeks earlier. Out of concern that Giraud might object to British involvement, it was disguised for this journey as an American vessel and sailed under an American captain.

On November 7, with the invasion less than twenty-four hours away, to the relief of all at the newly established Allied Forces Headquarters on the Rock, news came that Giraud had boarded the submarine after being spirited out to it aboard a fishing boat. The general had slipped and fallen into the sea as he was being transferred from one to the other and might have drowned had a sailor not caught him by the collar and hauled him aboard. A Catalina seaplane was sent to pick him up from the submarine in mid-Mediterranean and speed his journey to Gibraltar.

The British commando officer who was assigned to superintend Giraud's transfer to a canoe, and from the canoe to the seaplane, was Lieutenant James Foot, one of the three who had been with Clark on his secret mission to Algeria. Foot was jocularly warned that he would be court-martialed if the general fell into the water again during the transfer. Nevertheless, he could do nothing when Giraud refused to sit inside the canoe as advised but settled instead on its stern, with his legs inside. When they reached the seaplane, Foot, believing Giraud spoke no English, "advised the reception committee . . . that his passenger was a silly old bastard and that they were welcome to him." Once Giraud had been helped into the Catalina, he turned to Foot and in English thanked him for a very pleasant trip.

The Oran and Algiers Task Forces completed their crossing from the Atlantic into the Mediterranean by the predawn hours of November 7. It was an extraordinary feat of organization by the Royal Navy. Virtually all of the 340 vessels involved had arrived at Gibraltar in proper order and had passed uneventfully through the narrow Strait in proper order as well.

En route, the troops had learned of their destination and purpose and had been instructed in the specific missions of their units. Nervousness inevitably mixed with the bravado of men going into combat for the first time. The mood of American troops aboard British transports was not made easier by a troublesome adjustment they had to make. British cooks provided them with unfamiliar culinary concoctions to which their stomachs had to grow accustomed on the voyage; not something designed to improve their combat readiness.

Once in the Mediterranean, the huge flotilla proceeded almost due east, as if heading for Malta. Submarines of the Royal Navy's special Force H, patrolling the Mediterranean as backup for the Torch escort warships, were positioned in waters near Italian naval bases and off Toulon to detect any suspicious activity by Italian or French warships. As darkness fell on November 7, the various segments of the Center Task Force peeled off southward to assume positions off the three Oran assault areas—two west of the city, one to its east. The Eastern Task Force proceeded eastward until its ships were almost due north of Algiers before veering south to make for the beaches on either side of the Algerian capital that the troops they carried were to assault.

The German High Command still pursued mistaken ideas about what the Allies were up to. Enemy submarines, motor torpedo boats, and aircraft still awaited the Allied flotilla farther into the Mediterranean. Two individual vessels in the operation were attacked. HMS *Panther,* one of the Royal Navy's screening vessels, was damaged but not sunk by a U-boat, and the troop transport USS *Thomas Stone* was hit by a torpedo 150 miles off Algiers. It was left dead in the water with 800 men of the 2nd Battalion, 39th U.S. Infantry Regiment, aboard.

The battalion commander, Major Walter Oakes, had no intention of being left out of the operation because of this mishap. With the agreement of the commander of the *Thomas Stone,* he transferred his men to the ship's twenty-four landing craft so that they might proceed to their assigned landing beach, with the Royal Navy corvette *Spey* for escort. It was a reckless decision. Without the *Spey* for protection, the *Thomas Stone,* unable to move, was an inviting target for any passing German U-boat or aircraft until help arrived.

Of greater consequence for Torch, the landing craft into which the troops had scrambled at sea were not up to the 150-mile voyage they had to complete to reach the Algerian coast. One after another, they were stricken with mechanical problems. Each time it happened, all had to stop until repairs were made. Some of the landing craft collided and soon they were all being swamped. The troops were soaked, tossed about, and hardly in fighting trim. Finally it was realized that the endeavor had been misconceived.

The troops were crammed on board their *Spey* corvette escort, which then proceeded to carry them toward their assigned landing area, where they arrived some twelve hours after the invasion had been launched.

The Western Task Force completed its trek across the Atlantic to Casablanca uneventfully. But a belated close study of its charts aroused anxiety. The naval charts indicated that the coast of Morocco was a few miles west of where the operational charts showed it to be. More worrying was the question of timing. As the long ocean crossing drew toward a climax, convoy commanders were not certain they would arrive at their appointed places at the assigned time. They warned that the landings might have to be made in daylight rather than under the cover of predawn darkness.

Still worse, the weather showed signs of turning foul. If the winds whipped up a nasty surf on the shore—and forecasts of fifteen-foot breakers were being made—it would be impossible for the landing craft to negotiate safe passage to the beaches. If delay was unavoidable, the element of surprise would be lost and the entire Casablanca operation could be in trouble. German submarines, so far eluded, would have a greater chance to gather for the kill, and the French forces ashore, alerted by the landings at Algiers and Oran, if not prepared to cooperate would have time to organize and maximize resistance.

Task Force naval commander Admiral Hewitt contemplated resorting to the emergency alternative plan. That called for his flotilla to change direction, slip north to proceed through the Gibraltar Strait as the Algiers and Oran Task Forces had done, and head for designated contingency beaches on the Mediterranean shore. Troops landed there would then move inland through Algeria to Morocco to take Casblanca and its precious port from the rear.

However, the operation's weather officer disputed the grim radioed predictions from the meteorologists in Washington and London. He forecast that the surf at the landing beaches would abate by H-Hour. Risking fiasco, Hewitt chose to trust that prediction. He instructed the convoy to divide into its three invasion components at dawn of November 7 as planned, and for each to prepare to put its troops ashore at the specified landing points on either side of Casablanca less than twenty-four hours later.

* * *

The seaplane that had picked Giraud up from the submarine he had boarded in the Gulf of Lions off Le Lavandou reached Gibraltar on the afternoon of November 7. H-Hour was now only twelve hours away. If the French general was to be of any use in the operation, he would have to act quickly. The proclamation to be issued in his name had been prepared. It was to tell the people of North Africa that the United States was intervening to block a German invasion and to call on French officers and soldiers to assist the Americans. No reference was to be made to British involvement.

Eisenhower was not certain he could rely on Giraud. He had been rattled and soured by requests and demands for authority, equipment, and funds by the men who claimed through Murphy to speak for the general. Admiral Cunningham had no such concerns. Giraud, he said, had "thrown his coat over the fence. He will do as he is told." He was mistaken.

Giraud walked with a cane but his bearing belied his advanced years. Tall and straight-backed, he had a commanding presence, augmented by his cold gray eyes and his neatly trimmed mustache. Despite his tiring journey, he met with Eisenhower and Clark as soon as he arrived at Gibraltar and made it immediately clear that he did not intend to be told what his role would be. Instead, as the Torch commander reported to the Combined Chiefs of Staff, he proceeded to make a series of unacceptable demands, which were, in fact, little more than the stipulations that had earlier been made on his behalf through his intermediates.

> ... KINGPIN [Giraud] refused to issue any statement that could be broadcast ... either from here or from London or Washington. ... [He] flatly declined to participate in [the] operation except as Allied supreme commander in a position in which he could be completely independent to carry out his own strategic and tactical conceptions. Moreover he insisted that this position must be given to him at once. He stated categorically that by November 10 all forces then ashore must come under his control and that thereafter all forces landing in North Africa would have to come under his command upon debarkation ... [and] that he ... would make all decisions respecting the tactical and strategical employment of the troops. ... It was pointed out to him that until the Allied force can be well established in North Africa, there is no possibility of the two governments disrupting the present command and

staff arrangements that have been so laboriously developed for the control of large ground, air and naval formations. It was further explained that since the plan was already in the process of execution there were measures now going forward, including [the] movement of convoys, the landing of troops and the assignment of tactical objectives, that could not be changed overnight without the creation of great confusion and uncertainty. . . . He is obsessed with the idea of moving immediately into France and implied [that] if he were made commander, he would promptly use the entire air force coming into North Africa in neutralizing Sardinia and transporting troops into southern France. . . . Both EAGLE [Clark] and I urged him to go along with us temporarily . . . under all the assurances that the President has made respecting French sovereignty and territorial integrity. We pointed out that eventual command has already been promised him but that as a soldier he would realize that the establishment of secure bases and development of land and sea communications would require several weeks at least. To all of this he was completely deaf; nothing matters to him except personal command. . . . KINGPIN said that there was no possibility of his guaranteeing non-resistance to our attacks tonight, and would not make any attempt to do so. . . .

Not all of this could be attributed to Giraud's unreasonable stubbornness. In the intrigue that had accompanied Murphy's efforts to guarantee his active commitment to the Allied cause, the general had been given the impression through his intermediaries that it was agreed that he and not Eisenhower would be commander of the Allied forces in the operation. He was angered to learn that such a possibility had never even been considered. Eisenhower, in turn, was astonished to hear him insist that to take command was the only reason he had left Lyons and come to Gibraltar. The Allies were prepared to permit him to assume immediate command of all French forces in North Africa. Eisenhower was willing to go further and offer Giraud "the governorship, virtually the kingship, of North Africa." But Giraud could not be budged. He wanted the total and absolute Torch command he had been led to believe would be his.

His refusal to cooperate compounded the anxiety felt in Gibraltar as H-Hour approached. Both of Eisenhower's political advisers—the State Department's H. Freeman Matthews and the British Foreign Office's William Mack—believed that "the difference between public association and non-association of the Giraud name with the operation might mean the difference between success and disaster." That view was consistent with the emphasis Murphy had placed on the contribution the French general could make.

As the convoys closed in on the landing sites, hours of argument followed at Gibraltar. It was an unnerving experience for Eisenhower. The unpretentious, straight-talking soldier from Kansas who, despite never having commanded in combat before, was Supreme Commander of the most massive amphibious battle operation ever undertaken found himself facing a man whose background, rank, and self-regard had fashioned a kind of arrogance that led him to speak of himself in the third person. It was equally unnerving for Giraud, who, despite his advanced years, had been lured from Lyons mistakenly believing that certain agreements had been made. He now was being required to forget his own plans for action to save France and to act instead in a subsidiary role in accordance with what he believed to be the mistaken judgment of others. Through an interpreter (Colonel Julius Holmes, who had been with Clark at Cherchell), Giraud, not trusting his command of English and feeling slighted and ill-used, kept referring to questions of propriety, honor, and prestige rather than the blood-and-guts problems that worried Eisenhower. Despite Giraud's dignified military bearing, only the belief at Gibraltar that his cooperation could save lives, and perhaps turn the invasion of North Africa into a walkover, kept his regard for his reputation at this critical moment from appearing absurd in the eyes of those trying desperately to elicit his support.

Exhausted by his obstinacy, Eisenhower handed him over to Clark, who was less inclined to show respect to this elderly superior officer. Clark tried to cut things short. He bluntly informed Giraud that the time when his assistance would be useful to the Allies was running out. Either he would immediately offer the support that was required of him or he would have no role whatsoever in the operation. Giraud said he would choose the latter course. He maintained once more that his reputation, dignity, and pride did not permit him to accept a subordinate role, and if he could not be supreme Allied commander, he would not be involved in any way. He would instead be a mere spectator in the affair. Indeed, he would return to France the same way he had left it.

"Oh, no you won't," Clark told him. "That's a one-way submarine. You're not going back to France on it." He instructed the interpreter to inform Giraud, "From now on your ass is out in the snow." Presumably, Colonel Holmes found an appropriate French expression to convey that sentiment to the general.

Despite the exasperation of Eisenhower and Clark, Giraud's obstinacy was not the blind mulishness of an old man. He had genuinely harbored illusions about becoming supreme commander. But he now realized that Eisenhower could not hand that role over to him even if he wanted to. He didn't have the authority. Giraud was playing for time. Expecting at least some and possibly a great deal of resistance to Allied North Africa landings that were not under French command, he did not want to be held responsible for the shedding of French blood by siding with the Allies at that stage. It would destroy his hope of subsequently unifying the French Army against the Germans.

Though vexed by Giraud's behavior, Eisenhower did not completely despair of gaining his assistance. He expected him to prove more compliant if reports came in that the landings were meeting with success. Early reports did not reveal much. Many hours would pass before any clear picture would emerge of how the operation was proceeding. There was little for Eisenhower to do except wait, hope, and compose for himself a litany of "Worries of a Commander":

1. Spain is so ominously quiet that Gov. of Gib. reports himself uneasy. No word from any agent or Ambassador.

2. No news from Task Forces. Reports few and unsatisfactory.

3. Defensive fighting, which seemed half-hearted and spiritless this morning, has blazed up, and in many places resistance is stubborn.

4. No Frenchman immediately available, no matter how friendly toward us, seems able to stop the fighting. (Mast, et al.)

5. Giraud is in Gibraltar, manifestly unwilling to enter the theater so long as fighting is going on.

6. Giraud is difficult to deal with—wants much in power, equipment, etc., but seems little disposed to do his part to stop fighting.

7. Giraud wants planes, radios.

8. We are slowed up in eastern sector when we should be getting toward Bône-Bizerte at once.

9. We don't know whereabouts or conditions of airborne force.

10. We cannot find out anything.

President Franklin Roosevelt and Prime Minister Winston Churchill at the Casablanca Conference NATIONAL ARCHIVES

General George C. Marshall, Chairman of the U.S. Joint Chiefs of Staff (*left*), and General Sir Alan Brooke, Chief of the Imperial General Staff NATIONAL ARCHIVES

Torch Supreme Commander
General Dwight D. Eisenhower
NATIONAL ARCHIVES

General George S. Patton, bodyguards, and personal staff, going
ashore in Morocco after the initial
landings NATIONAL ARCHIVES

Torch naval commander Admiral Sir
Andrew Cunningham NATIONAL ARCHIVES

Torch deputy commander General
Mark Clark NATIONAL ARCHIVES

General Henri Giraud (*second from right*) while a German prisoner, before his
escape and involvement in Operation Torch NATIONAL ARCHIVES

(*Left to right*) General Dwight Eisenhower, Admiral Jean Darlan, General
Mark Clark, and American chargé d'affaires Robert Murphy in Algiers
NATIONAL ARCHIVES

General Omar Bradley, who assumed command of the U.S. II Corps during
operations in Tunisia, shown here aboard the navy flagship during the
subsequent invasion of Sicily   U.S. NAVY

General Charles Mast, who disobeyed instructions from Vichy and assisted the Allied landings at Algiers, shown here with his wife
NATIONAL ARCHIVES

Vichy chief of state Marshal Philippe Pétain (*left*) and Pierre Laval, Vichy's primary collaborator with the Germans
NATIONAL ARCHIVES

Soldier descending cargo net
during pre-operation amphibious
landing practice in Maryland
NATIONAL ARCHIVES

Equipment being prepared for
disembarkation following initial
landings at Fedala, Morocco
U.S. NAVY

Troops disembarking from transport
vessel into landing craft
NATIONAL ARCHIVES

Landing craft carrying troops
streaking ashore from transports
anchored off Moroccan coast
U.S. NAVY

Troops wading ashore at Oran, Algeria, on D-Day NATIONAL ARCHIVES

Troops storming ashore in Algeria were prepared to meet heavy resistance but met little. NATIONAL ARCHIVES

Troops in a landing craft en route to a designated landing beach near Oran
NATIONAL ARCHIVES

Amphibious activity by the Allied forces during the landings often attracted
the curiosity of local Arab civilians. NATIONAL ARCHIVES

Much equipment was landed on the wrong beaches by mistake or accident in the opening phases of the operation. Much of it was abandoned. NATIONAL ARCHIVES

Some troops commandeered local vehicles to advance when their own equipment failed to be put ashore where expected. NATIONAL ARCHIVES

Soldiers take a break near Oran while waiting for their unit to regroup.
NATIONAL ARCHIVES

The U.S. Army quickly made its presence known in Algiers, but only after a
pro-Allied coup had been crushed. NATIONAL ARCHIVES

The U.S. Navy provided aerial cover off the coast of Morocco for the armada that had crossed the Atlantic from Virginia. NATIONAL ARCHIVES

It was while traversing the rugged terrain of Tunisia that the U.S. Army learned that the road to Berlin would be long and hard. NATIONAL ARCHIVES

Wary troops in Tunisia examine a knocked-out German vehicle for booby traps. NATIONAL ARCHIVES

Virtually none of the more than a quarter of a million Axis troops in North Africa escaped death or capture by the time Operation Torch's mission was successfully concluded. Caring for the prisoners became a major logistical problem. NATIONAL ARCHIVES

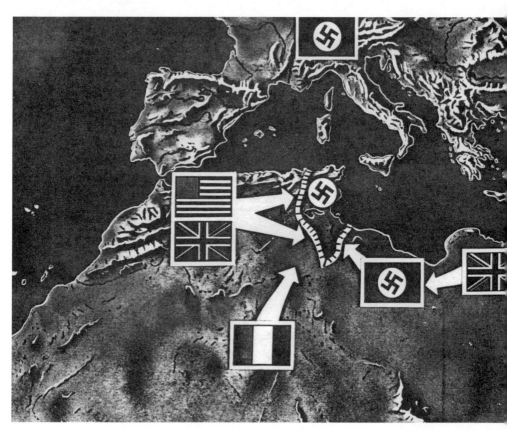

1943 U.S. Office of W[ar]
Information propagand[a]
showing American, Br[itish]
and French forces seali[ng]
trap on German forces [in]
Tunisia NATIONAL ARCH[IVES]

GENERAL HEADQUARTERS, U. S. ARMY

ARMY WAR COLLEGE

WASHINGTON, D. C.

LY REFER TO:

January 15, 1942.

MEMORANDUM FOR THE C.G., FIELD FORCES.

Subject: Future Operations.

1. The two inclosures herewith are intended to indicate briefly:
a. The reasons why Gymnast should not be undertaken. These
comments are the result of studies still in progress at this headquarters
by C.G., III Army Corps, and his staff, and by the staff of this headquarters.
b. A description of a plan with the same general objective as
Gymnast, but feasible and sound. This plan would be the basis of the
major effort of the United States against Axis.

2. While I do not know what transpired yesterday, I urge that the
necessary steps - whatever they may be - be taken to abandon Gymnast completely, and to embark on the substitute plan at the earliest possible
date entirely independently of Great Britain. All other plans for offensive action toward Europe likewise should be abandoned. The occupation
of Iceland is a dispersion of forces and preferably should be abandoned
as soon as possible. The expeditions to Great Britain must be viewed as
secondary and as weakening our main effort, and should be restricted in
every way possible. The reinforcement of the British in the Middle East
with combat units also should be avoided, since an offensive, or preparations therefor, in Northwest Africa would be simpler and probably more
effective. We must take the offensive in our own way, our own theater,
with the greatest possible force, and at the earliest practicable time.

L. J. McNAIR,
Lt. Gen., G.S.C.,
Chief of Staff.

Incls:
Comments on Gymnast.
Sub. for Gymnast.
Nat.Geo.Mag.map: Africa.

Secret memorandum, one
month after Pearl Harbor,
displaying aversion felt by
some in the U.S. War De-
partment to joint operation[s]
with the British forces
NATIONAL ARCHIVES

SECRET

Memorandum:

Subject: Operations in Western Europe.

1. Western Europe is favored as the theater in which to stage the first major offensive by the United States and Great Britain. By every applicable basis of comparison, it is definitely superior to any other. In point of time required to produce effective results, its selection will save many months. Through France passes our shortest route to the heart of Germany. In no other area can we attain the overwhelming air superiority vital to successful land attack; while here and here only can the bulk of the British air and ground forces be employed. In this area the United States can concentrate and maintain a larger force than it can in any other. A British-American attack through western Europe provides the only feasible method for employing the bulk of the combat power of the United States, the United Kingdom and Russia in a concerted effort against a single enemy.

Another, and most significant consideration is the unique opportunity to establish an active sector on this front this summer, through steadily increasing air operations and by raids or forays all along the coasts. This initial phase will be of some help to Russia and of immediate satisfaction to the public; but what is most important it will make experienced veterans of the air and ground units, and it will offset the tendency toward deterioration in morale which threaten the latter due to prolonged inactivity.

Finally, successful attack through Western Europe will afford the maximum possible support to Russia, whose continued participation in the war is essential to the defeat of Germany.

2. Decision as to the main effort must be made now. This is true even if the invasion cannot be launched during this year. A major attack must be preceded by a long period of intensive preparation. Basic decision is necessary so that all production, special construction, training, troop movements and allocations can be coordinated to a single end. Until this process of coordinated and intensified effort is initiated, it is difficult to calculate even the approximate date at which a major offensive can be undertaken. Decision now will stop continued dispersion of means.

Draft of a position paper presenting the views of General George Marshall and the U.S. War Department's Operations Division in an abortive attempt to overcome British resistance to an early invasion of France NATIONAL ARCHIVES

---

e #3 of Number 262, July 11, 1942.

My own position has been that if ordered to conduct an offen-

e this year an attempt at Sledgehammer in spite of its obvious risks

costs would be preferable to Gymnast or other major expeditions in-

ded to open up an entirely new front unrelated to this theater. I

not repeat not believe that the British rejection of Sledgehammer

ses from any lack of desire to take the offensive but from deep con-

tion that it is not feasible as a permanent invasion. THe fixed pur-

e among the staffs to adhere to a decisive purpose grows daily more

iceable and in my opinion they will oppose anything that they believe

l seriously interfere with mountings of the major plan. They realize

t overall planning for next year has not progressed as rapidly as is

uired and most individuals among them believe that one reason for this

clumsiness in their organization. This fact is one of the causes for

British pressure for early appointment of a supreme commander. I feel

tain that most of them believe such commander will promptly arrange

or command organization for the British forces assigned to him according

his own desires. Some British officers have been outspoken to me in

ir desire to have you as supreme commander even though they realize

t in view of the enormity of your present duties you would have to

rate largely by long distance methods for a considerable time.

Eisenhower

Part of a cable from General Eisenhower in London to General Marshall in Washington in July 1942 explaining his and the British position on Operation Sledgehammer that was about to be abandoned against Marshall's wishes NATIONAL ARCHIVES

PROCLAMATION

ARMY OF THE UNITED STATES

Headquarters of the Theater of Operations

_____1942

TO THE PEOPLE OF: FRENCH NORTH AFRICA

In keeping with the ancient and traditional friendship of the Government and people of the United States of America, for French North Africa and its people, the American forces have landed in your country. We come among you as friends, not as conquerors. We want you to receive us as friends.

Our purpose, as the President of the United States of America has proclaimed, is to protect your country from invasion by our common enemies, and to maintain your authority and to secure to your country and its people, the enjoyment of an orderly government, of its choice.

When conditions permit and the necessity for our presence shall have ceased, our troops will be withdrawn.

Your religious institutions and customs will be completely respected.

Your laws and regulations will remain in force, except insofar as they may be inconsistent with a state of war and military necessities, or with the safety of our forces.

The officers and employees of your government and its administrative districts will continue their duties as usual, and co-operate with the forces of the United States, for the security of its inhabitants, and the American troops, and in the maintenance of internal order. You are urged to continue your work, to keep open your churches, mosques, temples, and schools, and to follow as far as possible, the usual habits and customs of your lives and the business of your community.

All governmental officials and employees, including police, both local and state, and all officers and men of the Army, Navy and Air Corps, who co-operate with the American military authorities, will continue to receive at the same rate and in the same amounts, all salaries, pensions and benefits that they now enjoy, under the guarantee of the Government of the United States of America.

Your patriotic duty is clear; it is confidently expected that you will co-operate with the American forces and will observe such orders and regula- tions as your governing authorities, or I, as Commanding General of these forces may issue.

This observance is necessary to assure the safety and tranquility of your country and yourselves.

Dwight D. Eisenhower

DWIGHT D. EISENHOWER
Lieutenant General, U.S. Army
Commanding

Draft of General Eisenhower's D-Day proclamation to the people of French North Africa NATIONAL ARCHIVES

HEADQUARTERS 53D SIGNAL BATTALION
APO 302

SECRET

(EQUALS BRITISH MOST SECRET)

29 December 1942

SUBJECT: Lessons from Operation TORCH.

TO   : Commanding General, Center Task Force.

1. In compliance with 1st Ind., Letter, AF Hq, AG 370.2 /054-C 16 December 1942, the following report, based on the experience of this or- ization in operation TORCH, is submitted.

2. Movement

a. Embarkation. Movement orders received from British Movement were not identical with authorizations from CTF Headquarters relative to assignments of personnel and vehicles to transports and to the shipment equipment. Last minute changes in unit embarkation plans were necessit resulting in motor convoys not moving on schedule, westage of shipping and changes in the assignment of personnel to detachments.

b. Debarkation. Personnel from this organization were on the as long as 30 hours before the first vehicles and equipment were landed

c. There were instances of equipment being delivered at the po embarkation in good order which arrived at destination in bad order. S of the equipment shipped was not received at destination. Guards and m tenance details should accompany each shipment of vehicles and equipmen give reasonable assurance of arrival at destination in good order.

3. Operations.

a. Efficient operations has been hampered by the following:

(1) Lack of sufficient platoon, company and battalion trai

(2) Lack of training with the headquarters being served

(3) Lack of sufficient training with some of the equipment used.

(4) Lack of sufficient training with communication personnel other units participating in the operation. (Link-sign procedure a spe case)

(5) Lack of information necessary to keep the situation pos on a map. (Unless well informed, both as to the tactical and the commun situation, communication personnel are unable to act with the initiative and accuracy expected of them. It is believed that lack of information for the loss of an officer and two men who unnecessarily entered a dange area while on duty in connection with the delivery of an important messa

(6) Necessity of improvising ways to accomplish mission due lack of TBA transportation and equipment.

(7) Improper address on messages and lack of return address envelope.

Part of one of the many reports submitted by U.S. units concerning problems that arose during the North Africa landings
PUBLIC RECORD OFFICE, LONDON

★ 12 ★

SHOWDOWN IN ALGIERS

Here we are with a city on our hands. It is bizarre.

—CONSPIRATOR JEAN RIGAULT

Of the conspiracies afoot in North Africa, clandestine plans to ease the way for the invaders had been most highly developed in Algiers. Almost a thousand insurgents, many of them armed, some of them army officers, were supposed to be prepared to spring into action in the Algerian capital at the appointed time to seize control of the city and block resistance to the landings.

Teams of insurgents were set to seize the Algiers radio station, police headquarters, and other important public buildings and installations. They would take control of the telephone and other communications systems. Where possible, they would take into custody key military and civilian personnel who might prove obstructive. The French Navy, traditionally more conservative, had been generally far less restive politically than elements of the army officer corps. Senior French naval commanders had been considered unlikely to cooperate at first, so no serious effort had been made to draw them into the conspiracy. But plans had been made to sever the navy's communications system in North Africa to hamper armed naval resistance when the invasion began.

Much depended on timing. The insurgents had reason to doubt whether the senior army officers in Algiers would cooperate with the Allies. Though known to be anti-German, General Alphonse

Juin, the commander of French ground and air forces in North Africa, and General Louis Koeltz, XIX Corps commander, were expected to obey recently restated orders from Vichy that invaders of whatever stripe were to repelled. Indeed, Juin had clearly indicated to Murphy that he would obey those orders. Their own comparative weakness and the positions of authority of the people they were likely to be up against led the conspirators to accept their own limitations. They did not expect to be able to hold the key installations they planned to seize for more than a few hours. But the invading Allied troops were not likely to need more time than that to establish themselves and take control of the situation in order to keep the coup from being crushed by those acting in accordance with Vichy's instructions.

The landings at the beaches near Algiers were scheduled for 1:00 A.M., Sunday, November 8. But only a few of the senior French conspirators knew that in advance—and not till four days before had those few been informed. That left little time for detailed preparations. Having been told only that the invasion would not be long in coming, most of the others had assumed the landings were planned for much later in November at the earliest. Many of them still were under that impression.

For fear of a leak if word spread too early even in insurgent circles, necessary arrangements were not due to be made until nearer to what was thought would be D-Day. Unaware of the actual timing, many who were counted on to take part in the coup had left town for the weekend as they often did. Others could not be activated because the leaders of their particular sections were away. Though important tasks were to be assigned to various insurgents at the proper moment, fewer than four hundred were available to sweep into action when the critical moment arrived.

On the the evening of Friday, November 6, several of the key conspirators met at their secret headquarters, the Rue Michelet apartment of Dr. Henri Aboulker, a prominent Jewish eye specialist whose son José, a twenty-one-year-old medical student, was a leading figure among the young insurgents. At that time they learned from Colonel Émile Jousse, administrative officer of the XIX Corps, that they had little more than twenty-four hours to prepare to seize control of Algiers.

White armbands with black letters were distributed for use by the insurgents. They identified the wearers as belonging to a volunteer militia. They thus could be mistaken for thugs of the Service d'Ordre Légionnaire (SOL), the pro-Vichy official militia. It was expected to intimidate possibly obstructive police. The insurgents were informed where they were to receive weapons and vehicles. Gas, in short supply in Algeria, was to be provided by the American consulate, which was also holding back a thousand liters for a motorcade reception for Giraud.

Though the others did not yet know it, General Mast, the most senior of the conspirators, would not be taking part in the Algiers takeover. He was not much enamored of civilian insurgencies; his effort was to be directed toward preventing armed resistance to the invaders. He intended to make his way before H-Hour to the shore west of the city to assist the invaders by his presence.

At 10:30 on Saturday night, just hours before the landings were scheduled to begin, Murphy and the senior conspirators gathered anxiously at Dr. Aboulker's house-cum-HQ. Shortly before midnight, they heard a coded radio message broadcast from London on the French language service of the BBC: *Allo, Robert. Franklin arrive.* That allusion to Robert Murphy and Franklin Roosevelt, hardly the most indecipherable of messages, was the signal that the invasion was about to begin.

Elated that the moment they had long prepared for had finally arrived, the conspirators swept into action. As the troops offshore prepared to scramble down the cargo nets of their transport vessels and board their landing craft, teams of young men, some led by junior army officers, were dispatched to seize the Algiers radio station, police headquarters, and telephone centers. Communications lines with the naval command and coastal batteries were severed. As expected, General Koeltz refused to join the uprising unless ordered by superior authority to do so. He was placed in protective custody as were officials, their names drawn from a previously prepared list, who were thought capable of interfering with the proceedings. One of them, awakened by insurgents who burst into his bedroom, was so bewildered by what was happening that he kept protesting that he was loyal to Pétain and Laval. Meantime, as planned, guides were dispatched to lead the invading troops into the city as quickly as possible so that the military takeover could be achieved before any armed reaction to the coup could be organized.

The coup was remarkably successful. "The entire town of Al-

giers was actually in our hands," Vice-Consul Pendar later wrote,
"without people realizing that anything had happened." Murphy
had by then proceeded with his more delicate task. He had expected Giraud to be in Algiers by then, or at least to have issued a
suitably pro-Allied proclamation from Gibraltar. But Giraud was
still refusing to cooperate. Murphy realized he would have to do
without him, for the moment at least.

Around 12:30 A.M. on November 8, a half hour before the invasion at Algiers was scheduled to be launched, he drove to the Villa
des Oliviers in an outlying section of the Algerian capital, a sump-
tuous mini-palace that served as General Juin's official residence.
Juin, who received him in his pajamas, had been informed by
telephone that Murphy was coming to see him on a matter of great
urgency. He told the general that the landings were already taking
place. He urged him to order that they not be resisted because "you
desire above all else to see the liberation of France which can come
about only through cooperation with the United States."

Juin had known of the Allied convoys in the Mediterranean. But
like others, he had believed they were headed for Malta. He had
earlier been assured by Murphy that American forces would come
to North Africa only when invited. Murphy now said that such an
invitation had been issued—by General Giraud. Juin was not impressed. As far as he was concerned, whatever his other qualities,
Giraud was a retired officer with no official authority. Besides,
where was he? Murphy told him that he was expected momentarily
but what guarantee was there that Murphy was telling the truth?

Juin didn't appreciate being placed in so awkward a position. He
was not a political general. Like most senior French officers, regardless of what he thought of the Vichy regime, he accepted it as
the legitimate government of France whose orders he was pledged
to obey.

General Juin paced the floor for a number of minutes [Murphy later
wrote] making references to the grave situation which was thus presented and regretting vehemently that he had not been taken into our
confidence before. To these regrets [I] pointed to the fact that General
Juin had taken an oath of allegiance to the French Government and that
it had not been desired to place him in a situation embarrassing to an
army officer, but that knowing his sentiments we were confident of his
support when the time came.

Juin longed for the Germans to be driven from French soil and might have wavered under other circumstances. "If the matter was entirely in my hands," he told Murphy, "I would be with you. But . . . Darlan is in Algiers. He outranks me and no matter what decision I might make, Darlan could immediately overrule it."

That was true and presented Murphy with a problem. After the Allied command had concluded that Giraud was the French figure who would best serve their purposes in North Africa, the idea of dealing with Darlan had been put on hold. Now Murphy was left with no option but to explore what could be done with the admiral.

Darlan's presence in Algeria was unexpected. He had just gone back to Vichy after having completed an inspection of French military installations in France's African territories to determine how prepared they were to resist an attack from any quarter. But he had hurriedly returned to Algiers to be with his son, who had been stricken with polio and who, he had just been informed, was in critical condition. (It is, however, possible that that was an excuse, and that Darlan's presence was linked to an expectation of military developments in France's North African territories.)

As supreme commander of Vichy's armed forces, the admiral was in a position to do what Juin felt he himself could not do—order that no resistance be offered to the invaders wherever they came ashore. What was more, he could order French troops in Tunisia to resist the arrival of German forces there if they were dispatched—as they were likely to be—in reaction to the Torch landings.

Arrangements now had to be made for Murphy to confer with Darlan without delay. Juin agreed to contact the admiral by phone. He told him that Murphy was with him at his residence and had an urgent message for him. Darlan was staying at a villa about a mile away. He said he would be willing to see Murphy, and a car was sent to bring him to the Villa des Oliviers. When Darlan got there and Murphy told him what was happening, he exploded in fury. "I have known for a long time that the British are stupid," he snapped, "but I always believed Americans were more intelligent. Apparently you have the same genius as the British for making massive blunders!" He maintained that if he had been informed in advance and if the Americans had been prepared to wait a few weeks, he could have organized effective French cooperation not only for the landings in North Africa but for a simultaneous invasion of France itself. He said the American move, if it actually was taking place, was all the Germans would need to occupy Vichy France and the North African territories as well.

Murphy reminded the admiral that more than a year earlier, he had told Ambassador Leahy in Vichy that he would be ready to cooperate with the Americans when they were prepared to send half a million troops and fleets of aircraft to liberate France. Murphy told him, "That moment has now arrived." Darlan was not sure that it had. Murphy spoke of a huge invasion force, escorted by a powerful armada of warships. But where were the troops? Where were the noises of war? Where were the reports of landings? Murphy could not say. He did not know exactly what was happening. The Allied fleet had been instructed to maintain radio silence prior to the landings and he had been out of contact with his radio-equipped secret headquarters since just before the landings were supposed to have begun.

Unable to reach Admiral Jacques Moreau, the naval commander in French North Africa, by telephone—the insurgents had cut the lines—Darlan instructed one of his aides to go to him to determine if an American invasion was truly in progress. But the young, white-armbanded, armed insurgents who, under an army cadet, had now taken command of the military guard around Juin's residence would not permit the aide through. Not even Juin was permitted out. He and Darlan were effectively being kept under house arrest by a handful of youngsters.

Anxiously awaiting word that the landings on the beaches had successfully taken place and that the troops were about to enter Algiers itself, Murphy vainly persisted in his attempt to persuade the Frenchmen to throw in their lot with the Americans. But as far as Darlan could see and hear, despite Murphy's claims and assurances, the night was passing and no invasion was taking place. He knew it was unlikely that the American had invented the story, either for the benefit of the Allies or for the armbanded insurgents who presumed to prevent him from leaving Juin's villa. That would have been pointless and futile. But it could have been that a small, brief, Dieppe-scale commando raid was taking place somewhere along the coast.

Yet Darlan also understood that such an operation could serve no significant purpose without French acquiescence, and that would not be forthcoming if only because it would provoke the

Germans to more effective action. Unless proof was provided that a full-scale American invasion was actually in progress, Darlan had no intention of even considering an order to French forces not to resist.

Not till 3:00 A.M. did the sound of heavy guns shatter the silence of predawn Algiers. But even then Darlan, doubting the magnitude of the attack, refused to comply with Murphy's request for cooperation unless he first received Pétain's approval. Murphy suggested that he now seek such approval. Darlan agreed. He composed a cable that was to be sent to Vichy. It was put in a sealed envelope and given to Vice-Consul Pendar to take to French naval headquarters for dispatch. Pendar had accompanied Murphy that night and was permitted to pass through the cordon of insurgents around Juin's villa.

Not trusting Darlan, he took the cable back to Dr. Aboulker's Rue Michelet insurgent headquarters, where he had the envelope steamed open to determine what the admiral was actually up to. "Late at night," Darlan's message to Pétain read, "I received a telephone call to come to General Juin's house, where I found myself in the presence of M. Murphy. He told me that the American fleet was off the North African coast in force. I told him I had given my word to you, the Chief of State, that I would defend the Empire with our fullest force against anyone infringing upon it."

Darlan clearly was not yet willing to burn his bridges and commit himself to cooperating with the Allies. He was still keeping his options open. The cable therefore was not delivered to French naval headquarters for dispatch. It was now almost 4:00 A.M. The only thing to do was sit tight, keep Darlan in custody to prevent him from mobilizing resistance to the invasion, and wait for the tardy invaders to arrive. Murphy wrote a message for Western Assault Force commander General Ryder informing him that it was essential for at least some American troops to show up in Algiers quickly or things might get out of hand. But as the night slipped away, there was still no sign of them in Algiers. With each passing hour, the ability of Murphy and the insurgents to retain control of the situation was eroded. One of the leading conspirators informed Murphy he could not answer for what would happen after daybreak.

*　*　*

In fact, the invasion had begun as planned at around 1:00 A.M, though not without mishap. The landings, taking place on either side of Algiers, were divided into three sectors, code-named Apple, Beer, and Charlie. At Apple Sector, all went well. Seven thousand men of the British 11th Infantry Brigade Group went ashore at two sites near the coastal town of Castiglione west of Algiers and quickly secured their landing areas. They met no resistance. The only units of French troops they encountered told them they were under orders not to resist. General Mast had done his work well there.

At Beer Sector, also west of Algiers but closer to the city, 4,355 American infantrymen and 1,065 British commandos landed at two beach areas. While some were to secure the coastal area, others were to push inland and approach Algiers through its southern heights. For these troops, the operation was a mixed success. A section of the British 1st Commando met no resistance and many of its troops, after uneventfully wading ashore, marked the occasion of reaching Africa by sitting down on the beach to change their socks. Their good fortune did not end there. Assigned the task of taking Fort de Sidi-Ferruch and its heavy guns, and ready for a fight, they found the garrison there obeying orders to receive them amicably. Indeed, General Mast was there to welcome them personally.

For the British 6th Commando, things did not go as well. Problems with landing craft, some of which were in such poor mechanical shape that they should never have been brought along, delayed the first wave for two hours and the subsequent waves even longer. As a consequence, the main initial target of these troops, Fort Duperré on the western coastal fringe of Algiers, wasn't reached until after daylight. Its garrison refused to submit and British naval aircraft had to be summoned to deal with the problem. It would not be resolved for several hours.

Meantime, confusion had reigned for the 1st Battalion, U.S. 168th Infantry, which was supposed to make for the main western coastal road and a rapid entry into Algiers. Landing craft coxswains had been unable to find their assigned beaches. Through piloting errors, the troops were put ashore on the wrong beach and had no idea where they were or what they were to do next.

Suspicions would later be expressed by some Americans that the

208

Royal Navy deliberately landed troops at undesignated beaches for fear of treachery by French insurgents, some of whom knew by then where the landings were to take place. That was sour grapes. It definitely was not planned for some of the troops to be unloaded in water over their heads so that they had to struggle ashore as best they could with packs on their backs weighing sixty pounds or more. The consequences might have been grave, as one American officer later reported:

> We received no opposition whatsoever from the beach and if we had in that condition of landing, it would have been a complete failure in my opinion, as the troops in the wallowing boats and those in the water would have been helpless against enemy fire.

Little in the way of transport was successfully brought ashore for the troops. Vehicles and the men they were to carry had been loaded onto different landing craft and, after unloading, the latter had trouble finding the former in the darkness.

Communications equipment had been damaged during landing or proved unreliable for other reasons. That made it difficult for dispersed units to regroup rapidly. After landing, some battalions found themselves spread out along fifteen miles of the coast. Officers commandeered whatever vehicles they could find and raced up and down trying to locate their men and reform their units.

At Charlie Sector, the U.S. 39th Combat Team and the mixed 1st Commando, a total of 6,000 American and British troops, ran into a variety of problems. Originally Charlie Sector was to consist of four landing areas. But because men from the torpedoed *Thomas Stone* were out of the operation for the moment, it was decided to confine the sector to three beaches instead. Appropriate prelanding planning adjustments had to be made, with resulting snarls. In addition, fog delayed some of the landings and inexperience showed there as well. Some of the landing-craft crews misread directional markers and their craft went astray at first.

As dispersed units began piecing themselves together on the shore to trudge off toward Algiers and other strategic objectives in the area, a violent clash was taking place in the harbor of the city. At 3:00 A.M., two destroyers—HMS *Broke* and *Malcolm*—flying

American flags and carrying 665 American and British officers and men, all in American uniforms, raced in to seize the harbor and prevent French warships there from being scuttled. It was meant to be a surprise operation despite the fact that the French forces responsible for harbor defenses were likely to know of the troop landings hours earlier on either side of Algiers. It had been hoped that once alerted, port defense personnel would have been dispatched to help cope with those landings. At the same time, coastal batteries above the port were by then supposed to have been put out of action by an assault unit of commandos reaching the area from its landing beach. Finally, it had also been hoped that the French defending the port would not fire on Americans.

None of that convenient set of expectations was fulfilled. The commandos had not been able to reach the batteries, and as soon as the destroyers were spotted by searchlight beams, the coastal guns let loose a withering barrage of fire. Those were the sounds that finally persuaded Darlan that it was possible an invasion was actually being attempted. The *Malcolm* was hit, its engine room was badly holed, and it was forced to withdraw. However, the *Broke* ran the gauntlet of fire, smashed through a boom blocking entry to the harbor, managed to berth successfully despite heavy machine-gun fire, and disgorged its troops. They quickly seized the pier, the port's electric power station, and other installations in the immediate vicinity and established control of the area.

The batteries that had opened fire had awakened the city. Officers, most of whom had known nothing of the coup until then, began arriving at or contacting French Army headquarters, which had been taken over by insurgents. Those officers quickly realized that something very strange was happening. Reports circulated that key centers in Algiers were not functioning as they normally did. Troops and police were sent to investigate. General Koeltz threw a note from the window of the building in which he was still being held in custody by the insurgents. Within minutes, soldiers came to his rescue, dispersing his captors.

From that point on, the coup, which would have had a good chance of succeeding had the invading troops rolled into Algiers in the middle of the night, quickly collapsed. General Mast was ordered relieved of his command and the orders he had issued that the invaders were not to be resisted were countermanded. Uncertain of how to deal with a situation that was yet to be clarified and hoping to avoid a bloody clash with the Americans, General Juin ordered French forces to defend their positions but to limit their action to "elastic but nonaggressive" contact with the invaders.

Calls flooded in to coup headquarters from insurgents at various positions in Algiers. They wanted to know whether they were to continue to hold out or surrender. In fact, few of them had much choice. Those who had seized the radio station, police station, and other key installations were soon taken prisoner or scattered. Some were killed. A detachment of Gardes Mobiles police armed with submachine guns had already arrived at Juin's residence to disperse the cordon of youthful insurgents there, free Darlan, and take Murphy prisoner.

The troops landed by the destroyer *Broke* who had seized the port area were still in control there. Indeed, a delegation of French police officers and civilians had been received by them soon after daybreak and told them that Algiers was ready to surrender to the Americans. But French troops, newly ordered to resist, closed in on the port invaders, who had begun running low on ammunition. A few managed to return to the *Broke* before it was forced by artillery fire to withdraw badly damaged from the harbor. The others were compelled to surrender.

The assault on the harbor had not been well thought out. It was excessively daring. The troops landing on the beaches hoped for a welcome but knew they might meet stiff resistance. In contrast, the mission to seize the harbor had been premised on the unwarranted assumption that resistance in the port would be weak or nonexistent. Once strong resistance developed, it was doomed. In a report on the assault on the harbor, one of the U.S. infantry officers involved later said the mission had been "by its very nature, ill conceived, foolhardy, and well nigh impossible of accomplishment. In its adherence to the correct principles of warfare, it should be placed in the same category as Pickett's Charge at Gettysburg, and the Charge of the Light Brigade in the Crimean War." As if in a mocking commentary on the incident, the *Broke*, disabled, lingered outside the port until it sank to the bottom the following day.

Though the attempt to seize the harbor had failed, the landing operations on either side of Algiers continued to meet only light resistance. However, the advance of the invaders on the city was delayed until daylight. By then Murphy, whose months of intrigue and conspiracy had almost been capped with triumph, was a captive of the Gardes Mobiles who, bewildered by what had transpired during the night, thought he was a German and contemplated shooting him.

Ironically, the failure of the coup was in part a result of one of the achievements of the conspirators. A barrage by the coastal battery at Cape Sidi-Ferruch against the Task Force could have provided the noises of war around 1:00 A.M., at the time of the first landings. That might have convinced Darlan that the massive invasion of which Murphy spoke was indeed under way. But its gunners had been ordered or persuaded to hold their fire and that graphic message was therefore not delivered. Instead, the gunfire in Algiers harbor erupted too late for Murphy to intimidate the wavering admiral into capitulating. By then, Darlan had gathered his wits and had begun examining alternative possibilities and considering his future.

☆ 13 ☆

ORAN

This place gives me the goddamned creeps!
—AMERICAN SOLDIER ON THE SHORE

The coup in Algiers probably would have succeeded if American troops had reached the city during the night rather than during the late morning. But the uprising planned for Oran two hundred miles to the west, which was to take place at exactly the same time, fizzled out before it began.

Oran was a far less important center than the Algerian capital and from the start had fewer well-placed conspirators to draw upon. Several who might have been among its leading activists had shifted to Algiers well before D-Day and were active there instead on the night of the invasion. Included among them was a French Air Force major who had been strategically placed to assist the Allied seizure of an Oran airfield. He had been transferred a few days earlier to an assignment at an airport near Algiers where he was not in a position to offer as much help.

Colonel Paul Tostain, chief of staff of the Oran Division, was also a disappointment. Tostain was supposed to be the senior insurgent in the city. He was to arrange for the seizure of key military installations so that they would not be used against the invaders. He was also to arrest his commanding general, if he proved hostile, before orders could be issued to resist the landings. But Tostain felt isolated. Without the comforting support of a large group of like-minded conspirators, he felt unable to undertake such grave acts of insubordination or to collaborate with the invaders in any other way. Informed in advance, American Vice-Consul Ridgeway Knight sent a warning message to Gibraltar that the Allies could expect serious resistance at Oran.

As at Algiers, landings were to be made at 1:00 A.M. at three sectors on either side of Oran. After securing their landing beaches, the troops were to converge on the city. As at Algiers, inexperience and bad luck were much in evidence. Because of a pesky current and a variety of miscalculations and mishaps at Mersa Bou Zedjar west of Oran, the second wave went ashore before the first. The troops met no resistance and the beach was quickly secured. But the *Bachaquero,* a supply vessel carrying tanks with which the men planned to advance on Oran, was able to get no farther than a quarter mile from the shore of the shallow bay, and a pontoon bridge laid by the 16th Armored Engineers didn't at first quite reach land. Vehicles that were put ashore elsewhere with less trouble found the soft sand of the beaches difficult to negotiate. Many had to be manhandled onto terra firma before they could move off toward the city, a time-consuming process.

Troops landing at the beaches of Les Andalouses, closer to Oran, also met no resistance at first but they too ran into difficulties. The rungs of the ladders of the troop transport *Monarch of Bermuda* were two feet apart and provided no easy descent to the landing craft for men burdened by heavy backpacks. Some of the landing craft encountered a sandbar some distance from the shore. Believing they had reached shallow water, their crews quickly began disembarking troops and unloading equipment, only to discover that the water depth plummeted again up to five feet between the sandbar and the beach. Jeeps and equipment were lost as the men found themselves having to swim to shore, fearing they might become targets of gunfire if French resistance materialized on the dry land toward which they struggled with their rifles and packs.

Fewer problems were encountered at the main Oran landing beach, at the Gulf of Arzew, east of the city. A Royal Navy officer later described a first-wave landing there as having been as peaceful an invasion as could have been hoped for.

214

[W]e beached very quietly indeed; there was hardly a sound. The Americans went off excellently and very quietly, so quietly in fact that once they were on the beach, the sound of their feet on the sand woke one of the inhabitants of a cabana who opened his door letting out a flood of light and who was completely bewildered by soldiers running past him on either side and he stood there in trousers and shirt scratching his head and wondering what was happening.

It was at Arzew that most of the Oran Task Force went ashore, including a U.S. Ranger battalion assigned to securing two nearby French coastal batteries. That was quickly and efficiently accomplished. But trouble was yet to come both on shore and during an attempt from the sea to seize the port of Oran intact so that it could be quickly converted into the primary supply port for the Allied forces.

Nothing was to be risked at Oran on the possibility that cooperation would be forthcoming from the French military. The naval base of Mers el-Kébir, which the Royal Navy had attacked in 1940, was just a few miles away. Memories of that raid were fresh in French minds. It was feared that once the French realized that the invasion had been launched, they might destroy the port before it could be secured. To prevent that, an operation was planned that was so hazardous and chancy that U.S. Rear Admiral Andrew C. Bennett, commander of the Advance Group of the Amphibious Force, Atlantic Fleet, considered it both suicidal and likely to be futile.

The exploit was undertaken by the *Walney* and the *Hartland,* former U.S. Coast Guard cutters that had been transferred to the Royal Navy the previous year. Aboard the two vessels now was a small American assault force. The ships were to dash into the port of Oran under the cover of darkness at 3:00 A.M. and disgorge those troops, who were to then capture the fort at the end of the harbor, prevent French ships there from being scuttled, seize the docks before they could be damaged, and if possible, knock out a gun battery perched on a cliff overlooking the harbor.

It was accepted that the operation obviously could not be a complete surprise. Amphibious landings on either side of Oran had been scheduled to begin some two hours earlier and the alert had already been given. But it was thought that French defenders of the harbor would consider such a raid so unlikely that they would have taken no special precautions and the element of surprise would be sustained.

As the *Walney,* with the *Hartland* not far behind it, headed for the port, clinging to the shadow of the cliffs above the harbor as long as possible, Oran was blacked out in expectation of trouble. Sirens had sounded across the city. Though now a British vessel, the *Walney* flew an American flag as well as a British ensign, and as it closed on the port, its loudspeaker called out in French that the vessel was on a friendly mission.

The French were not convinced. A searchlight beam picked out the vessel. An instant later a shell from a shore gun struck it, making bitter nonsense of a message it had just received from the *Largs,* the operations headquarters ship, that there was "No shooting thus far; landings unopposed. Don't start a fight unless you have to." The *Hartland* still following in its wake, the *Walney* made for the harbor at full tilt despite the damage it had sustained. It took further damage from shell and machine-gun fire but smashed through a floating boom that had been positioned to block the harbor entrance, almost ramming a French sloop that raked its decks as they slid past each other.

By now, many of its crew and the troops on board had been killed or wounded and its engines had sustained serious damage. It drifted deeper into the harbor to be met by a devastating fusillade from the sides and straight ahead. The ship was ablaze. Ammunition exploded. Only one ship's officer, wounded, remained alive on the bridge. As the vessel began to go under, troops and members of the ship's company still alive abandoned it. Those who managed to reach dry land were taken prisoner.

The *Hartland* didn't get as far as the *Walney* but it suffered a similar fate. After first colliding in the darkness with a jetty south of the harbor entrance, it entered the port only to pass directly in front of the French destroyer *Typhon.* The destroyer unleashed a ferocious point-blank barrage that touched off a series of fires on the *Hartland* and sent the vessel drifting out of control. It too was abandoned. Survivors piled into two motor launches on which they managed to escape back out to open sea.

Nine of the 17 army officers engaged in the operation and 180 of 376 enlisted men were killed. Five officers and 152 enlisted men were wounded. The Royal Navy lost 113 killed and 86 wounded. The U.S. Navy lost 5 killed and 7 wounded.

Ironically, while this bloody escapade was being played out, the landing parties were still encountering little trouble on the shore on either side of Oran. That accounted for the hopeful message from the *Largs* to the two cutters as they headed to their doom. The beaches were for the most part being uneventfully secured. Troops meeting no resistance were relieved not to be fired on. If this was war, it wasn't too bad. All was serene around them. The moon was out. The surf rolled in. But the heavy gunfire in the distance made it seem spooky as they prepared for the trek that was supposed to have them converging on Oran by dawn.

At the time, the United States had no experience with airborne operations. But the War Department, like the War Office in London and everyone else familiar with the dramatic successes of German airborne troops in the conquest of Norway, Belgium, and Holland two years earlier, had been impressed by the possibilities. In July 1940, less than a month after France capitulated to Hitler, the U.S. Army began a modest experiment with airborne ground operations, assigning an infantry platoon to begin training for parachute drops. But the Army Air Force—from which the U.S. Air Force as a separate service would later evolve—was so short of aircraft that it had trouble finding any that could be earmarked for training even so small a unit. Not until March 1942, almost a year after the conquest of Crete by German paratroops, was the U.S. Army's Airborne Command established. Early in the summer of 1942, two battalions of paratroops were dispatched to Britain, along with other U.S. troops, to prepare to participate in the invasion of France.

After Operation Torch was given precedence, problems related to airpower came under close scrutiny. The French air force in North Africa was a threat, capable of damaging Allied chances of a quick victory. The only Allied land-based aircraft that could provide cover for the invasion forces would be at Gibraltar, a good distance away. The attention of the invasion planners focused on La Senia, five miles south of Oran, and Tafaraoui, which was ten miles south of La Senia. As the only good airfields between Algiers and the Atlantic coast, they were of much potential significance to the invasion. What was more, Tafaraoui boasted the only hard-surface runway west of Tunis and east of Casablanca. French aircraft based there could pose a serious threat to the invaders. Conversely,

217

Allied aircraft operating from them could provide aerial cover for the opening phase of the operation.

Suggestions that the two airfields be bombed prior to the invasion, and the French planes based there destroyed, had been dismissed so as not to antagonize the French while there was a chance to gain their cooperation. Bombing the fields might also limit their use as transit bases as the Allied forces moved east to take Tunisia. The more sensible alternative seemed to be to employ paratroops as surgically as the Germans had in their blitzkrieg. They would be dispatched from England to take the airfields by force if necessary without causing excessive damage or arousing excessive hostility, or they would be welcomed as friends if prior arrangements were successfully negotiated with the French.

The 2nd Battalion, 509th U.S. Parachute Infantry Regiment, was given the job. Its men were to be the first American paratroops ever to be engaged in combat. Officers who had promoted the formation of U.S. Army paratroop units were anxious to see what they could do. Yet doubts were raised from the outset. Algeria was more than one thousand miles away by air, but as far as was known, no paratroop operation had ever been attempted at a distance of more than four hundred miles from takeoff point. The troops would hardly be in the best of shape to go into combat after a ten-hour flight in cramped conditions in C-47 transports flying at heights that reduced their oxygen intake. Not many navigators could be expected, with the limited navigational aids then available, to guide aircraft to an unfamiliar target after a flight made in darkness so as to avoid the attention of enemy fighter planes, and to land at the appointed time.

The British did not like the idea at all. Air Marshal William Welsh said the danger that the C-47s would get lost was too great to be risked. If planes were forced down en route and men were captured, the Germans might get wind of the amphibious landings hours before they were due to be made and take action accordingly. Welsh also strongly believed that the transport aircraft, in short supply like everything else, should be reserved for the crucial follow-up step to the Torch landings—the dash into Tunisia.

Colonel Hoyt Vandenberg, chief of staff of the Morocco end of Torch's air operations (and much later U.S. Air Force Chief of Staff) thought that such a long-range airborne operation would have little chance of succeeding. Lieutenant Colonel Lauris

Norstadt (later Supreme Allied Commander in Europe), also a member of the planning staff, felt the same way. Even Eisenhower thought the idea "hare brained." But General Doolittle was enthusiastic about the idea. Esteemed for his recent Tokyo bombing-raid exploit, he and his opinions carried much weight.

The plan was not revealed to Colonel William Bentley, commander of the Paratroop Task Force, until early September. Until that time, he was under the impression that his men were training for a drop on Normandy to seize a beachhead there. He was now informed that a battalion of his paratroops was to head south of Oran to seize the Tafaraoui and La Senia airfields. The men would bail out over Tafaraoui. One company of them would immediately dash to La Senia airfield ten miles away to immobilize French combat aircraft there before returning to Tafaraoui. They would then assist the remainder of the battalion, which would have seized that field by then, to defend it until troops landed by sea at the Arzew beach area arrived to reinforce them.

The Royal Air Force provided aerial photographs of the airfields and British intelligence supplied information on ground conditions. Nevertheless, how the transport aircraft would be able to find and pinpoint the target for the drop after flying all the way from England remained a problem. The British came up with the answer. They had been doing pioneer work in the development of radar. Among other things, they had produced "Rebecca" and "Eureka," two devices that would suit the circumstances admirably. They permitted a signal sent from the ground to be picked up in aircraft aloft and thus guide them to designated locations.

The difficulty was that someone had to be on the ground at or near Tafaraoui airfield south of Oran to operate the "Eureka" signaling instrument at the proper moment so that "Rebecca" aboard the C-47s could receive its signals and be guided by them to the drop. That job fell to a certain Lieutenant Hapgood, a young U.S. Signal Corps scientist who had shortly before arrived in Britain. Hapgood—code-named Bantam—was trained by the British to operate the "Eureka" device. For security reasons, he was then formally discharged from the army and sent back to the United States. There he was taken in charge by the OSS, which arranged for his entry into Algeria as a civilian carrying "Eureka" in a suitcase.

Local insurgents organized by the OSS were to take up positions near the airfield to light ground flares when the signal was given, to indicate where the paratroops in the incoming transports were to bail out. The Royal Navy was to help as well. It was to position a ship, the *Alynbank,* in the Mediterranean thirty-five miles northwest of Oran to transmit radio homing signals to help direct the transports toward Tafaraoui.

Once they received their orders, the paratroops who were to take part in the operation went into intensive training. They made repeated practice drops and received exhaustive instruction in what each man's job would be—which hangars, plane blast shelters, and airfield buildings they were to assault. Models of Tafaraoui and La Senia were built and studied. Not told where they were, some of the men grew convinced they were going to jump over Berlin in an operation designed to kidnap Hitler.

The men made training flights at 10,000 feet to condition them to the thinner air they would have to breathe on their journey. On September 16, the entire battalion jumped together in practice and every man landed in the drop zone. But full-dress maneuvers in Northern Ireland ten days later proved less auspicious. Two companies dropped on the first day and all the men landed in a bog two miles from their objective, after which bad weather prevented further jumps.

It was decided that the C-47s would fly over Spain en route to Algeria, violating Spanish neutrality. The plan was risky. If the C-47s were detected or forced to land, the Germans might receive advance notice of the operation. It might also contribute to Spain's being goaded into entering the war on the side of the Axis. But the speedy capture of the two Algerian airfields was considered to be of great importance and the alternative was the greater risk of being intercepted over France or getting lost by taking the much longer all-water route.

The transports, thirty-nine of them, were to take off from St. Eval and Predannack in Cornwall, airfields as close as possible in Britain to North Africa. They were to assemble in four flights—one of nine aircraft, three of ten—in the air over Portreath. They would then fly west over the Scilly Isles, turn south toward the Bay of Biscay, traverse Spain and the Mediterranean, and cross the Algerian coast near Oran. They would have an escort of Spitfires and Beaufighters at the start of their journey, while RAF fighter-bombers would sweep over Brittany to distract Luftwaffe fighters that might present a challenge as the transports lumbered south off the coast of France.

A new consideration was introduced as a result of General Clark's clandestine mission to Algeria. Clark had received assurances that U.S. aircraft would be able to land unopposed at Tafaraoui. That meant the paratroops would not have to jump to capture that airfield. The C-47s would be able to land safely with them still on board. They and the planes would be immediately available to assist and perhaps even spearhead the drive to take Tunisia. The news was welcome but it complicated matters. Could the assurances Clark received be trusted? There was no absolute guarantee that the invaders would not be fired upon. Alternative plans had to be prepared. (Indeed, though the Allies did not know it, the French officer who was to make the arrangements at Tafaraoui was the one just transferred out of help's way from Oran to Algiers.)

Takeoff from Cornwall was originally scheduled for 5:00 P.M. on D-Day eve, November 7. That would mean the transports would be flying only the first half hour in twilight, with an RAF escort, before darkness set in, and the men would be bailing out over Tafaraoui in the dark hours of the early morning of November 8. But if there was to be no resistance to them at the airfield, they would be able to land more safely in the C-47s by morning daylight instead of jumping in the dark and could, therefore, depart Cornwall four hours later than planned.

The decision would be made at the Torch forward command post on Gibraltar, from which the signal to Cornwall would be either "Advance Napoleon," which meant that resistance was to be expected, or "Advance Alexis," which would mean that the paratroops would meet no resistance and could leave late. Just before the original planned takeoff time, the "Advance Alexis" peace-plan message was received from Gibraltar. The planes would be able to land safely at Tafaraoui. They would not be fired upon. There was no need for the paratroops to jump. Takeoff could be delayed until 9:00 P.M. In the confusion, some of the troops who had already boarded were left waiting in the aircraft on the ground for two hours before being told and disembarked. It was a portent of what was to come.

There had been indications days before that problems would arise. The paratroops were based at Ramsbury in Wiltshire; the aircrews of the 60th Troop Carrier Group who were to fly them to Algeria were based at Aldermaston in Berkshire twenty-five miles away. That made liaison between them difficult in the run-up to takeoff. In addition, while the paratroops were intensively trained, the aircrews were not. For security reasons, it was decided not to brief them until their planes had been shifted to the departure bases in Cornwall.

But on November 5, two days before takeoff, recurring bad weather indicated that flight movements prior to the operation might be restricted, so some of the aircrews based at Aldermaston were given an impromptu briefing. That briefing and some of the subsequent ones bordered on the preposterous. One briefing officer thought Gibraltar was the destination and instructed the aircrews on how to get there. Charts and maps were in short supply and could be provided only to the four flight leaders, which meant that if formations split up, other aircraft might be left with only a limited idea of where they were. The other aircraft had to keep in formation in the dark all the way to Algeria if they were to be certain of getting to where they were supposed to be.

Fourteen of the thirty-nine C-47s used in the operation did not arrive from servicing until the afternoon of November 6, little more than twenty-four hours before takeoff. That left time enough for them to be only partially tested for their long journeys. On the night before takeoff it was realized that only four sets of navigational instruments were available for the mission. British equipment was installed instead, but the American C-47 crews were unfamiliar with how it worked.

The takeoffs and early part of the flight were uneventful and for the most part the formations kept in remarkably good order. But when the planes reached the Bay of Biscay, they began to scatter. Some planes climbed to dodge dense clouds or squalls. Strong easterly winds, which had not been forecast, tossed the planes about. Crews had little or no experience in using newly installed VHF radios to maintain contact with one another. Some tried Aldis lamps or even flashlights to keep in touch.

By the time the aircraft, which had been flying low to evade detection, had risen to 10,000 feet to soar over the Spanish mountains, no more than three planes in each flight were still in formation. Navigators had fallen back on dead reckoning to find their way. One plane, out of fuel, was fortunate enough to find Gibraltar and glide in for a safe landing there. When the others crossed the Mediterranean, ground fog over the Algerian hills further complicated the situation. One paratroop officer scanned the skies as his aircraft crossed the Algerian coast but was unable to spot any of the other planes that were supposed to be in his flight. He was jolted by the thought that "we were invading Africa alone!"

Whatever their difficulties aloft, the paratroops—having received the "Advance Alexis" signal from Gibraltar—had been led to believe that they would receive a friendly welcome from the French upon arrival in Algeria. A more realistic assessment of the possibilities had subsequently been made at Gibraltar. A message had been sent to inform the planes that the paratroops might in fact be given a hostile reception. Communications being what they were, that message was not received.

The efforts of the *Alynbank,* the ship whose radio signals were to direct the aircraft toward their target, proved to be a total waste. Arrangements had been made for it to transmit at 440 kilocycles. Instead, it was transmitting on a different wavelength and its signals were not picked up. One plane, straying westward, found itself homing in on a lighthouse in Spanish Morocco. As for Bantam, the young scientist who had been smuggled into Algeria with the "Eureka" device, he had successfully positioned himself near Tafaraouri during the night to send the signal that would guide the C-47s to the airfield. No one had thought of informing him through OSS contacts that the operation had been delayed for four hours. When the aircraft did not arrive at the predawn arranged time, Bantam destroyed his "Eureka" set and, wearing an Arab burnoose as disguise, disappeared into the darkness.

Some of the planes did manage to regroup as they approached the Algerian coast. But three aircraft, completely lost, landed in Spanish Morocco, two hundred miles from their objective, and the men aboard were taken prisoner. The troops aboard a fourth aircraft jumped out by mistake over Spanish Morocco and were taken prisoner too. The crew of another C-47 that landed in Spanish Morocco realized the error and, in a scene worthy of an adventure movie, took off again, pursued by armed Moroccan tribesmen on horseback. Two of the C-47s landed in French Morocco rather than Algeria. The troops held in Spanish Morocco were not released for three months; those who landed in French Morocco where held until November 13, five days after D-Day.

Many of the thirty-two transports that did reach Algeria flew back and forth trying to locate their formations. Spotting an aircraft in the distance, and suspecting it might be an attacking fighter, the men in one plane were ordered to remove plugs from the windows, shove the muzzles of their rifles through them, and prepare to fire when the aircraft came within range. The passing aircraft turned out to be another lost C-47.

The troops were weary from the long flight in cramped conditions. Most were aware that their pilots had little idea of where they were. The planes all were running out of fuel. Some of the men began inflating rubber life rafts in case they were forced to ditch in the sea. One plane flew through French ground fire in Algeria, was attacked and damaged by French fighter aircraft, and landed near Oran, where it was surrounded by French troops to whom the paratroops, outgunned and outnumbered, surrendered. Two other planes were also forced down by French fighters.

Spotting a C-47 on the ground with tanks moving threateningly toward it, men in six of the C-47s sought to help out and jumped onto what their commander thought was flat terrain. The terrain proved to be anything but smooth. In landing, the commander cracked two ribs against a jagged rock. The tanks proved to be American. They had come ashore earlier near Oran. Troops aboard twelve of the planes jumped near Lourmel, southwest of Oran, and began making their weary way toward Tafaraoui, not getting there till the next day, by which time the airfield had long been in the hands of troops landed by sea. Despite their specialized assault training, all they were assigned to do was guard French prisoners.

Sixteen of the planes landed on a sebkha, a vast dried salt lake near Oran, and the men aboard set up defensive positions there. As the heat of the day began to take its toil, they set about removing the long-john underwear they had donned for the flight from England in their unheated C-47s. Troops on three other planes that landed not far away were arrested by the French police.

So much of a blunder did the operation prove to be that only 300 of the 556 paratroops who had flown from Cornwall could be gathered by November 15, a week later, at Maison Blanche airfield near Algiers to participate in the move against Tunisia. Of the thirty-nine aircraft that had set off on the operation, only fourteen were still operational.

☆ **14** ☆

CASABLANCA

The grinding of ship's engines dies away, and the
quiet seems strange after so many days at sea. . . .
The anchor chain rattles loudly. There is suddenly
the sound of many footsteps and voices topside;
gear being kicked around; sailors stumbling over
army equipment and cursing all landlubbers; . . .
power winches starting up preparatory to lowering
craft into the water; clanging, apparently meaningless
bells; orders shouted in that strange Navy idiom. . . .

—HAL BOYLE, ASSOCIATED PRESS CORRESPONDENT

As the Western Task Force started on the final leg of its transatlantic voyage from Virginia to Morocco, insurgents in Casablanca prepared to spring into action. As in Algiers, when given the signal by the U.S. consulate, they were to seize key installations, paralyze military communications, and take noncooperative officers and officials into custody.

However, three days before the landings, Murphy sent fresh instructions to his local vice-consular Disciples. Civilian insurgents, not as well organized or as well led as in Algiers, were to be held in check. General Béthouart, commander of the Casablanca Division, who was unreservedly committed to the Allied cause, was to be entrusted with the task of minimizing resistance to the invaders. In a position to work through the military, he was considered better able than an assortment of civilians, however strongly motivated, to influence the course of events.

At 2:00 A.M. on November 8, two hours before the first Morocco landings were to take place, Béthouart launched his attempt to do exactly that. Having driven from Casablanca to the Moroccan capital of Rabat fifty miles away, he had a message delivered there to

General Noguès, Vichy's resident-general in Morocco. Noguès was informed that an American invasion was about to take place. Béthouart told him that its purpose was to install General Giraud in command in French North Africa as a first step toward liberating France from enemy occupation. Noguès was either to cooperate or, if he felt he could not agree to do that, to discreetly remove himself from the scene so that he could more easily give formal acceptance later to what was about to happen.

Béthouart had prepared well. He had the support of a battalion of infantry, mostly troops who had escaped from France and who wished to resume the fight against Germany.* Some of those soldiers were detailed to throw a cordon around Noguès's official residence. Béthouart himself proceeded to army headquarters in Rabat to inform his superior, Major General Georges Lascroux, army commander in Morocco, of developments and solicit his assistance. When Lascroux proved hesitant, he had him placed in custody.

He then approached Major General Louis Lahoulle, French air force commander in Morocco. Lahoulle was uncertain about what to do but finally agreed to order that there be no air-force resistance to the invaders, provided the French army also did not resist. Lahoulle then telephoned Vice Admiral François Michelier, commander of the navy in Morocco, to persuade him not to resist the landings either.

Michelier had by then received a message from Béthouart similar to the one delivered to Noguès, informing him that the Americans, with General Giraud's backing, were landing to begin the liberation of France. The admiral had immediately contacted French naval installations along the Moroccan coast to ask how the defenders were coping. His request was met with surprise. He was informed that no invasion was taking place. None of the coastal air and submarine patrols had detected the American fleet. What was more, a rough surf along the coast appeared to rule out any amphibious landing attempt, if that was indeed what the Americans had in mind.

---

*Béthouart assumed the main landing in Morocco would be at Rabat, the capital, as had been contemplated before Patton was persuaded that Muslim sensibilities might be offended if the city was attacked. Those troops were with him in Rabat to assist the invaders. The Casablanca episode might have been different if a landing had been made there.

226

Reports had not yet begun arriving from Algiers and Oran of the developments there. Michelier was convinced that Béthouart was the victim of a hoax, possibly designed by German intelligence to give Hitler an excuse to take over France's African territories. Or possibly only a small-scale American hit-and-run commando raid was intended, which would also give the Germans an excuse to move in. The admiral had no intention of being a party to such foolishness. Instead of being persuaded by Lahoulle to join the coup, he convinced the air force commander to reverse his position and back out of it. Faced with this setback, Béthouart felt he had no alternative but to take Lahoulle into custody and issue orders in his name that all French aircraft were to be grounded.

By then, however, the initiative was passing from his hands. Admiral Michelier instructed the deputy commander of the Casablanca Division to countermand Béthouart's order that the troops remain in their barracks. Instead they were instructed to take up defensive positions in the city and the port. Meantime Noguès, also having had no independent confirmation of an American invasion, had concluded as well that Béthouart had been hoaxed into acting foolishly and traitorously.

Astoundingly, no one reported to Noguès or Michelier the announcement of the landings and message of friendship broadcast by Roosevelt:

We come among you to repulse cruel invaders who would remove forever your rights of self-government, your rights to religious freedom, and your rights to live your own lives in peace and security. We come among you solely to defeat and rout your enemies. Have faith in our words. . . . We assure you that once the menace of Germany and Italy is removed from you, we shall quit your territory at once.

The message had first been broadcast at 1:00 A.M. and then repeated every half hour. Possibly no one in authority in French North Africa bothered to monitor radio broadcasts after midnight. For the troops waiting on the vessels that had carried them across the Atlantic, still some four hours away from landing, the president's message appeared to serve only as a warning to the French that they were coming. Those who knew of it roundly cursed their Commander in Chief for risking their lives that way.

Béthouart was in a quandry. His reputation, his career, and

perhaps his life were at stake. He had been led to believe the landings would commence at 2:00 A.M. They had actually been scheduled to commence two hours later and did not get started until 5:00 A.M. Noguès had now reissued the standing order to the French armed forces in Morocco to resist all would-be invaders. All advantage Béthouart had earlier gained by acting decisively was lost. Fellow officers he had recruited to the Allied cause were discovering that while valor had its place, there was much to be said for discretion. Removed from command of the Casablanca Division, his main source of strength, Béthouart gave himself up to Noguès in order to prevent a clash between troops still loyal to him and those he could no longer command. He was placed under arrest and ordered to stand trial on charges of treason.

Aboard ship offshore, Task Force commanders had no idea of the developments on land or of what had led up to them. They knew only that either their forces would be welcomed as friends or given no quarter as enemies. According to navy historian Samuel Eliot Morison, who was an officer on the battleship *Brooklyn* taking part in the operation, "On board ship we anticipated a 100 percent solution; either everyone would receive us with open arms, or everyone would fight."

Three Morocco landing points had been chosen; two of them north of Casablanca, one south. Nineteen thousand men, under the command of Major General Jonathan Anderson, were to storm ashore at Fedala, the main landing point, some fifteen miles north of Casablanca. Nine thousand men, under the command of Major General Truscott, were to land near the beach resort of Mehdia farther north to seize the town of Port Lyautey fifteen miles upriver from the coast. At the coastal town of Safi, 120 miles south of Casablanca, 6,500 troops, under the command of Major General Ernest Harmon, were to secure the area and join in the pincer move on the city. The capture of Safi was important because it was near an important communications junction. Troops in control there would be able to block French reinforcements who might be summoned inland from Marrakesh to reinforce troops garrisoned at Casablanca if they put up a fight.

Sea conditions at all three Moroccan landing areas proved Admiral Hewitt's optimistic meteorologist almost right. The surf was far from calm but it was not as turbulent as reports from afar had forecast. The alternative plan of shifting the Casablanca Task Force into the Mediterranean for a landing there instead would not have to be implemented.

Nevertheless, problems arose immediately. In the waters off Fedala, a strong current had shifted some of the troop transports as much as five miles from their designated debarkation stations. Greater difficulties were in store when the landing craft were finally loaded with troops from the transports and made their delayed runs in to the shore. The surf proved troublesome to the inexperienced coxswains, some of whom were disoriented by the problems they had already faced loading men into their craft while they were being buffeted by high waves. Some of the landing craft broached to when they reached the beaches and had to be abandoned. Some were holed on rocks. Others capsized, dumping troops into the water. (Sixty percent of the landing craft employed in the assault phase of the operation were lost. Ninety percent failed to turn around.)

The men's backpacks weighed them down so heavily that they had trouble struggling ashore when knocked over by waves. Some drowned. Some stumbled onto land having lost their weapons. Some boats collided and others put troops ashore well away from where they were supposed to be. Men wandered along the beach trying to find their units. The lack of trained beachmasters to coordinate activity on the shore was sorely felt.

Advance scout boats, which were positioned close to the shore off Fedala to help direct the landing craft to their assigned beaches, had not been informed of a delay. No one remembered about them in the turmoil. They were left wondering what had gone wrong. They blinked messages at each other through the dark, trying to find out what was happening. If the French had been better prepared to resist the landings, those light signals, visible from the shore, might have caused even greater difficulties than the Casablanca Task Force was about to face.

Similar problems arose in the assault on Mehdia. Some of the troop transports assigned to the Mehdia beaches were also out of position. Each had been assigned a place facing the beach the troops it carried were to storm. But several were found to have broken formation in the predawn darkness while positioning themselves for the landings. The resulting confusion was compounded by the fact that some of the larger vessels in the convoy had transported landing craft that were to be lowered in the dark and boarded by troops from other specified ships.

To the planners back in Washington and Norfolk, that had seemed a straightforward procedure: Once lowered into the water, such-and-such landing craft would make directly for such-and-such troop transport to be boarded by troops it would then deposit on the shore. But it was to prove anything but simple in the dark at boarding time. The location of some of the troop transports was in doubt and could not easily be determined because no radio communications existed between most of the vessels and radio silence was to be maintained in any case. An extraordinary exchange took place between General Truscott, commanding troops that were to land at Mehdia, and the captain of the ship he was on, just hours before the landings were to commence.

"Well, Commodore, where are we?"

"Well, General, to be perfectly honest, I am not rightly sure exactly where we are."

It was not much better when the landing craft were finally lowered into the water, as a post-operation report testified.

Boat crews were drifting aimlessly from transport to transport and megaphoning "Is this the *Ancon?*" "Is this the *Leonard Wood?*" "Where is the *Bliss?*" It would have been difficult to distinguish between enemy and friendly boats.

Truscott boarded a landing craft and went from ship to ship, calling out to discover which was where. But his visits were unexpected and security-conscious personnel aboard, who had only his word for who the man shouting up to them from below was, were reluctant to tell him anything. When he was able to convince them he was not a spy, they could only tell him they didn't know where other ships had positioned themselves. Order was eventually more or less established through the limited radio facilities available and signal lamps.

Then, to the scorn of the navy, which was anxious to unload and pull back, the troops took longer than anticipated descending the nets to reach the landing craft. The swells tossed the landing craft against the sides of the transports. Even when the troops had made their way down the cargo nets and were aboard, many of those craft milled about as they sought to position themselves properly in the dark for the run in to the shore. With all of that happening, there was no chance whatever that the landings would occur on schedule.

The same trouble was met at Safi, where other difficulties cropped up as well. On one of the cargo vessels, improperly loaded heavy equipment had to be laboriously shifted to get at vehicles and artillery four decks down but needed quickly ashore. Two speedboats that had been lowered from a tanker for rescue work were mistaken in the dark for French torpedo boats and fired upon. Greater damage might have been done to them if the men on the transports had been better marksmen.

Five army scouts, delivered by submarine, had earlier been put into a rubber boat in the dark to paddle landward to serve as a beacon for the invaders but were mistakenly dropped off too far out at sea. After paddling toward shore for six hours, they arrived on location just as shooting there started. A flare designed to light up the sky with the image of an American flag, to identify the invaders as friends, served only to outline the invaders as targets.

Despite all of that, the Safi landings were successfully achieved. The invaders met comparatively light resistance, which they soon overcame. French shore batteries that might have done great damage were quickly silenced by the heavy guns of the battleship *New York* and the cruiser *Philadelphia* as the venerable destroyers *Bernaudou* and *Cole* streaked into Safi harbor and put troops ashore. They quickly routed the surprised Foreign Legionnaires defending the harbor.

At Fedala too, light resistance to the landings was rapidly overcome. Shore batteries that opened up on the troops at the break of day were silenced by escort warships. Fedala town itself was taken before midday and the invaders there prepared to advance on Casablanca. An unexpected obstruction encountered by the troops on the beaches was crowds of fascinated local Arabs, mostly children, who gathered to see what was happening and who appeared not to be troubled either by small-arms fire exchanges between invaders and defenders or by the naval shelling.

The quick successes at Fedala and Safi did not yet signify an easy victory at Casablanca. Nor was it duplicated at Mehdia, the coastal appendage of the upriver town of Port Lyautey, which was the real target of the third prong of the Casablanca operation. The prime immediate objective at Port Lyautey was the airfield, a short distance from the coast, up the Sebou River. The intention was to put troops ashore on either side of the river mouth at Mehdia while a French river pilot, who had earlier been spirited out of Morocco by Donovan's OSS operatives, guided the destroyer *Dallas* up the winding river to the airfield. Troops would be put ashore to secure the field so that Allied aircraft could be flown in safely and quickly to operate from it in support of the operation to take Casablanca.

But the *Dallas* was driven off by heavy gunfire, and General Truscott looked on in dismay as the "combination of inexperienced landing craft crews, poor navigation, and desperate hurry resulting from lateness of hour" turned the disembarkation of his troops from their transports "into a hit-or-miss affair." So hit-or-miss was it that the first-wave landings—some of which would turn out to be miles from assigned beaches—were delayed until after sunrise. As a consequence, heavy guns zeroed in on the invaders and French aircraft were able to spot and strafe landing craft and troops. Fighter planes from the carriers were able soon to eliminate that aerial threat. When a biplane appeared over the area during the morning, it was greeted with a barrage of fire from the ships offshore and was shot down. It turned out to have been a British reconnaissance craft dispatched by Eisenhower for a progress report on the operation.

Despite the might of the Task Force's warships, intermittent fire from French coastal artillery plagued the invaders at Mehdia. The captain of one of the transport vessels, fearing for its safety, ordered disembarkation to be halted and instructed his crew to "stand by to move out to sea." Only with difficulty was he persuaded that the troops still on board were needed ashore. Nevertheless, some vessels did pull back for fear of being hit. As a consequence, one battalion of troops failed to have its artillery delivered on D-Day and was at one point in danger of being overwhelmed by the defenders.

Resistance ashore, at first effective but sporadic, grew better organized during the course of D-Day. Moroccan troops under French officers and Foreign Legionnaires put up increasingly strong resistance as the invaders struggled to resolve persisting landing confusions and related difficulties. Some of the follow-up waves of troops were put ashore at different beaches. The sand in several places proved much softer than had been expected. Vehicles, some of them deposited on the wrong beaches, dug deep into the shore and had to be left where they were until well into the day. Engines of tanks had been dampened by sea air on the journey across the Atlantic and were not easy to spark into ignition. Some were also found to have faulty batteries. Troops did not easily adjust to some of the newly supplied equipment with which they had received little training. The shell of a bazooka, fired in combat for the first time that day, hit a tree instead of the French tank at which it had been aimed.

So few troops were put ashore in organized fashion at Mehdia during the early hours of the invasion that plans for maintaining a combat reserve had to be abandoned. Even soldiers with normally noncombatant tasks—mechanics, cooks, company clerks—were mobilized for combat and put through quick weapons drills. At one point, General Truscott picked up a rifle and prepared to fight alongside his men.

Truscott was partly responsible for the failure to make better headway at Mehdia. Not trusting the accuracy of naval gunfire, he feared pulverizing fusillades to eliminate resistance would cost the lives of his own forward troops. He therefore declined to call for as much naval firepower support as could have been provided.

By then it was obvious that a bid to cut short the confrontation at Mehdia had failed. Two Task Force officers, Colonel Demas T. Craw and Major Pierpont M. Hamilton, had been put ashore early in the day to seek out the French commander at Port Lyautey. They were to tell him that the Americans were coming as friends of France and persuade him to order that there be no resistance to the landings. Nothing more would be heard of them until two days had passed, when it was learned that, proceeding toward Port Lyautey in a jeep flying the American and French flags as well as a flag of truce, they had been directed toward the French headquarters by some soldiers but had then been fired upon by others. Craw had been shot dead and Hamilton had been taken prisoner.

*   *   *

At the insistence of President Roosevelt, General de Gaulle continued to be kept in the dark about Allied invasion plans. Through hints from British sympathizers, he knew the invasion was in the cards but he had been given none of the details. When he was awakened in London at 6:00 A.M. to be informed of the landings by his chief of staff, he bitterly snapped, "I hope the Vichy people will fling them into the sea! You don't get France by burglary!"

Not until noon that day did de Gaulle receive a briefing on Torch from Churchill. By then he had swallowed the worst of his anger, though he still criticized the prime minister for letting the Americans make key decisions in the operation. "I cannot understand," he told him, "how you British can stand aside so completely in an undertaking of such primary concern to Europe." Nevertheless, he broadcast a message of support for Torch to France and its territories through the BBC that evening.

His plea had no effect on the course of events on D-Day morning. General Giraud's obstinacy in Gibraltar remained of far greater significance. Giraud's refusal to play a role in Torch had provoked much rancor. It compounded the anxiety felt by Eisenhower and his staff as they awaited reports on the resistance the invaders were encountering and what progress they were making. Mason-MacFarlane, the governor of Gibraltar, jokingly suggested to Eisenhower that he could provide "a good body disposal squad if needed" to deal with the recalcitrant French general. The idea of "a little airplane accident" for him occurred to some of those present.

But Giraud was in a more accommodating mood in the morning as reports, exaggerated by Eisenhower's staff, were passed to him of the progress made by the landing parties. They were said to have met virtually no resistance at Algiers and Oran while the Casablanca landings, about which very little was then known at Gibraltar, were reported to be proceeding as planned. Giraud was still considered a figure of potentially great importance for the operation. It was thought that even at that stage, he could persuade French officers in North Africa to order their troops to cease all resistance. His changed attitude when his talks with Eisenhower were resumed aroused much relief.

After renewed consideration of details, Giraud agreed to accept what he had been offered the night before. He would be commander of all French forces in North Africa and supreme civil administrator as well. He would fly to Algiers the following day to bring French forces there into the Allied fold in the fight against the Germans.

Near the Algerian capital meantime, the invaders were making belated headway. By midday, having secured the landing beaches, advance units were proceeding through the outskirts of the city against sporadic, for the most part halfhearted, resistance. French civilians cheered them on. Insurgents, having finally made contact with the troops, were guiding them into town. After meeting token resistance at Algiers's Maison Blanche airfield, the 1st Battalion, 39th Infantry Regiment, had taken control of the base early in the morning and a squadron of British Hurricanes flew in from Gibraltar to assist in the operation.

Meantime, there had been little that Murphy, his coup plans in ruins, had been able to do. He had been freed from the porter's lodge at Juin's residence where he had been incarcerated that morning and was no longer in danger of being shot by the Gardes Mobiles. But he was still confined to the residence as Darlan and Juin monitored the developing situation. Reports they received as the morning wore on finally convinced them that American troops, supported by a strong naval force, and now by aircraft as well, had indeed been landing in significant numbers. Only a score of American troops had reached the center of Algiers by midday but they appeared to be the vanguard of a much larger presence.

By early afternoon, Darlan accepted that further resistance in Algiers was pointless. He informed Vichy that he was left with no alternative but to surrender the city to the Americans. He asked Murphy to arrange a meeting for him with General Ryder for that purpose. Murphy was provided with a car flying French and white flags to take him through advancing units of suspicious American troops to a beach about ten miles west of the city where Ryder was said to be. With the help of Captain Randolph Churchill, the prime minister's son, whom he met on the beach attired in the uniform of an American Ranger, he found the general and returned with him to the city.

Word of these developments was not received in Gibraltar until hours after Eisenhower had reached agreement with Giraud on the role he was to play as the situation unfolded. The news that Darlan not only was in Algiers but wanted to negotiate came as a surprise, as did subsequent word that Darlan and Ryder had met and agreed on a cease-fire, though only for Algiers, not for Oran or Casa-blanca. Armistice talks between them would take place the follow-ing morning, on D-Day plus one. That was when Giraud was due to fly from Gibraltar to the Algerian capital where Eisenhower had agreed that he—not the unexpected Darlan—would assume the position of senior French figure in North Africa. Clearly, further complications were in store.

As the Torch convoys had begun positioning themselves off the coasts of Morocco and Algeria, Hitler had other things on his mind. He was distracted by something that had nothing to do with the war. It was true that German aircraft and U-boats were ready to attack the Allied flotillas steaming through the Mediterranean when they had proceeded farther east, as the Germans still ex-pected them to do. But Rommel's panzer army, including what was left of the elite Afrika Korps, was by early November in full retreat in the Libyan desert after having been driven out of El Alamein by Montgomery's reinvigorated Eighth Army. At the same time, intel-ligence reports arriving at Hitler's East Prussia headquarters from the Eastern Front, where the latest German advances had petered out, indicated that a Soviet offensive was in the making near the key center of Stalingrad. Soviet units were moving into position there for a major assault.

The German Führer chose to neglect those portentous develop-ments to devote himself to one of the main events on the Nazi calendar, the anniversary of his abortive Munich beer-hall putsch in 1923, which had ended with him in a prison cell. On the after-noon of November 7, just hours before the North Africa landings, Hitler and some of his senior staff boarded his special train for a journey from East Prussia to Munich, where he was to deliver a speech at the annual gathering of Nazi party veterans the following evening. At major train stations on his way there, each successive communiqué reaching Hitler's staff through telegraph linkage de-scribed the Allied convoys that had streamed through the Strait of Gibraltar into the Mediterranean as being bigger and stronger. Informed, Hitler was impressed. "This is the largest landing oper-ation that has ever taken place in the history of the world," he said. But he seemed detached from the situation, except to leave his aides with the impression that he was flattered to be "the cause of enterprises of such magnitude."

He still did not imagine that North Africa was the destination of that great flotilla of vessels. He remained convinced that it had been sent to reinforce Montgomery, or perhaps would put troops ashore in central Italy. Asleep on the train when the invasion was launched, he was awakened to be informed of it early in the morning as the train passed through Thuringia. By the time he reached Munich, reports of how the landings were proceedings were filtering through to him.

He found those reports encouraging. They told of fierce French resistance. It was said that the attacks had been beaten off at Algiers and Oran and that Admiral Darlan, who had previously proved himself useful to the Germans, was personally organizing the defense of French North Africa. Nevertheless, it was an extremely serious development. There was as yet no way of knowing for certain that the Allied operation would fail or how the Vichy regime would react. As the first troops had gone ashore, Marshal Pétain had received a message from President Roosevelt saying that the action had been taken because Germany and Italy had been planning to invade France's African territories. Roosevelt told Pétain that such action by the Axis powers would have constituted a threat to the security of the United States and Latin America. He had therefore dispatched "powerful American armed forces to cooperate with the governing agencies of Algeria, Tunisia and Morocco in repelling this latest act in the long litany of German and Italian international crime."

Within hours, the elderly Pétain, who had been allowed to sleep on until later in the morning, reacted sharply—though he did so only in an effort to dissuade the Germans from acting against Vichy France. He indicated to American chargé d'affaires S. Pinckney Tuck that he was not at all unhappy with the Allied invasion but, so as not to provoke Hitler, he felt obliged to break diplomatic relations with the United States and issue a strong response to Roosevelt's message.

It is with stupor and grief that I learned during the night of the aggression of your troops against North Africa. . . . You invoke pretexts which nothing justifies. . . . I have always declared that we would defend our empire if it were attacked. You knew that we would defend it against any aggressor whoever he might be. You knew that I would keep my word. . . . France and her honor are at stake. We are attacked. We shall defend ourselves. This is the order I am giving.

Recovering from the euphoria that had momentarily overtaken him during his Munich excursion, Hitler began to examine the likely consequences of Operation Torch. It seemed possible that Vichy might react to the Allied aggression by finally being drawn into the Axis military alliance. Nevertheless, he instructed Field Marshal Gerd von Rundstedt, commander in chief of German forces in the West, to prepare to implement the long-planned Operation Anton—the occupation of Vichy France. Von Rundstedt was to await further orders before sending his troops across France's internal armistice frontier.

Instructions were also issued that Giraud was to be kept under heightened surveillance. Word had not yet come through that the general had already fled to Gibraltar and was preparing to go on to Algiers to begin the process of bringing France back into the war against the Axis.

☆ 15 ☆

NEGOTIATIONS

Why do soldiers have to get mixed up in things like
this when there is a war to be fought?

—GENERAL MARK CLARK

As dawn rose on November 9—D-Day plus one—communications between Allied Forces Headquarters at Gibraltar and the assault forces were still too patchy for Eisenhower to assess the situation with any precision. Algiers had surrendered but it wasn't clear what was happening at Casablanca and progress at Oran appeared to be uneven at best. General Giraud would be leaving for Algiers that morning, having agreed to do what he could on behalf of the Allies. But it was frustratingly uncertain whether Admiral Darlan was prepared to cooperate and order all French forces in North Africa to cease hostilities.

Darlan refused to negotiate with Murphy. He would talk only to someone more senior, preferably Eisenhower himself if he would come to Algiers. With the battle still continuing elsewhere, the Supreme Commander did not intend to abandon his command post. But Clark, his deputy, had already been scheduled to fly to the Algerian capital that day to initiate the process of establishing a communications center so that Allied Forces Headquarters could be shifted there from the Rock. Eisenhower instructed him to meet with Darlan and settle things with him.

That would not be easy. Eisenhower had been convinced by Murphy that if there was any chance that all of French North Africa

239

could be brought over to the Allies without further struggle, Giraud was the man to do it. He had agreed that Giraud was to become commander of all French military forces in North Africa and its governor as well, and he saw no reason to renege on that agreement. However, Darlan had made it clear that he would have nothing to do with Giraud. "He is not your man," he had told Murphy. "Politically he is a child. He is a good divisional commander, nothing more." Once again, French military politics tried Eisenhower's patience. Writing to General Smith in London, the Torch commander confessed:

> I've promised Giraud to make him the big shot, while I've got to use every kind of cajolery, bribe, threat and all else to get Darlan's *active* cooperation. All of these Frogs have a single thought—"ME." It isn't this operation that's wearing me down—it's the petty intrigue and the necessity of dealing with little, selfish, conceited worms that call themselves men. Oh well—by the time this thing is over I'll probably be as crooked as any of them.

Eisenhower had even greater reason to be displeased with French behavior. Hoping to appease Hitler and thereby dissuade him from occupying Vichy France, Marshal Pétain agreed that the Germans should send troops to Tunisia—they would have done so anyway—ostensibly to help French forces there resist the Allied invaders. And the Germans were authorized by the marshal to use Tunisian airfields for that purpose.

Blida airport near Algiers had been neutralized by British troops the previous day. When Giraud arrived there from Gibraltar in the morning, he expected a ceremonial welcome. He had come to save France. To his profound humiliation he was virtually ignored by the French despite—more probably because of—an Allied proclamation announcing his impending triumphal arrival. The senior French officer at Blida insultingly claimed never to have heard of him. The situation was made even more distressing for the general by the failure to locate the luggage containing his uniform. Despite his dignified bearing, he appeared to be just another old man.

The pro-Allied proclamation that had belatedly been issued in his name was having no noticeable effect. It was Darlan who had arranged the surrender of Algiers, and resistance to the invading troops was continuing around Oran, where General Fredendall wanted to build up his forces before moving on the city, and at Casablanca, where General Patton's troops were delayed because too few of their vehicles and support weapons had been brought ashore. Senior French figures in Algiers whom Giraud met later in the day made it clear they did not recognize his authority. Despite Eisenhower's expectations and hopes, he apparently had nothing to contribute to the Allied cause. He could not order a cease fire. He could not save lives. He could not help Torch fulfill its mission. It was hard to determine what he could do.

Giraud may have been acclaimed as a war hero in days gone by but it was apparent that he no longer had even an honorary place in France's military hierarchy or establishment. He exercised no formal or personal authority over the French officers in North Africa whose collaboration Eisenhower desperately sought and who were unlikely to be impressed by a foreigner appointing him their commander. "This really messes things up," Clark told Murphy when he was apprised of the prevailing situation after he arrived in Algiers from Gibraltar later that day. It was apparent that the loathsome Darlan rather than the untainted Giraud was the Frenchman who could influence the course of events.

As Commander in Chief of Vichy's armed forces, Darlan was accepted by French officers and officials in North Africa both as their superior and as speaking for Pétain, to whom they had pledged allegiance. He alone was in a position to issue effective orders to end resistance. Even after hostilities were ended, the Allies wanted the support or at worst the acquiescence of the French in order to sweep quickly on to take Tunisia before the Germans established themselves there. Otherwise they might find themselves bogged down in a protracted struggle and, at the same time, probably lumbered with cumbersome occupation duties.

However, Darlan did not appear anxious to be of assistance. He had surrendered Algiers because there had seemed no alternative. But he was not about to volunteer any favors while the situation with regard to Vichy France and his own personal position remained to be clarified.

For Eisenhower, stuck in Gibraltar and anxious to get on with winning the war, bitterness over what he saw as French perversity was becoming an obsession. "I am so impatient to go eastward and seize the ground in the Tunisian area," he wrote to General Marshall, "that I find myself getting absolutely furious with these stupid Frogs."

Algiers was quiet under the armistice but as Clark took his bearings upon his arrival there, he found the atmosphere of the city clouded by a "feeling of uncertainty" stronger than he had ever before experienced. Resistance to the Allies had ceased in the immediate area, but the French were beginning to realize that the occupying force was not nearly as large or as well equipped as they had been led to believe. In fact, just a few thousand troops were then ashore in the area, and very little equipment. The weather had turned, delaying troop reinforcement and the unloading of tanks. The Allied commanders feared they could still run into problems if, despite the Algiers armistice, organized resistance developed. Taking his bearings in the city, Clark believed the situation remained precarious.

Murphy advised him to march some troops and run some tanks down the main street of Algiers, both to impress the French with a show of force and divert them with a parade. It would help persuade them that the Allies, while meaning them no harm, were in charge. Clark didn't like the idea, largely because he still had no more than three tanks at his disposal. "Why do soldiers have to get mixed up in things like this," he wanted to know, "when there is a war to be fought?"

For an ambitious soldier like Clark, who had his eye on a senior field command, that question was heartfelt. His immediate assignment had little to do with coming to grips with the enemy on the battlefield. That was the job of the British First Army under Lieutenant General Kenneth Anderson. Some of its units were still to come ashore near Algiers but it was already beginning to make its way up the coast toward Tunisia. In addition to starting the process of shifting Allied Forces Headquarters to Algiers, Clark was to confine himself to the irksome, unrewarding task of sorting out relations with the French in general, and Darlan in particular. He had been reminded by Admiral Cunningham before he had left Gibraltar that Churchill had said, "Kiss Darlan's stern if you have to, but get the French Navy," most of which was at anchor at Toulon across the Mediterranean.

Never one to humble himself, Clark chose a different approach when the two met on the morning of November 10—D-Day plus two—at the Hotel St. George. Instead of flattering or pleading with

Darlan, he treated him with so little regard to his rank and position that during a break in their talks, Darlan woundedly asked Murphy to remind the general that he was a five-star admiral. It was not right, he complained, for anyone to make demands of him as if he were a lieutenant junior grade. One of the group of senior French generals and admirals who attended the meeting later described Clark as a "big American who does nothing but shout and pound the table."

At his first meeting with them, Clark had, "for psychological effect," posted armed U.S. naval guards around the hotel. It was to demonstrate from the start that he, and not Darlan, was in charge of the situation. Despite his brusque display of authority, Clark was greatly impressed by the array of senior officers—excluding Giraud—Darlan had brought with him to the meeting. Though some had fought against the Germans before France's capitulation, they all unreservedly accepted subordinate status to the admiral who everyone knew had been a Nazi collaborator. In his reports to Eisenhower during the next few days, Clark referred to one or another of those officers by the codeword YBSOB, which stood for Yellow-Bellied Son of a Bitch. Eisenhower later observed that Clark "quickly ran foul of the traditional French demand for a cloak of legality over any action they might take."

> Without exception every commander with whom [he] held exhaustive conversation declined to make any move toward bringing his forces to the side of the Allies unless he got a legal order to do so. Each of them had sworn an oath of personal fealty to Marshal Pétain. . . . None of these men felt he could be absolved from that oath or could give any order to cease firing unless the necessary instructions were given by Darlan as their legal commander, to whom they looked as the direct and personal representative of Marshal Pétain.

General Mast and other officers who had rallied to the Allies were regarded by them as traitors who deserved severe punishment for disobeying explicit orders to resist any and all invaders. Some, like General Béthouart in Morocco, were already under arrest and awaiting court-martial.

Clark began the meeting at the Algiers hotel by demanding that Darlan agree to an immediate armistice to cover all of French North Africa. The admiral responded evasively. He agreed that all hostilities between the French and Americans should be ended as soon as possible, but he said he required authorization from Vichy to order a cease-fire. He told Clark he had sent a summary of armistice terms to Vichy for approval and was awaiting a reply. That would not come before the Vichy Council of Ministers met in the afternoon.

Clark was not prepared to wait. There was no guarantee that the Council of Ministers would approve the armistice terms, or even acknowledge them. "What you propose," he told Darlan, "is not possible." Under the circumstances, he said, there was no reason for the meeting to continue. He would call it to a halt and deal instead with Giraud.

Darlan said that would be pointless. He said French forces would not obey Giraud and therefore fighting would continue. But Clark stood fast. Darlan offered a compromise formula. He would issue a proclamation to the French forces saying that further battle was futile and might cost France its North African territories. Added would be an explanation that the Americans had not accepted his reluctance to declare an immediate armistice until he received orders from Vichy to do so. Clark turned that down. He wanted nothing less than an unambiguous order to all French troops, as well as to the French Navy and Air Force, that all resistance was to be terminated at once.

Darlan's alternative was to refuse all cooperation, remain in American custody, let the Americans get on with their invasion, and leave it to Vichy to decide what to do about it. The admiral realized, however, that such a course of inaction on his part would be futile, possibly disastrous, and very likely would be to his personal disadvantage. Faced with continuing French resistance at Oran and Casablanca, the Allies might resort to intensive naval bombardment and air attacks. Extensive damage and heavy French casualties might result for which those not willing to cooperate with the Allies might be held responsible. Vichy could no longer hope to control the situation. French forces in Morocco and Algeria could do no more than delay the victory of the invaders, and not for long.

No matter how deeply Clark's bullying tactics upset Darlan, he bowed to what appeared to be the only reasonable choice available to him and agreed to issue the instructions the Americans demanded. He ordered all French land, air, and sea forces in North

Africa to cease firing against Allied troops immediately. They were to return to their bases and remain there until they received further instructions. He also instructed the French fleet at Toulon to prepare for an emergency departure if the Germans invaded Vichy France in response to the latest developments. "In no circumstances," he promised Clark, "will our fleet fall into German hands." In the name of Pétain, whom he informed of his actions by cable, he announced he was assuming supreme authority in North Africa and instructed all officers and officials to remain at their posts.

Accepting that matters were slipping beyond his control and realizing that a decisive moment in the war had been reached, Pétain was tempted to endorse Darlan's submission to the Allies. He even considered ordering his diminutive Armistice Army to take to the hills and woods of unoccupied France. But by now, the Germans were closely monitoring the situation. They intercepted Darlan's report to the marshal and warned of dire consequences for Vichy unless the admiral and his surrender to the Americans were disavowed. Pétain once more felt obliged to submit. He dismissed Darlan as Commander in Chief of Vichy France's armed forces and reaffirmed orders that North Africa was to be defended against attack. There was to be no armistice between the French defenders and the Allied invaders. General Noguès in Morocco, where the French were still stubbornly resisting the Americans converging on Casablanca, was named by Pétain to replace Darlan as Commander in Chief in North Africa.

Pétain's disavowal deeply dejected Darlan. He feared he was being marginalized. To Clark, he seemed to be "like a king who had suddenly had his empire shot out from under him." He told Clark it left him no choice but to revoke the North Africa cease-fire order he had issued. Clark told him he would not be permitted to do so. Darlan then suggested to Clark that the Americans put him under arrest so that he would remain a factor in the ongoing equation. Clark obliged by having a squad of infantrymen thrown around Darlan's Algiers residence.

He then called a meeting of senior French generals in Algiers, this time including Giraud. His aim was to resolve differences among them so that French resources in North Africa could be efficiently harnessed to the Allied cause despite Pétain's orders. Confirmation had been received of the arrival of the first German troops in Tunisia the previous day. It reminded Clark of how peripheral the squabbling in Algiers was to the nuts and bolts of Operation Torch's mission.

Abashed by his unenthusiastic reception in Algeria, Giraud was no longer the unbending, headstrong figure who had confronted Eisenhower with impossible demands at Gibraltar three days earlier. He now was prepared to forgo the governorship of French North Africa that Eisenhower had promised him and was willing to settle for command of the French military forces. Indeed, Giraud claimed to want nothing more than that. With Darlan appearing to withdraw from active involvement, the situation, though still confused, seemed to favor a renewed Allied effort to back this shilly-shallying septuagenarian as prospective leader of France's return to Allied ranks.

Not having considered an Allied invasion of North Africa likely, the German High Command had no detailed contingency plan for coping with it or with the failure of Vichy military forces in Algeria to resist the Torch invaders more vigorously. But as a precautionary measure, Field Marshal Kesselring, the German commander in Italy, acting on his own initiative, had concentrated aircraft and whatever troops he could spare in the south of that country. He had acted swiftly once word reached him of the first landings. Within thirty-six hours, while the situation still remained unclear, Kesselring had begun flying troops he had immediately available into El Aouina airfield near Tunis. These included his own headquarters guard and a unit of paratroops. They set about securing the airfield and its perimeter as a prelude to further action. At that stage, the French command in Tunisia could easily have repelled the Germans. But it obeyed orders from Vichy to offer no resistance to them.

On the morning of November 10, when Clark began his talks with Darlan, Hitler still had little idea of what exactly was happening in French North Africa. He soon realized, however, that whatever resistance the Vichy forces there might be prepared to mount, they would be no match for the invaders. As the day wore on, word reached him that it appeared the Allies had consolidated their landings, were in control in Algiers, and probably would soon be in control in Oran as well, if they weren't already. Urgent measures against the invaders were imperative. The Führer ordered that action by his armed forces to prevent the Allied capture of Tunisia should take priority over all other German operations in the Mediterranean area. Kesselring was instructed to establish a bridgehead to block the expected Allied offensive in that direction. After deploying the necessary forces in Tunisia, Kesselring was to advance into Algeria to drive the Allies into the sea.

However, with Rommel's outnumbered and outgunned Panzerarmee Afrika struggling to avoid annihilation at the hands of Montgomery's Eighth Army more than a thousand miles to the east, the Axis powers had few resources for achieving such an ambitious aim. It was entirely possible that the Allies would soon have unchallenged mastery of the southern rim of the Mediterranean.

A heavy burden was thus added to the Wehrmacht's strategic planning. What Churchill hankeringly called the soft underbelly of Europe would be exposed to invasion unless the Allies were driven out of North Africa, and that might not be achievable. Vichy's army on the mainland could not be relied upon by Hitler to repel an Allied incursion into southern France from across the Mediterranean. Its commanders could not be trusted and, as a matter of policy, the Germans had made certain that their Armistice Army had been kept weak and poorly equipped.

Only German troops could be relied upon but they were excluded from southern France by the armistice terms negotiated with the Vichy regime two years earlier. Hitler now decreed that the armistice had outlived its usefulness. Operation Anton was activated. Before dawn on November 11, ten divisions of German troops crossed the border between occupied France and Vichy France to occupy the rest of the country. They met no resistance and moved in largely without incident. At the same time, six Italian divisions marched into the southeast corner of France and occupied the island of Corsica, which Mussolini had long coveted.

The occupation of Vichy France and the elimination of its illusion of independence brought Darlan back into the picture in Algiers. Armed with a secret message of support from Pétain, he was able to maintain that the marshal was effectively a prisoner of the Germans. The admiral informed Clark that he now considered himself free to act on behalf of France in its North African territories. On November 11—D-Day plus three—he agreed to command all French forces in North Africa to cease resistance and to join the Allies in their fight against the Axis forces.

Anxious for an end to the political wrangling and for French military cooperation, Clark was delighted. Thus were planted the seeds of the notorious Darlan deal that was soon to subject the Allied Command to much vilification and cause it much grief.

Though Clark had not yet known it, Oran, which had been encircled during the day, had fallen to the Americans even before Darlan had issued his disputed cease-fire order the day before. Center Task Force headquarters were already being shifted from the HMS *Largs* to the city-center Grand Hotel. The French were not to be humbled when they were about to rally to the Allied cause. Their troops retired to their barracks but were allowed to keep their weapons. French officials retained administrative and policing responsibilities. However, work was begun immediately to clear Oran harbor of obstructions that might delay the unloading of supplies and equipment for the Allied push into Tunisia.

In Morocco, the situation had also moved toward a climax, though more slowly. General Noguès, Vichy's newly appointed military commander for North Africa, had also decided that further resistance to the invaders was futile. His troops had sustained heavy casualties and the Americans appeared to be about to intensify their offensive to seize Casablanca. He issued instructions for arrangements to be made for a meeting with Western Task Force commander General Patton.

But Patton's forces had also suffered heavy casualties and he would tolerate no prolonged negotiations over terms. He demanded quick agreement from the French to suspend all hostilities at once. He ordered a massive assault on Casablanca to be launched on the morning of November 11. That attack would take place if agreement was not reached. Patton's command post received word of Noguès's compliance only minutes before a coordinated bombardment of French positions in and around the city was to be launched by artillery, aircraft, and warships. One artillery commander did not receive word in time. His guns opened up but he quickly ordered a cease-fire when the scheduled synchronized naval and air attacks failed to materialize and alerted him to the change in plans.

Some isolated bursts of gunfire still were offered by French units that hadn't received cease-fire orders, but the fighting in Algeria and Morocco was effectively concluded. Formal armistice agreements had been reached for Algiers, Oran, and Casablanca. The landings had been successfully secured and initial objectives had been realized. The first stage of Operation Torch had been a success.

News that the operation had been launched, and exaggerated reports of the success of its opening stage, had been received with acclaim and relief wherever people longed for the destruction of Nazi Germany. Following hard upon news of Montgomery's success at El Alamein and coinciding with premature but soon to be confirmed reports of Red Army triumphs against German forces at Stalingrad, it appeared that the Allies had finally started winning the war.

It was, of course, an occasion for Churchillian oratory. "I have never promised anything," the prime minister told guests at the Lord Mayor of London's annual luncheon on November 10, "but blood, toil, tears and sweat. Now, however, we have a new experience. We have victory—a remarkable and definite victory. The bright gleam has caught the helmets of our soldiers, and warmed and cheered all our hearts." The prime minister said the British victory over Rommel and the American-British North African landings established a "new bond between the English-speaking peoples and a new hope for the whole world."

For Americans, whose troops were engaged for the first time in the European Theater and who constituted the bulk of the invasion force, the news was equally exhilarating. At a football game in Washington, a voice over a loudspeaker called for play to stop and then proclaimed, "The President of the United States announces the successful landing on the African coast of an American Expeditionary Force. This is our second front." People rose from their stadium seats, cheers bursting from their throats. The football players whirled in joyous somersaults across the field. Similar scenes were acted out elsewhere across the land. The invasion had an effect in other countries too. In Sweden, for example, where industry was doing nicely out of the war, stocks fell sharply at suggestions that it might end sooner than expected.

No public disclosure was made of the muddles and mistakes that had characterized the Torch landings. Morale was one of the weapons with which the war was being fought and it was not going to be needlessly damaged. Besides, little was known yet of the difficulties the troops had encountered on those remote shores. All that was publicly announced was that the Allied move to roll back Hitler's armies was at last being inaugurated.

However, the men who planned, organized, and commanded the operation had no illusions about what had transpired. A report subsequently made by the Historical Branch of the U.S. General Staff bluntly stated, "Neither the British nor the American General Staffs would care to offer Torch as a model of planning." A report to the Ministry of War in London observed, "The planning of the operation was based on the political background and it is of vital importance to note that the taking of similar risks in circumstances that are less favourable from the military and political point of view would lead to disaster." While conceding the low level of training for the personnel involved, Admiral Cunningham attempted an explanation.

> No officer commanding a unit will ever be satisfied . . . until his unit is trained and equipped down to the last gaiter button. There are times in history when we cannot wait for the final polish. . . . [F]or Torch particularly, we could not afford to wait, . . . the risk of embarking on these large-scale operations with inadequate training was deliberately accepted in order to strike while the time was ripe.

The operation produced a long catalog of detailed shortcomings. "The individual officer and soldier was woefully overloaded. Men were so burdened by weapons, ammunition and equipment as to be virtually immobilized." Combat communications proved inadequate at best and in most places virtually nonexistent. At a fortified point of resistance near Algiers, it took two hours for a call for carrier-based aircraft support to be answered. A U.S. Navy assessment of the operation by Captain A. G. Shepard emphasized how precarious it had been.

> The entire operation was blessed by an almost providential good fortune. . . . [W]ithout this good fortune [the amphibious] part of the operation would not have been successful and might have been so unsuccessful as to jeopardize the whole. Secrecy in advance, and concealment, or evasion, in movement succeeded beyond all justifiable hope. The weather was far more favorable than could possibly have been hoped for. Shore resistance, [e]specially shore-based air resistance, was much weaker and more disorganized than anyone had a right

to expect, based on information available. Resistance at sea, particularly by enemy submarines, was weaker and slower in developing than could have been expected. On the strength of this, and without any intention to detract in the slightest from the admiration I feel for the success that was achieved, I must say seriously and emphatically that I do not believe that under identical conditions of organization and training, this feature of the operation could be repeated as successfully once in ten tries.

Though Captain Shepard attributed the success of the landings to "almost providential good fortune," General Patton believed there was nothing "almost" about it. He told Admiral Hewitt, "It is my firm conviction that the great success attending the hazardous operations carried out on sea and land . . . will only have been possible through the intervention of Divine Providence."

★ 16 ★

ON TO TUNISIA

I'm no reactionary. Christ on the mountain! I'm as
idealistic as hell!

—GENERAL DWIGHT D. EISENHOWER

For Vice Admiral Jean-Pierre Esteva, the white-bearded resident-general of Tunisia, life had become very complicated. What had been an undemanding, dignified sinecure had become a nightmare. He was not accustomed to being awakened in the middle of the night. But in the early morning hours of D-Day, he received a visit at his residence in Tunis from Hooker Doolittle, the American consul general in Tunisia. Doolittle handed Esteva, who except for his bedroom slippers had donned his full naval uniform to receive him, a message from President Roosevelt. It advised him that the landings had begun, that it was undertaken to preempt Axis aggression, and urged that no resistance be given to the Allied invaders.

Esteva, who had commanded the French fleet in the Mediterranean at the beginning of the war, received Doolittle cordially. He did not conceal his hope that the Axis powers would be defeated. He pointed out, however, that he was under standing orders from Pétain to repel any attack. He said that all he could do was forward to Vichy the message Doolittle had brought and await further instructions. When the Germans began arriving at El Aouina airfield at noon the following day, the order he received and obeyed was not to interfere with them in any

252

way. After the liberation of France, a French court would sentence the unfortunate Esteva to life imprisonment for "national unworthiness."

For their part, the arriving German forces had been instructed to establish "close and friendly relations" with the French in Tunisia. They were, however, not certain what to expect from Esteva or from General Georges Barré, commander of Vichy's Tunis Division, who also was known to be not especially fond of the Germans. They were instructed to disarm Barré's men if questions arose about their intentions. Shaken by the pace and direction of events and under orders not to resist, Barré decided to withdraw his troops into the mountains southwest of Tunis to retain freedom of action, though initially they could easily have overwhelmed the Germans. For much of the first week, senior German officers on the scene had no idea which of their units had arrived or where they were.

Had Clark been able to get what he wanted from the French in Algiers more quickly, Esteva might have swung over to the Allied cause. But by the time the cease-fire order for all of French North Africa had been extracted from Darlan, the resident-general was left with no room to maneuver. The advance party of Germans had been reinforced, was still being augmented, and he was being closely chaperoned. "I now have a guardian," Esteva reported in a phone conversation with an official in Algiers. When orders from Darlan finally reached Admiral Edmond Derrien, French naval commander in Tunisia, to repel the Axis forces, he explained that he couldn't do so because his coastal guns pointed out to sea and the newly arrived Germans and Italians were already entrenched behind them.

While the Americans had been winding up the fighting at Oran and Casablanca and striving to sort out French military politics in Algiers, the completion of Operation Torch's mission had become the responsibility of the British. General Anderson had flown to Algiers from Gibraltar on November 9 to take charge of the Eastern Task Force. Under his command, the British First Army was to spurt eastward, "with all possible speed," more than five hundred miles to seize Tunis and Bizerte before the Germans could establish themselves there. The distance to be covered was marked by rugged terrain that boasted few good roads and only one arthritic railway line. Forward momentum was to be assisted by subsidiary landings along the coast and by paratroop drops.

Armed French support, which had been hoped for, or at least tacit French military backing, could not be counted on, at least not yet. As First Army troops began their overland trek on D-Day plus one, plans for flash raids by commandos and paratroops to seize positions far forward were abandoned as too risky under the circumstances. But two days later, on November 11, troops of the British 36th Infantry Brigade were put ashore at the small Algerian port of Bougie, 100 miles closer to Bizerte. The day after that, commandos landed at Bône, 125 miles still closer.

On November 13, Blade Force, an assortment of armored units, was landed at Bône to press inland into central Tunisia. On November 14, other British units were sent east from Bône along the coast road. On November 15, troops of the U.S. 509th Parachute Infantry Regiment—the same unit whose planned capture of Oran's Tafaraoui airfield had ended in fiasco and which was now under General Anderson's control—dropped on the small airfield at Youks-les-Bains near the Algeria-Tunisia border farther south to a friendly welcome from the French. The British 1st Parachute Battalion took the railway hub of Souk el Arba the following day.

The forward airfields quickly occupied by Allied forces were small and far from ideal, but aircraft were flown in to operate from them to shield the advancing Allied forces that, together with supply vessels, were already under attack from German planes flying from bases near Tunis and in Sicily.

The Tunisian border was crossed at two points and contact was made with General Barré's Tunis Division, whose poorly equipped troops were now prepared to fight alongside the Allied forces. On November 17, British troops clashed with a forward German unit just inside Tunisia. American paratroops in the south, aided by the French, tangled with Italian patrols. The battle for Tunisia had begun.

An Axis command headquarters had been established in Tunis under General Walther Nehring. Nehring had been recuperating in Germany from wounds he had received in the Egyptian desert, when he had been ordered to rush back to Africa to weld the forces gathering in Tunisia into effective battle groups and establish a bridgehead reaching as far as the Algerian border if possible. As usual, Hitler had even more far-reaching aspirations than that. He declared that the objective would be to eradicate totally the Allied threat in French North Africa.

Back in Algiers, the French continued to exasperate the Americans. "First the Germans had taken their pride away," diplomat-spy Kenneth Pendar noted, "now the Americans wanted to dictate to them too. They sulked and grew shifty, as people will when their pride is hurt."

Despite the cease-fire that Darlan had ordered and the successful completion of Torch's opening phase, the political climate in Algeria and Morocco remained plagued by the absence of unified French leadership. Having been led to expect significant French backing in its pursuit of Torch's wider mission, Allied Forces Headquarters became obsessed with the belief that such leadership was essential and the need for it urgent.

Senior French figures with whom Allied officers dealt in Algiers agreed that once Vichy France had been overrun by the Germans, Pétain had effectively become Hitler's prisoner. That nullified their oath of allegiance to the marshal. But differences persisted between those ready to join the Allied cause and those whose morale had been shattered by Germany's earlier defeat of France and who preferred to sit on the sidelines until the dust settled.

The Americans still hoped that Giraud, to whom they had promised much, would emerge from the confusion as the authoritative figure with whom they would be able to deal constructively. But the general was still regarded with contempt by other senior officers in Algiers for having prematurely collaborated with the Allies. Noguès, who had never objected to dealing with the German Armistice Commission in Morocco, refused even to shake his hand and called him "traitor" to his face.

Nevertheless, Clark pressed the French to resolve their differences and get on with the war. Meeting with little success, he warned that he would brush them aside and establish an Allied military government to administer North Africa. Murphy, for whom the proprieties of civil administration appeared to weigh more heavily than Torch's military mission, feared that he might do exactly that:

> I tried to imagine what would happen if Americans undertook to fight Germans in North Africa and simultaneously to govern twenty million

assorted civilians in a vast territory, without knowing any Arab dialects or even, in the case of most Americans, the French language.

Stranded at Allied Forces Headquarters in Gibraltar, still the nearest place with adequate communications facilities, Eisenhower was frustrated by the failure of the French generals to reach agreement.

> If they would only see reason at this moment, we could avoid many weeks of later fighting and have exactly what we will then gain at the cost of many lives and resources, but I fear . . . they are not thinking in terms of a cause but of individual fortunes and opportunities.

On the morning of November 13, the Supreme Commander flew to Algiers for a quick on-the-spot review of the situation and to do "a bit of table pounding" of his own. He arrived just as the French generals finally recognized the absurdity of squabbling at a time when critical developments both in North Africa and in France threatened to reduce them to an irrelevance.

A compromise had finally been hammered out among them, and between them and the Americans, to establish a provisional government for French North Africa. It was to work with the Allies for the defeat of the Axis powers. Former Nazi collaborator Darlan would be political and civil leader while Giraud would command the French armed forces in North Africa. Those forces would participate in the Allied advance into Tunisia—thus was General Barré's belated cooperation with the Allied forces legalized—as well as the liberation of France from German occupation.

Eisenhower, who quickly approved the accord before flying back to Gibraltar, was greatly relieved and gratified. The distraction that had prevented him and Clark from concentrating as they should have on the push into Tunisia was finally eliminated—or so they thought. The Supreme Commander did, however, realize that Darlan enjoyed neither the respect nor the admiration of any senior Allied figure. Expecting criticism, he issued a warning to his staff.

> None of you should be under any misapprehension as to what the consequences of this action may be. In both our nations, Darlan is a deep-dyed villain. When public opinion raises the outcry, our two governments will be embarrassed. Because of this, we'll act so quickly that

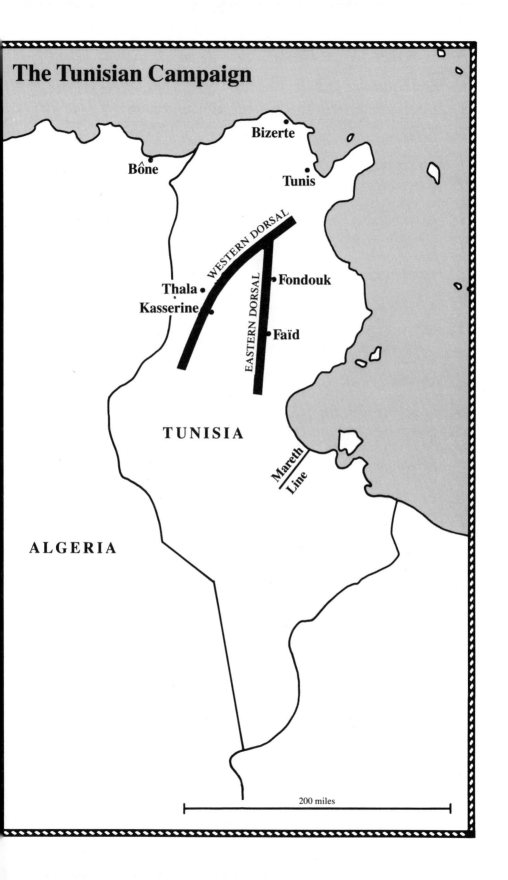

The Tunisian Campaign

Bizerte

Bône

Tunis

WESTERN DORSAL

EASTERN DORSAL

Fondouk

Thala

Kasserine

Faïd

TUNISIA

Mareth Line

ALGERIA

200 miles

reports to our governments will be on the basis of *action taken.* I'll do my best to convince our governments that the decision is right. If they find it necessary to take action against this headquarters, I'll make it clear that I alone am responsible.

Eisenhower was grievously mistaken in thinking that accepting responsibility for what soon came to be known as the Darlan deal would defuse the condemnation it aroused. Neither he nor Murphy, who was serving as his Algiers-based political adviser, appreciated how bitterly an agreement that left the Vichy-appointed administration in North Africa intact would be received in London and Washington. Nor did they have any idea of how piercing, pervasive, and persistent would be the howl of outrage that rose as word spread of the agreement forged with such difficulty in Algiers.

Darlan's collaboration with the Nazis had been widely and consistently reported in the Allied countries for more than two years. Failing to comprehend the depth of contempt for him, Murphy had advised Eisenhower that the agreement was purely a military matter. Much as the Supreme Commander wished that to be true, it was not. It had powerful political overtones, as was made clear when the first public disclosure of the accord came from Darlan himself in a radio announcement. Its reception in London and Washington was hardly improved by Darlan's hint that Pétain—who, after the war, at the age of eighty-nine, would be tried and imprisoned for war crimes—had himself secretly sent approval from German-occupied Vichy France where the marshal was still chief of state.

The depth of the bitter reaction in Britain and the United States to the Darlan deal flabbergasted Eisenhower. Instead of lightening his load as he expected, it tied him in knots. On November 14, only one day after the Algiers agreement had been reached but with condemnation already erupting, he attempted to spike it in a message to the Combined Chiefs of Staff.

The actual state of existing sentiment here does not repeat not agree even remotely with some of prior calculations. . . . Foremost is the fact that the name of Marshal Pétain is something to conjure with here. Everyone from highest to lowest attempts to create the impression that he lives and acts under the shadow of the Marshal's figure. The civil governors, military leaders and naval commanders will agree on only one man as having an obvious right to assume the Marshal's mantle in North Africa. That man is Darlan. . . . All concerned profess themselves to be ready to go along with us provided Darlan tells them to do so, but they are absolutely not repeat not willing to follow anyone else. . . . I realize that there may be a feeling at home that we have been sold a bill of goods, but I assure you that these agreements have been arrived at only after incessant examination of the important factors and with the determination to get on with military objectives against the Axis. . . . Without a strong French government of some kind here we would be forced to undertake complete military occupation. The cost in time and resources would be tremendous.

In his message, Eisenhower stressed that the untainted Giraud fully approved of the arrangement with Darlan and was assigned a key role under its terms. He indicated that in view of the admiral's shady reputation, Murphy would keep a sharp eye on whatever the admiral got up to. He warned that if Darlan was repudiated, Allied military operations in the region would stagnate, and that they would be subjected to passive and perhaps even active resistance from French forces. Whatever else Darlan had been before, to Eisenhower he was now the individual with whom he was obliged to deal in order to avoid all sorts of problems that had nothing to do with confronting and defeating the enemy.

As a result of the agreements we have made [he wrote Marshall] we have secured an opportunity to press our concentration toward the east for battle in Tunisia without worrying about the rear. At every principal port we would be badly handicapped without the assistance cheerfully rendered us now by French military, naval and civil groups. . . . What I am trying to point out is that even if we should only have passive resistance, our operations would be sadly slowed up and our position badly weakened.

Churchill was sympathetic. But he was embarrassed. He had to face the fury of the British press and Parliament, which reacted with bitterness and bewilderment to the elevation of a man long seen as a Nazi stooge to the position of effective head of a recognized French government in exile, while de Gaulle, the head of a genuine Free French movement, was excluded from Allied councils and considerations. Some allowed that Eisenhower had acted for military reasons but protested that the agreement with Darlan had far-reaching political implications, an area in which the Torch commander was empowered with no authority. The Foreign Office in London was livid. Foreign Secretary Anthony Eden denounced the Algiers agreement at a meeting of the War Cabinet. In a message to Washington, Eden said that the people of Britain felt that a magnificent military victory had been tarnished and defiled.

Aside from the moral question, it was feared that the arrangement could disrupt clandestine espionage and sabotage activity by underground fighters in occupied Europe who were stunned by the Allied agreement to deal with an arch Nazi collaborator. Lord Selborne, head of the Special Operations Executive, complained that the Darlan deal had "produced violent reactions on all our subterranean organizations in enemy occupied countries, particularly in France where it has had a blasting and withering effect."

Churchill warned Roosevelt that dealing with Darlan could damage public morale. He cabled the president, "A permanent arrangement with Darlan or the formation of a Darlan Government in French North Africa would not be understood by the great masses of ordinary people, whose simple loyalties are our strength." More important, the prime minister feared that Vichyites who were being left in place in North Africa as a result of the Darlan deal might rally to the side of the enemy if the Allies suffered military setbacks. He pointed out that despite the nuisance de Gaulle often proved to be, the British government had recognized him as the leader of Free France, was obligated to him, and could not lightly drop him. Churchill feared that Washington and London might find themselves backing French leaders who were bitter rivals.

Some in the Foreign Office credited the U.S. government with greater powers of long-range calculation than it possessed and scornfully suggested that the Darlan deal was part of a deliberate bid to establish overriding postwar American influence in France by sustaining the Vichy regime as a counterpoise to British-backed de Gaulle.

Many Americans shared the British view that accepting Darlan as an accomplice in the struggle against fascism was a mockery of the ideals for which the war was being fought. In a CBS broadcast from London, Edward R. Murrow said, " . . . there is nothing in the strategic position of the Allies to indicate that we are either so strong or so weak that we can afford to ignore the principles for which this war is being fought."

Prominent figures in Roosevelt's administration were outraged. Treasury Secretary Morgenthau threatened to resign over the affair. Morgenthau warned Roosevelt that people employed in war-armaments factories across the country would wonder why they should bother to work hard to win the war against fascism and oppression if a person like Darlan was going to be put back into power when it was over. Wendell Willkie, who had been the Republican candidate for president in the last election, was only narrowly persuaded, for the sake of the safety of American troops in North Africa, to refrain from publicly condemning the arrangement made with "Hitler's tool."

Roosevelt, who considered Darlan a "stinking skunk," was reluctant to complicate Eisenhower's already difficult mission, especially since the Supreme Commander reported that the complaints about the consequences of the Darlan deal were based on exaggerated reports. But so strong was the outcry that the president felt it necessary to make a public explanation of American policy, pointedly stressing the interim nature of the arrangement.

> The present temporary arrangement in North and West Africa is only a temporary expedient, justified solely by the stress of battle. The present temporary arrangement has accomplished two military objectives. The first was to save American and British lives, and French lives on the other hand. The second was a vital factor of time . . . to avoid a "mopping-up" period in Algiers and Morocco which might have taken a month or two to consummate. Such a period would have delayed the concentration for the attack from the West on Tunis. . . . Temporary arrangements made with Admiral Darlan apply, without exception, to the current local situation only.

Roosevelt assured Eisenhower of his full support. He told him that he understood the problems he faced and did not doubt that he had acted properly. But he warned him, "[I]t is impossible to keep a collaborator of Hitler . . . in civil power any longer than is absolutely necessary," and instructed him to keep Darlan's actions and communications under surveillance.

The president's public announcement that the Algiers accord

was mere expediency understandably irked the admiral. He complained to General Clark that he appeared to be no more than "a lemon which the Americans will drop after they have squeezed it dry." Allied military officers were apprehensive about the possible consequences of disdainful treatment of their new collaborator. Admiral Cunningham warned, "With our forces strung out as at present in the race for Tunisia we simply cannot afford a renewal of hostile feeling."

The controversy dragged on. Criticism was directed at Eisenhower personally, some of it in harsh terms. He was said to be responsible for transforming this first major military campaign in the crusade for freedom against fascism into just another squalid clash between antagonists of whom neither could be seen to hold the high moral ground. In addition to accusing him of political incompetence, some of his more extreme critics went so far as to call him a fascist. That wounded the Supreme Commander deeply because he abominated everything Hitler stood for. "I can't understand why these long-haired, starry-eyed guys keep gunning for me," he complained. "I'm no reactionary. Christ on the Mountain! I'm as idealistic as Hell."

Though Eisenhower was reluctant to appear to be passing the buck, he was persuaded by his staff to refer the agreement with Darlan to the Combined Chiefs of Staff in Washington for approval. They, in turn, used the excuse that it was a political matter to pass it on to Roosevelt and Churchill for judgment. Both leaders recognized that despite the uproar, a deed so widely publicized could not be repudiated without repudiating Eisenhower as well, just after he had been acclaimed for achieving victory in the North Africa landings. Accordingly, they signaled their concurrence with his decision on Darlan. It relieved him of some of the pressure the controversy had generated. However, the uproar distracted Eisenhower and consumed his energies at the critical moment when phase one of Torch was being transformed into phase two.

The Darlan deal was a fluke. It emerged from a sequence of developments in which wider political factors were neglected—a big mistake during a conflict in which political considerations played so great a role.

Though unsullied by Nazi collaboration, Giraud had been at first unwilling and then unable to bring French North Africa over to the

Allies. Found to be on the scene by chance, Darlan, who could do so, was pressed to cooperate and did so reluctantly.

So far, so good. The immediate situation in Algeria and Morocco was thus addressed. But when the French in Algiers subsequently were unable to reach agreement among themselves acceptable to the Allies, they embroiled the Americans on the spot in their deliberations. The result was that Eisenhower lost perspective and failed to appreciate the options at his disposal.

By the time Darlan was finally persuaded to cooperate fully, Vichy France had been invaded by the Germans. The claim that Vichy was an independent state could no longer be sustained. The liberation of all of France was now the only logical objective of patriotic French military commanders, wherever they were. General Juin, who had earlier declined to throw in his lot with the Allies, knew this. So did many of his colleagues in North Africa, some of whom would distinguish themselves in battle against the Germans before the war was over. Pro-Allied conspirators in North Africa—some of whom were still under arrest—had known it all along.

It was convenient but no longer essential for the Allies to gain the assistance of men like Darlan and Noguès who were dithering about what course to follow and who had shown no great fondness for the Allied cause. With the Germans effectively in charge in Vichy as well as Paris, arrangements could have been made to legitimize alternative French cooperation in North Africa. The main concern need not have been to gain the reluctant assistance of individuals whose only alternative was to bow out and hope to avoid being arrested themselves. The main task was to help get the British First Army to Bizerte and Tunis before the Germans were entrenched in Tunisia. For that, the Allies had to rely exclusively on their own limited resources as that campaign got under way.

Inexperienced, poorly advised, and wearied by the haggling to which he and Clark had been exposed, Eisenhower was unable to grasp the situation fully. Appalled by the bickering in Algiers, the Supreme Commander's only interest was winning the war. It was, as he wrote his brother, "my whole doctrine and reason for existence." First mistaken about Giraud, he had now been led to believe that Darlan was the only Frenchman who could facilitate completion of the second phase of Operation Torch by maintaining the civil and military administration of French North Africa, sparing the Allies occupation duties that he was told would otherwise await them.

Eisenhower also still hoped Darlan would bring the French fleet over to the Allied side. But Darlan was unable to do that: To his most recent request that the fleet leave Toulon, cross the Mediterranean, and make for the Allied-controlled port of Oran before the Germans broke their promise to Pétain to keep their hands off it, Admiral Jean de Laborde, commander at Toulon, had dismissively, succinctly replied, "Shit!"

Nor was there much reason for Eisenhower to take satisfaction from Darlan's order that remaining armed French resistance to the Allied invaders be terminated. By the time the admiral had finally been persuaded to issue his comprehensive cease-fire order, Oran and Casablanca as well as Algiers had already fallen to the Allies. Aside from some small-arms sniping, all resistance to the invaders had ceased.

Darlan did prove useful by assuming command and maintaining the continuity of the established administration. But the arrangement made with him meant leaving the quasi-fascist Vichy regime in place in Algeria and Morocco, which was not what the war was about. More to the point at that critical moment, Eisenhower became so preoccupied with French military politics and coping with the fallout from the Darlan deal that only belatedly did he recognize how much trouble was building up for the Allies as the British First Army pressed forward into Tunisia.

☆ 17 ☆

BOG DOWN

The dead were buried in the mud and the living were in it up to their knees. They were wet to the skin all day and all night. They had mud in their hair and mud in their food. When the mud dried, it set like iron and had to be beaten off the boots with a hammer or a rifle-butt. Before the astonished eyes of the commander, tanks went down to their turrets in mud.

—ALAN MOOREHEAD

General Anderson had a textbook plan for seizing Tunisia. His forces would drive a wedge between the two main port cities of Bizerte and Tunis. He would then take Tunis, upon which Montgomery's Eighth Army would soon be advancing from the east, and push the remaining Axis forces back around Bizerte where they would be trapped and destroyed.

Anderson proceeded cautiously. He did not intend to launch his offensive until he had gathered sufficient forces and concentrated them to administer irresistible blows against the enemy's defensive positions. He explained to London, "My forces available for the rush on Tunis are woefully weak and before committing them I must be sure of a good start and have a clear understanding of the odds against them."

Anderson's caution was understandable. His British First Army was an army in name only. It consisted so far of little more than one division—the 78th—plus elements of the 6th Armored Division and a smattering of American units. Much of the terrain his troops had to traverse was mountainous and covered with dense scrub. Its few good roads were soon rutted and cracked by the heavy military traffic they were never meant to carry.

265

The most serious problem Anderson faced was German supremacy in the air. With its bases in Sicily, and now in Tunisia as well, the Luftwaffe was able to attack Allied forces and supply ships as and when it liked. Algiers itself was being bombed almost every night. The Allies, for whom comparatively few attack aircraft were at first available at the front, had little opportunity to install radar, for which hardware was in any case still hard to come by. Signaling equipment was also in short supply, and what there was of it was mostly inadequate. As a result, coordination of air and ground action left much to be desired. In some areas, Allied forward movement had to be confined to hours of darkness to avoid aerial attack.

Despite the difficulties, Anderson launched his offensive to wind up the campaign in Tunisia on the night of November 24–25, a little more than two weeks after the North Africa landings. The 36th Infantry Brigade advanced along the coast; Blade Force moved forward in the center; the 11th Infantry Brigade advanced in the south. All were to be supported by U.S. armor but the rough landscape limited the advance of tanks and thus favored the Axis defenders in their rapidly established positions. Anderson hoped to overcome that difficulty by deploying his artillery, of which the Allies had a marked superiority for the moment. Despite a few minor setbacks, his forces at first made steady, if slow, progress. His foward units came within fifteen miles of Tunis by November 28, raising hopes of an early victory. But there they were brought to a halt by the enemy and by the elements.

Incessant rain, torrential downpours that had begun soon after the Allied offensive was launched, turned the countryside into a vast mud swamp. The glutinous soil clung to the men's boots, clothes, and vehicles. Even when there was a break in the weather, five days of continuous sunshine—which didn't happen often— were needed before any sustained attempt could be made at cross-country movement. Meantime, long stretches of highway, inadequate for large-scale troop activity at the best of times, simply dissolved.

Allied air operations also had to be sharply curtailed. Unlike the hard-surfaced airfields the Germans had seized in Tunisia and those in Italy and Sicily, the ones the Allies had commandeered in their advance were little more than strips of grass. Even at Algiers's Maison Blanche airport, B-17 bombers flown in to wreak havoc upon the enemy had to have props under their wings to keep them from sinking in the mud. Most of the time, fighters could not take off to attack enemy positions, a frustrating circumstance made more agonizing by reconnaissance reports that German combat aircraft were parked practically wingtip to wingtip at airfields in Tunisia. Even when weather permitted, the closest usable Allied airfield was more than one hundred miles from the front while the bases controlled by the Germans were only twenty miles away.

Meantime, German U-boats had begun trying to compensate for their failure to detect the Allied convoys prior to the initial Torch landings. They, and German bombers when the weather permitted, took their toll of Allied cargo ships as they ventured eastward from Algiers to supply Anderson's troops along their line of march through small coastal ports. It cost Anderson quick access to much of the equipment he needed to maintain his momentum while the enemy was growing increasingly organized, confident, and aggressive.

Soon after the Allied offensive had been launched, Field Marshal Kesselring visited General Nehring at the newly established Axis forces headquarters in Tunisia, housed in what had been the American consulate in Tunis. Kesselring scolded Nehring for being overly cautious and confining his operations to the defensive perimeters he had set up around Tunis and Bizerte. Holding the First Army back was not to be enough. He was instructed to drive it back into Algeria. The Führer would expect nothing less.

Despite improved communications between Gibraltar and Algiers, Eisenhower's sense of being isolated on the Rock from developments in North Africa had grown increasingly galling to the Supreme Commander. The continuing repercussions of the Darlan deal and the paucity of news from the Tunisia front intensified his wish to be where things were happening rather than stuck hundreds of miles away across the Mediterranean. He was much relieved when communications facilities were finally well-enough established in Algiers for Allied Forces Headquarters to shift there on November 24.

Able at last to take command on the spot, he hoped to turn the focus of his attention from the miasma of French politics to the race into Tunisia. He was distressed by how disorganized it appeared to be. Instead of a major thrust at the prime objectives,

Allied forces were thinly strung out along a wide front. Instead of engaging as planned in a coordinated advance, units were being committed to the attack in a piecemeal fashion. There appeared to be no coherent battle plan. To make matters worse, communications had remained so unreliable on the line that Anderson had difficulty keeping track of the positioning and movement of his forces.

Eisenhower held Anderson responsible for permitting such a situation to develop. He believed him to be "imbued with the will to win, but [he] blows hot and cold, by turns, in his estimates and resulting demands." The British on the other hand felt that as Torch deputy commander based in Algiers, General Clark, who, like Eisenhower, had found himself immersed in French factional politics, should have overseen this difficult operation which was being undertaken with very limited resources. They felt Clark should have tied the loose ends of the stuttering Tunisia campaign together. Air Marshal Sir Arthur Tedder, who was called in to examine the situation soon after Eisenhower had shifted over from Gibraltar, was "deeply disturbed" by what he saw.

> [C]ommunications for all Services were practically non-existent except for the archaic French telephone system. The aerodromes were inadequate . . . the degree of congestion [on the airfields] almost unbelievable. There seemed to be little drive to remedy the situation, which was to my mind dangerous in the extreme. . . . As for the control of operations, any semblance of a Combined Headquarters had gone. Eisenhower and huge American staffs filled a large hotel [in Algiers]. . . . Cunningham . . . chose to live in his ship, because it alone had good communications with the outside world. Air Marshal Welsh and his headquarters were some miles out of Algiers, and Doolittle, commanding the U.S. Air, had a separate headquarters in the town. The U.S. Air was running a separate war, and there was an incident on 27 November . . . when the U.S. Air refused to assist General Anderson's First Army's operations in the north. . . .

That last incident had resulted from a confusion in command duties, which Eisenhower, at Tedder's suggestion, quickly moved to resolve. As he should have earlier, he ordered that all forward air units respond immediately to Anderson's operational needs. He also took steps to accelerate the straggly flow of armored equipment to the front.

In one case, armored personnel carriers meant for the front had been held back because rail facilities had been found to be unsuitable for transporting them. Quartermaster officers had calculated that to send them cross-country would greatly shorten the useful life of their half-track treads. Hearing about it, Eisenhower angrily demanded, "What are we saving them for?," and had them dispatched at once. He also ordered General Patton to accelerate the shipment eastward of medium tanks that had been landed in Morocco and were squatting there doing nothing.

Eisenhower wanted Anderson's forces quickly regrouped and reinforced so that the offensive in Tunisia could be relaunched. But it was concluded that not all Allied forces in North Africa could be devoted to that purpose. A German attack through Spain and across the Strait of Gibraltar was now extremely unlikely but was not yet completely ruled out. Exaggerated suspicions also persisted about whether the largely Arab populations of the French North African territories would cause problems. Away from the main urban centers, the Arabs were considered at best "semi-hostile" to the Allies and their mood potentially explosive. General Patton, never one to underestimate his requirements, claimed from Morocco that if they turned against the Americans, he would need 60,000 troops to maintain order and he had nowhere near that number.

Nazi propagandists made a determined effort to stir up Arab resentment against the Allied presence. Under Vichy, to Arab satisfaction, the small, long-established Jewish community in Morocco—numbering 300,000 among 11 million Muslims—had been subjected to repressive legislation. Now from Berlin, "Arab leaders chosen for their eloquence" radioed claims not only that those laws were being repealed but that a Jewish government would be installed to rule over the Muslims. They spread rumors that Eisenhower was Jewish and had been sent to their lands by another Jew—Franklin Delano Roosevelt. Eisenhower's political staff took the possible consequences so seriously that information was fed to local newspapers about their Dutch (Roosevelt) and German (Eisenhower) ancestry.

The situation was bewildering for Eisenhower, who had previously had no direct experience of the depth of historic ethnic antagonisms. As he later wrote, it further complicated the befuddling political disarray:

Through all this period the tangled political situation kept worrying us; it was difficult to pierce the web of intrigue, misinformation, misunderstanding, and burning prejudice that surrounded even the minor elements of the whole problem.

He was astonished when, while he was being pressed from Washington to repeal anti-Jewish Vichy legislation, Darlan brought him a message from the rabbi of the Jewish community in the Algerian city of Constantine, who urged that when the authorities relaxed the anti-Jewish laws, they should do so slowly. Otherwise, it was suggested, the Arabs "would undoubtedly stage a pogrom!" Meantime, fears arose that repeated German bombing raids on Algiers might lead to a rebellion by the populace of that city, which had suffered no such attacks before the Allied invasion. It was thought that despite the cooperation afforded by the retained Vichy administrative structure, troops had to be held in reserve to deal with this wide assortment of dangers, whatever the needs at the front.

All along the front, meantime, the enemy, strongly supported by attack aircraft, struck back at Anderson's offensive. Colonel General Jürgen von Arnim, a more daring commander than General Nehring, had been brought in from the Russian Front and took command of the Axis forces on December 9, a month after the landings. Battered by a series of von Arnim's counterattacks, Allied advances in Tunisia staggered to a halt and withdrawals had to be made in several places. Plans for resumed offensive action were repeatedly postponed or canceled because of air raids, preemptive enemy ground action, or ground conditions. Instead of driving on to Tunis and Bizerte, Anderson warned Eisenhower that he might soon have to go over to the defensive.

The possibility of enemy airborne raids behind Allied lines by the Germans remained a worry. Troops of the U.S. 34th Division were posted as a precaution along a key line of supply for the forward forces. But there was so much territory to cover that even before French troops were considered reliable, they were called upon to guard bridges, tunnels, and other strategic positions.

The Tunisia campaign had become haphazard. Writing to General Handy in Washington, Eisenhower tacitly accepted the blame:

I think the best way to describe our operations to date is that they have violated every recognized principle of war, are in conflict with all operational and logistical methods laid down in text-books, and will be condemned, in their entirety, by all Leavenworth and War College classes for the next twenty-five years.

A new offensive in Tunisia was scheduled for December 24. The British 78th Division and 6th Armored Division with elements of the American 1st Infantry Division were to press forward, if not to wind up the battle, then at least to secure dominant positions before the worst of the winter weather set in. A preliminary assault was to be made to capture an elevated perch code-named Longstop Hill, which could command the lowland approach to Tunis. Launched December 22, it quickly turned into a series of back-and-forth clashes fought under a hammering of torrential rain, which had prevented adequate preliminary reconnaissance. In a four-day struggle to claim control of the site, the 1st Battalion, U.S. 18 Infantry, and the British Coldstream Guards took heavy casualties.

By Christmas Eve, even before that clash had ended in defeat, Eisenhower realized the plan to renew the offensive had to be scrapped. Having received reports of what the rainstorms were doing to the terrain the troops would have to cover, he had torn himself away from the political concerns that were consuming so much of his time in Algiers and had finally gone to the front to see conditions for himself. They proved to be as wretched as he had been told they were. At one point, he saw four soldiers struggling to extricate a motorcycle that was stuck in mud at the side of a road. Despite their exertions and the comparative lightness of the motorcycle, they were unable to shift it and had to leave it even more deeply embedded than before. That incident "as much as anything" convinced Eisenhower "of the hopelessness of an attack." He ordered that the offensive be indefinitely postponed and reported to the Combined Chiefs of Staff that he believed that further progress could not be expected in "less than two months."

[We] have discovered that we cannot maneuver any type of vehicle off the roads and, since our real hope of victory lay in the skillful maneuver and use of our artillery to provide the punch necessary to

271

blast enemy's armor, the original plan has met an impasse. . . . The evidence is complete, in my opinion, that any attempt to make a major attack under current conditions in Northern Tunisia would be merely to court disaster.

The fulfillment of Operation Torch's mission was thus suspended. Further forward movement would have to await the end of the winter rains. It was a particularly depressing turn of events for Eisenhower. It was an open admission of failure made doubly disheartening because mounting the Christmas Eve offensive had been his first major battlefield command decision.

The news of the setback was grimly received at the War Department and the War Office. The British Chiefs of Staff were unhappy about the limited information they were receiving about what was going on in Tunisia and pressed Eisenhower for further details. They feared: "Owing to the thinness of our defenses and lack of reserves the Allied forces may well be driven back well into Algeria."

At that moment, it was not only the U.S. War Department to whom Operation Torch seemed a liability. "News from Tunisia not too good," General Brooke noted in his diary, understating his concern. "I do not like much the way things are going there." While General Sir Harold Alexander, chief of British forces in the Middle East, was having his already well-established reputation as an able commander enhanced by Montgomery's successes over Rommel, Eisenhower, whom the British had come to admire personally, began to appear to the War Office in London as a rank amateur when an experienced professional like Alexander or Germany's Field Marshal Kesselring was what was needed. Churchill cabled Roosevelt, "I am most anxious about the military situation."

A quick Allied victory in Tunisia might have shifted attention from the unresolved political problems in North Africa. And had Darlan been able to persuade Admiral de Laborde to send the French fleet at Toulon to North Africa to be put at the disposal of the Allies, his value to the Allied cause would have been difficult to question. But instead, de Laborde scuttled the fleet at its moorings on November 27 when the Germans tried to seize it.

Still, the shabbiness of doing a deal with Darlan might have been soon forgotten if French troops had provided greater support to the advancing Allies at the start of the Tunisia campaign when they could have altered the course of the battle. But they had stayed clear until it was too late for them to influence developments in any important way.

The British were reluctant to be openly critical of Eisenhower's handling of the political situation, but with so little to show from the laboriously won French agreement to cooperate, Allied Forces Headquarters in Algiers, and Eisenhower personally, were subjected to streams of requests from Washington for proof that the vestiges of Vichy rule were being eradicated. They clearly were not. Despite censorship on political subjects as well as on classified military information imposed on American and British correspondents, reports filtered back to the United States and Britain that pro-fascist French officials remained in positions of authority in Algeria and Morocco.

Some French soldiers who had shot pro-Allied insurrectionists during the Torch landings were awarded the Croix de Guerre. A number of Frenchmen who had conspired in favor of the Allies prior to the landings were still languishing in jails. Others were harassed by the authorities and by members of the Service d'Ordre Légionnaire, the pro-Vichy militia, which had not been disbanded. They were menaced in the streets and ugly abuse was scrawled on the doors of their homes. French censors who had earlier faithfully served Vichy remained in place and unabashedly suppressed pro-Allied editorials written for newspapers in Algiers and Morocco. They went so far as to ban newspapers from reporting official Allied statements to which they objected, including those made by Roosevelt and Churchill.

American and British correspondents demanded that officers at Allied Forces Headquarters explain why this state of affairs was permitted to continue. They were told that the situation was not as bad as it seemed, and in any case, it was important to maintain stability and civil order while the troops at the front were fighting the Germans. They considered that explanation unsatisfactory. John MacVane, in Algiers as a correspondent for the National Broadcasting Company, was among the newsmen who grew bitter because "we were collaborating with the wrong Frenchmen."

An American officer summed up our situation graphically [MacVane later wrote]. "When we came to North Africa, my boss was an English general. He called a meeting of all the French officials that had anything to do with his particular line of work. When the Frenchmen arrived, the English general was sitting in his dirty, mud-smeared battledress behind a desk. On the desk lay his big, loaded forty-five pistol, pointed towards the Frenchmen. Behind him stood a group of rough-looking officers armed to the teeth. The British general pointed to one after another of the French officials. 'You do this,' he said, 'you, this; and you, the other thing.' They jumped to it. Everything went like clockwork. We never had a complaint or a hitch. Then I got a new boss. An American general took over the job. Now we must never command the French to do anything. So he asks them to drop into his office if they have a moment to spare. They come in and he asks them very gently, would they please do this and so. They say, 'Of course, General. Vive l'Amérique.' Then the Facist bastards go outside and screw us. Now everything is all balled up. Snafu."

Leland Rounds, one of Murphy's pre-invasion diplomat-spies, who had been ordered to London prior to the landings, returned to Oran to serve as political adviser for Center Task Force commander General Fredendall. It proved a delicate assignment. In the run-up to the attempted coup, Rounds, like Murphy's other Disciples, had dealt and sympathized with French insurgents who longed for the day when pro-fascist officials in North Africa, some of whom were known to have been in the pay of German intelligence, would be forced out of office. Upon his return to Oran, he discovered that had not happened. Great bitterness had developed openly between them and those of their colleagues who had favored the Allies. Some of the latter had risked much prior to the invasion by sympathizing undisguisedly with the Allied cause. They had expected the Allied command to cleanse the region of Nazi collaborators. Instead, they found themselves harassed as traitors. Rounds wanted something done about it.

The situation was awkward for Fredendall. Unlike many professional British officers who had served in far reaches of the British Empire, American officers had no experience of and little liking for political administration. Fredendall found the determination of his political adviser to get involved in local wrangles a nuisance. He preferred not to know that French liaison officers assigned to U.S.

units were scolded by their superiors for "fraternizing" with the Americans. He ignored a report that nineteen French soldiers had been court-martialed and imprisoned for responding to Roosevelt's invasion eve "we come as friends" radio appeal by dismantling the breach bolts of their guns so they could not be used against the invaders. A. J. Liebling, a correspondent for *The New Yorker* magazine, reported, "Members of uniformed [Vichy] fascist organizations . . . reappeared in the cafés [of Oran] wearing their capes, monocles, and high boots and talking loudly about the day of revenge, not against the Germans, but us."

Demands that French North Africa be quickly de-Vichyfied annoyed Murphy. He had no sympathy for fascists, but he was interested in avoiding what he considered unnecessary convulsions during the transition period in North Africa. He was miffed that proprieties were not being observed. In his Algiers office, he found himself receiving "a continuous parade of Very Important Persons—or those who thought they were" from the United States who took to passing through Algiers "because they wanted to participate in this first American campaign in World War II."

> Many of the newcomers assumed that Americans, not Frenchmen, were entitled to decide how French Africa should be administered while our soldiers were there. That assumption was entirely contrary to arrangements we had made with French officials before and during the landings, and it was contrary to promises which had been given with the full approval of Roosevelt and Eisenhower.

In Morocco too, controversy arose over how far the United States should go in interfering with the French administration. Patton's personal intervention had been required to get General Béthouart released from custody into which he had been placed, probably prior to execution, for organizing the abortive pro-Allied D-Day coup. But Patton had developed friendly relations with Resident-General Noguès, who had remained the senior French official there.

Noguès had been a central figure in crushing Béthouart's coup. He had then made no effort to end French resistance to the American landings. That resistance had been sustained even after Darlan had ordered a cease-fire in Algiers. Noguès thus was primarily responsible for the greatest number of casualties the Americans had suffered in Operation Torch's opening phase. Eisenhower considered him devious and unreliable.

But after establishing his headquarters in Casablanca, Patton found Noguès cordial and cooperative in controlling the "native population" and was impressed with the pomp that went with French colonial administration. According to a British official, Noguès fascinated "backwoods American generals with his dinners and hunting parties." Patton was prepared to overlook the fact that he still declined to free from prison a number of Frenchmen who had abortively conspired with Béthouart on behalf of the Allies. The simple fact was that it was easier to maintain the status quo than hand the administration of Morocco over to anti-Vichy figures—people with whom American diplomat-spy David King had been conspiring for more than a year—though they were anxious to cooperate fully with the Allies.

Word that Moroccan radio was still broadcasting pro-German propaganda reached the Allied capitals, as did reports that the old crowd was still very much in charge throughout the part of French North Africa supposedly liberated from Nazi collaboration. Churchill informed Roosevelt of his concern. "Well-known German sympathizers who had been ousted," he told the president, "have been reinstated. Not only have our enemies been thus encouraged, but our friends have been correspondingly confused and cast down."

Eisenhower felt required repeatedly to turn his attention from the Allied reverses in the Tunisia campaign to answer demands from the War Department that he explain what was going wrong in Algeria and Morocco. He saw even more trouble in store when Darlan indicated his intention, in view of the German occupation of Vichy France, to declare himself the repository of French sovereignty—in effect, the legitimate government of France in exile. That threatened to reinflame the smoldering row over the Darlan deal. The Supreme Commander had Murphy instruct the admiral that he would not be permitted delusions of grandeur. He was to tone down whatever claims he made to national authority and was told that the Allies recognized him only as de facto head of the local administration.

I think sometimes [Eisenhower wrote a friend] that I am a cross between a one-time soldier, a pseudo-statesman, a jack-legged politician

276

and a crooked diplomat. I walk a soapy tight-rope in a rain storm with a blazing furnace on one side and a pack of ravenous tigers on the other. . . . In spite of all this, I must admit that the whole thing is intriguing and interesting and is forever presenting new challenges. . . .

A senior British official who visited Algiers during this period made a depressing report to the War Cabinet in London. He had been struck by "a certain lack of assurance at the Allied headquarters."

The strongest impression he had received was that the greater part of the attention of both British and American senior officers was taken up with matters of French politics. In two long interviews, General Eisenhower had talked of little else. During these conversations there had been frequent interruptions by senior officers who came in to take General Eisenhower's instructions on some questions bearing on French politics, such as the relationship between General Noguès and Admiral Darlan, and whether Admiral Darlan could be persuaded to remove from office the mayor of Constantine. . . . The General thought that our ability to capture Tunis quickly was entirely dependent on French cooperation.

Problems that should have been sorted out by staff officers at Allied Headquarters often made their way to the top. General Walter Bedell Smith, who had arrived in Algiers to take up his position there as Eisenhower's chief of staff, provided much help. But Smith was a man with an easily inflamed, scalding temper and now his ulcer was acting up, making him even more of an ogre to officers with problems. Some who should have brought those problems to him chose not to, with the result that many ended up finally on Eisenhower's desk for sorting out. Though known for his readiness to assume responsibility and though famous later for his composure under pressure, the Supreme Commander took to muttering that he would gladly give his job to anyone who wanted it.

As the outcry against the extensive persisting Vichyite influence in Algeria and Morocco grew in intensity, Roosevelt felt obliged to make a public gesture of friendship toward General de Gaulle, whom the president continued to dislike and distrust. The general's Free French movement was still barred from participating in any aspect of the North Africa operations and in the political readjustments taking place there. But the American as well as the British press continued to portray de Gaulle, rather than Giraud or Darlan, as representing the true spirit of France. He remained widely regarded as the Frenchman who most embodied the ideals for which the crusade for freedom had been undertaken.

The president, therefore, grudgingly permitted arrangements to be made for him to be granted an audience at the White House to take place just after Christmas in 1942. It was to be done in a way that would not confer the formal American recognition that de Gaulle had long sought, an act that might have complicated Eisenhower's problems even more. But some sort of diplomatic acceptance would clearly be implied by the meeting. However, as the general was preparing to be driven from London to the airport for his trip to Washington, his visit to the United States was postponed. Word was passed along of a serious development in Algiers that would totally transform the North Africa situation.

On December 24, Fernand Eugène Bonnier de La Chapelle, a twenty-year-old Frenchman, had gained entrance to the Summer Palace in Algiers on a pretense and had hidden there. When Darlan returned from lunch to his office in the palace, Bonnier took out a pistol and shot him. Darlan died that afternoon as doctors at a nearby hospital tried to save him. Suddenly, the Darlan conundrum that had plagued the Allies from the day Operation Torch had been launched was resolved.

Whether the assassination was organizationally inspired was never positively determined. What is known is that Bonnier was one of four young Frenchmen who had participated in the abortive coup in Algiers on D-Day and who believed Darlan was an obstacle to the liberation of France. All four volunteered to kill the admiral and agreed to draw straws for the honor. Bonnier drew the shortest straw.

The youthful assassin was a monarchist and may have been motivated by his wish to see the Count of Paris, the pretender to the French throne, mount the long-vacant throne of France. The count had arrived in Algiers from his residence in Spanish Morocco shortly before, claiming to be the only individual who could unite the French people during those difficult times.

Bonnier had been in training at a camp set up in Algeria by the British Special Operations Executive after the Torch landings, leading to suggestions that he had acted on behalf of British intelligence, or perhaps had been encouraged by a British SOE agent acting on his own initiative. The possibility was also raised that the assassination was performed on behalf of the OSS to relieve the United States of the burden Darlan had become, or on behalf of the Gaullists. The White House believed the Free French were behind the assassination and that it was designed to eliminate the figure the Gaullists considered the greatest obstacle to their own assumption of leadership of the French in the struggle against the Axis powers.

Darlan's assassination was not a complete surprise. A month earlier, a report from Algiers to the British Foreign Office observed, "No one expects Darlan to be allowed to end his days in peace. There are too many people who want his blood."

The speed with which Bonnier was disposed of after the assassination precluded any serious investigation of who else might have been involved. A secret French military tribunal was convened in the middle of the night thirty-six hours after Darlan died and quickly sentenced Bonnier to death for his crime. He did not appear to be overly distressed by the decision of the court-martial, as if convinced that he would be reprieved. He is reported to have cryptically commented to his jailer that he had no concerns because "London has been advised," which, if true, might have pointed to either British or Gaullist involvement. He was found to be in possession of a regulation identity card and valid passport in the name of Morand. The passport had a visa permitting him to enter Spanish Morocco, which pointed to a monarchist conspiracy.

Had Bonnier been persuaded by monarchists that with Darlan dead, the Count of Paris would immediately come to power and reward him for his brave act? Had he been led to believe that senior figures among the French military and civil authorities in Algiers countenanced the assassination and would protect him?

Shortly after dawn on December 26, within hours of his hasty, brief trial, Bonnier was put before a firing squad and executed. It might have been understandable for the military men who passed sentence on him not to delay administering justice to an assassin whose guilt could not be denied. But it suspiciously ruled out investigation of a statement he allegedly made implicating other monarchists. That alleged statement strangely did not come to light until several days later.

A year later, on the anniversary of Bonnier's execution, a large group of people, including several officials, placed wreaths on his tomb and observed a minute of silence in his memory. In 1945, the Court of Appeals in Algiers exonerated Bonnier posthumously, ruling that "the act for which [he] was condemned was accomplished in the interests of the liberation of France." He was adjudged to have been a national hero.

Whatever motives and persons might have been behind Darlan's removal from the scene, it aroused few regrets. Despite official expressions of condolence to the admiral's family, his passing came as a great relief to the Allied command. General Clark, still trying to sort out the byzantine confusions of French politics, was hardly grief stricken by the assassination.

> Admiral Darlan's death was, to me, an act of Providence. It is too bad that he went that way, but, strategically speaking, his removal from the scene was like the lancing of a troublesome boil. He had served his purpose, and his death solved what could have been the very difficult problem of what to do with him in the future. Darlan was a political investment forced upon us by circumstances, but we made a sensational profit in lives and time through using him.

The British saw the elimination of Darlan not only as a fortunate development but as a satisfying one as well. De Gaulle, their troublesome but chosen French instrument, now was likely to have a clearer run. Monitoring their response to the assassination, the State Department asked through the U.S. embassy in London if they would "please calm down their gloating."

Despite the relief over Darlan's departure, it was soon apparent that the disagreeable vestiges of earlier official practices and procedures had not been eliminated. An immediate roundup of suspects involved in what might possibly be a wider assassination conspiracy took place. That was to be expected. The situation was tense and confused. But less understandable was the arrest of individuals who were rounded up only because they were known to hold pro-Allied and anti-Vichy sentiments. Among them was Dr. Aboulker, in whose home the abortive D-Day pro-Allied coup had been planned with Robert Murphy. It was there, though it now seemed a grotesque irony, that Murphy had left his black homburg the night of the coup, saying he would be back for it later. Despite Aboulker's advanced years—he was seventy-eight—and a leg damaged by an injury he had sustained fighting for France in World War I, the doctor had been hustled away by the police without being permitted to don his trousers or take his cane.

Others who had participated in the conspiracy with Murphy were also picked up, including one young man who had waded into the water near Cherchell to help steady the canoe in which General Clark had made his departure after his pre-invasion secret conference. Lack of evidence that these men had anything to do with the assassination did not save some of them from being transported to a concentration camp at Laghouat, two hundred miles away in the Sahara Desert. It was some time before they were released. Efforts to ask Murphy to intercede on their behalf were fruitless. Those who sought to appeal for his help found they could not get through to him. It may be that he considered the general situation too complex and too delicate for him to intervene.

The political climate in French North Africa was now substantially altered. Two days after the assassination, the French Imperial Council, which had been established in North Africa under Darlan, met to deal with the new situation. But the council's grand title belied its actual powers. Under pressure from Eisenhower, who was in turn acting under stepped-up pressure from the White House, it was obliged despite strenuous objections from Noguès to recognize Giraud as high commissioner in French North Africa and commander in chief of French armed forces there. That was the position and rank Eisenhower had agreed the general should assume seven weeks earlier, at Gibraltar.

For several days after the assassination, rumors of a conspiratorial death squad at work spread through Algiers. A "trusted French agent" reported to Allied Forces Headquarters that Murphy and Giraud were high on an assassination list. But though security was tightened around those said to be targeted for murder, the report appeared to have been a fabrication.

With Darlan out of the picture and the drive into Tunisia suspended for the moment, the much-harassed Allied Forces Headquarters could begin to put things in perspective. Dismayed by what had been happening in Algeria and Morocco, Churchill had to insist to Roosevelt that the Americans accept a senior British adviser at Allied Forces Headquarters. Harold Macmillan, under secretary of state at the British Colonial Office, arrived in Algiers shortly afterward to join Murphy in relieving Eisenhower of much of the confusions and anguish associated with political and diplomatic problems.

The persistence of the war correspondents in getting details of what was happening in Algiers and Morocco through to the United States and Britain gradually brought results. The most blatantly disagreeable residue of times past was gradually eliminated. Spared those distractions, and with Macmillan as well as Murphy fielding political aspects of the situation, Eisenhower, to his immense relief, could finally concentrate on consolidating Allied military gains and preparing for the renewal of the Tunisia offensive when the rains stopped and Allied troops could press forward again.

★ 18 ★

CHARTING THE WAY AHEAD

We came, we listened, and we were conquered.

—GENERAL ALBERT WEDEMEYER

For the Allies not to have successfully completed all phases of Operation Torch before the winter set in was a great disappointment. But the Axis powers had even less to cheer about. At Stalingrad, the German Army was in the process of suffering one of the most monumental routs in history. In Libya, Montgomery's Eighth Army was slowly but relentlessly driving Rommel's Panzerarmee toward a terminal trap in Tunisia. The American and British air forces had launched a bombing campaign against German cities and strategic targets. In the Pacific and on the Asian mainland, the Japanese advance had ground to a halt.

Nevertheless, the war was still far from won and the Allies had no blueprint for winning it. British and American strategic thinking was still at odds. Agreement hadn't even been reached within the American High Command on how best to proceed in the pursuit of victory, while to the U.S. War Department, the British still seemed determined to play around the edges of the conflict rather than getting to the heart of the matter. It was time to examine the situation in detail, overcome differences, and chart the way forward. A summit conference of the leaders of the Western democracies was arranged for mid-January for that purpose.

Iceland and other locations where security for Roosevelt and

Churchill and their entourages would cause little concern were considered suitable venues for the gathering. But for personal and political reasons, the president was much taken with the idea of reviewing American troops overseas. The site chosen for the conference was Anfa, an upmarket suburb in the hills above Casablanca with exquisite views over the Atlantic shore. The modern three-story hotel at Anfa and eighteen luxury villas adjoining it were commandeered, a wire fence was thrown around the area, and armed guards—both troops and personal bodyguards of the senior figures—were assigned to patrol it. In view of the Darlan assassination, security was particularly tight.

> I have never seen so many sentries armed with such terrifying weapons [Harold MacMillan wrote in his diary]. The rifle is almost forgotten here. There are machine-guns and Tommy guns and sawn-off shot-guns and all sorts of weapons of that kind. Every time you go in and out of the circle you are in danger all the time of being shot.

Roosevelt and Churchill, accompanied by their chiefs of staff, met at Anfa on January 14. They had hoped that Stalin would take part in the summit session, and the American and British leaders had even considered proposing that the meeting be held in Moscow. But Churchill felt that his uncomfortable experience with Stalin in the Russian capital the previous August suggested that the Western Allies were likely to find themselves at an awkward disadvantage dealing with the Soviet leader on his home ground and, with important developments all along the Russian Front, Stalin felt he could not leave Moscow at that time. It may also have been that Stalin thought it likely that what he wanted most from the Western Allies—the long-promised second front in Europe— would still be denied him and that he preferred not to be in attendance when that happened. As it was, the second front controversy was again high on the agenda when the chiefs of staff of the two countries conferred at the conference.

Proceeding with a cross-Channel invasion of France in 1943 (Operation Round-Up) and the buildup of American forces in Britain for that invasion (Operation Bolero) were still Allied policy. At least they were policy to the extent that no official move had been made to cancel them. But as General Marshall had predicted, Operation Torch had effectively preempted both and the failure to

284

bring Torch to an early, victorious conclusion had made their implementation even more remote.

In view of how forces had been committed, the first priority in the European Theater had to be crushing Axis resistance in Tunisia and gaining complete, unchallenged mastery of the southern rim of the Mediterranean Sea. Marshall was concerned that even after that had been achieved, the British would continue to pursue their close-the-ring-around-Hitler strategy and would propose further "sideshows" in the Mediterranean. They had already suggested as much. Even worse, so had Roosevelt. Well before the conference, Churchill, in his communications with the White House, had urged the president to recognize the importance of "using the bases on the African shore to strike at the under-belly of the Axis in effective strength and in the shortest time." Roosevelt had replied favorably.

The role the United States was playing in the war had the overwhelming support of the American people. In less than a year, the public mood in the United States had shifted from isolationism to firm determination to defeat the Axis powers. However, in congressional elections two months earlier, Roosevelt's Democratic party had suffered a major setback, almost losing control of the House of Representatives. It may have been because great numbers of young men, traditionally Democratic, were in the armed forces and most of them had been unable to vote. Whatever the reasons, the president had to take account of political factors in his direction of the war. It was difficult for him to avoid concluding that a Mediterranean strategy was not to be spurned, if only because it was likely to result in far fewer American casualties than an early frontal assault on Europe across the English Channel.

Besides, moving forward from Operation Torch to operations in southern Europe appeared to be eminently logical. There seemed to be little sense in throwing away the advantage to be derived from the concentration of Allied ground and air forces in North Africa. With the Mediterranean removed from Axis control, conditions would be ideal for using the area as a springboard for action that would knock Italy out of the war, exert pressure on the enemy in the occupied Balkans, and perhaps draw Turkey into the conflict on the Allied side. According to this scenario, Hitler would be hard-pressed to protect his southern flank when it was so vulnerable to Allied assault. Indeed, the Germans saw North Africa as a "springboard for a thrust into the groin of Fortress Europe, a naturally weak and practically unprepared south flank."

General Marshall was in an awkward position. Roosevelt continued to admire him personally and respect his judgment as Army Chief of Staff and Chairman of the Joint Chiefs. Churchill also regarded him highly. Yet he was unable to win his argument on the central plank of the strategy he favored and pressed with great vigor. He continued to maintain that an early invasion of France from England would bring the war to a speedier, and ultimately less costly, conclusion. He remained convinced that Churchill's Mediterranean strategy was a mistake that would serve only to further fritter away resources required to win the war without needless delay. A member of the British team at the conference said that some of the Americans at Casablanca regarded "the Mediterranean as a kind of . . . dark hole into which one entered at one's peril. If large forces were committed . . . the door would suddenly and firmly be shut behind [them]."

Marshall objected also to what was developing into a strategy of improvisation, of making-it-up-as-we-go-along. It made nonsense of long-range planning. Aside from the danger of being drawn into ill-prepared undertakings, it diverted resources from, and could endanger, long-planned operations. Operations would be undertaken simply because the circumstances appeared suitable at the time rather than because they fitted into a carefully preformulated strategy.

Marshall was at a distinct disadvantage at Casablanca. Not only was Roosevelt receptive to the British-promoted Mediterranean strategy, but the British were far better prepared than the Americans to argue their case. For one thing, the Americans were divided in their views. As before, Admiral King was far more interested in the Pacific than operations either against France across the English Channel or across the Mediterranean. General Arnold, the U.S. Air Force chief, was much taken by the idea of establishing Allied bomber bases in Sicily and perhaps even Italy to help bring the war home to the enemy in an ever-increasing crescendo. Even Marshall had to concede that the concentration of Allied forces in the Mediterranean region was a strong argument in favor of continuing to employ them there. And no one could forget how much of a disaster the cross-Channel Dieppe raid had been the previous summer, even though it was a miniature undertaking compared to what a full-scale invasion of France was to be.

In contrast to the diversity of American views, the British spoke with one voice at Casablanca. In preparing for the summit, their Chiefs of Staff had conferred closely with each other and with Churchill not only on military strategy but also on tactics to employ in rebutting American arguments. They continued those consultations between themselves during the conference to make certain they maintained a unified approach on the issues raised. That was in striking contrast to American disharmony. Field Marshal Dill, who had established a warm and close working relationship with Marshall while serving on the Combined Chiefs of Staff in Washington and who had warned Marshall that the British would be well prepared to deal with them, had been brought to Casablanca to advise on "how best to tackle the Americans."

What was more, Churchill had arranged for a command ship to be docked in Casablanca harbor to service and provide communications backup for the staff he had brought along from London. The British were thus able to present updated and greatly detailed analyses of strategic objectives and possibilities while the Americans arrived in Casablanca expecting that both sides would rely on comparatively generalized presentations of their views.

> They swarmed down upon us like locusts [General Wedemeyer complained] with a plentiful supply of planners and various other assistants, with prepared plans to insure that they not only accomplished their purpose but did so in stride and with fair promise of continuing in the role of directing strategy the whole course of the war. . . . If I were a Britisher, I would feel very proud. However, as an American, I wish that we might be more glib and better organized to cope with these super-negotiators. . . . It was apparent that we were confronted by generations and generations of experience in committee work, in diplomacy, and in rationalizing points of view.

The arguments Marshall and like-minded American planners presented in favor of an invasion of France across the Channel within the next few months were met with a storm of facts and figures that challenged the premises on which those arguments were based. Up-to-date maps, charts, and statistical analyses on enemy strengths were produced, leaving the Americans with little more than opinions to offer in rebuttal.*

Once more, some of the Americans grew suspicious of British motives. Once more they grumbled to each other that the British were interested in a Mediterranean strategy primarily "to improve their over-all Empire position." Their fraternal feelings for the British were not improved by General Brooke's manner. A small, sharp-faced, quick-thinking, fast-talking man, the Chief of the Imperial General Staff was constitutionally incapable of respecting or pretending to respect the views of those who differed with him on key questions. His low regard for the intelligence of the Americans is revealed in his diary accounts of conference sessions. "It is a slow and tedious process as all matters have to be carefully explained and re-explained before they can be absorbed. And finally the counter-arguments put forward often show that even then the true conception has not been grasped, and the process has to be started again."

Only with difficulty did Dill persuade Brooke to attempt to convince the Americans rather than force his opinions upon them. He recognized the need for tact and stressed that the Americans "must be made gradually to assimilate our proposed policy."

Much was at stake at the Casablanca Conference. It was generally recognized by all concerned that, advisable or not, what followed would by no means be a sideshow. This was a turning point. Now that the Allies had taken the initiative on the field of battle, the strategy to be agreed at Casablanca could determine how the rest of the war would be fought.

The British rebuttal of Marshall's cross-Channel invasion arguments was mostly a repeat of what they had said before. Doubts were expressed on whether sufficient bomber strength was available to soften up German forces deployed in France to make a success of the landings there and subsequent beachhead consolida-

---

*The Americans were determined afterward not to be caught short again. According to an official U.S. Army historian, at the Quebec conference of the Combined Chiefs of Staff later in the year, they "made particularly careful preparations to present their views. They analyzed at length the procedure of previous conferences, the debating techniques of the British, and even the precise number of planners required to cope on equal terms with British staffs."

tion. Not enough shipping and landing craft were available for the massive operation the Americans had in mind. The troops were insufficiently combat-tested for the long haul that would follow a landing in France and there weren't enough of them. It was calculated that only twenty-one divisions could be assembled in Britain for a cross-Channel assault by August 1943, as compared to the forty-eight originally thought necessary. With the Germans and Italians about to be sent reeling in the Mediterranean area where the Allied forces were more strongly placed, conditions were right for further operations there. Finally, the British maintained that such operations would provide greater relief than was possible anywhere else at that time for the Soviets, who, despite what appeared to be happening at Stalingrad, were still in trouble.

Confronted with a meticulously organized, well-documented, strongly reasoned presentation of the British case, the Americans, unable to make adequate rebuttal and believing that Roosevelt had been largely won over by Churchill already, had to concede its merits. However, having to give ground in the European Theater, they were determined that it would not be at the expense of the war in the Pacific. Though the forward momentum of the Japanese in the Pacific had been broken, Japan's forces were in the process of trying to establish a defensive line from which it would be difficult to eject them.

The British knew that having been bulldozed into Operation Torch, the War Department had not been overly meticulous in adhering to the agreed Germany First policy. During the previous year more American troops had been deployed in the war against Japan than in the European Theater (nine of seventeen divisions overseas). And almost as many U.S. aircraft (1,910 to 2,065) were deployed against the Japanese as against the Germans. By pressing at Casablanca for acceptance of the Mediterranean strategy, the British had risked goading the American Joint Chiefs into further diluting their commitment to the Germany First approach.

They relied on Churchill's ability to persuade Roosevelt, the disharmony of the American planners, and the bird-in-the-hand logic of employing the forces already concentrated to best advantage. But hints of renewed pressure for the Pacific Alternative among the Americans made the British uneasy and led them to agree reluctantly at Casablanca to the commitment of greater Allied resources to fighting the Japanese. Nevertheless, a member of

Churchill's staff observed at Casablanca, "[I]f I had written down before I came what I hoped that the conclusions would be I could never have written anything so sweeping, so comprehensive, and so favourable to our ideas. . . . "

Despite agreement on a Mediterranean strategy, plans for the invasion of France across the English Channel were not to be abandoned. Indeed, all senior figures at the conference expressed continued confidence that it would ultimately be undertaken and that it would lead to the liberation of Europe and the destruction of the Third Reich. Churchill suggested "a 'Sledgehammer' of some sort" before the end of 1943 "if Germany shows definite signs of collapse." But Round-Up—the main cross-Channel invasion—would be put on hold. For the time being, the Mediterranean would be the main theater of operations for the Western Allies. After the enemy had been vanquished in North Africa, the next step would be the invasion of Sicily. To a cynic like Admiral King, it seemed like "merely doing something just for the sake of doing something."

Eisenhower's views on Allied strategy had undergone fundamental transformation during his tenure as Operation Torch's Supreme Commander. Almost a year before, as head of the Operations Division in Washington, he and his staff had devised the plans for Sledgehammer and Round-Up. Six months earlier, in London, he had declared that the decision to mount Torch instead might turn out to be one of the greatest mistakes in history. But by the time the Casablanca Conference took place, he had been persuaded that it had been the right move to make and, furthermore, that it made sense to move forward from it with another operation in the Mediterranean.

Once more, Eisenhower was pained by how far his views had come to differ from those of his former colleagues at the Operations Division at the War Department. Many of them were bitter over how the British had once more been permitted to overrule the Americans. Aware of that sentiment, Eisenhower wrote to General Thomas Handy urging him to believe that he had not done so. "One of the constant sources of danger to us in this war," he wrote, "is the temptation to regard as the first enemy the partner that must work with us in defeating the real enemy." Handy considered that admonition patronizing and was offended by it.

* * *

Dealing with the question of who truly represented the people and interests of France and its overseas territories provided a dramatic finale to the Casablanca conclave. The Americans had dismissed the possible contribution of France to the Allied war effort as very much of secondary significance. The country had been defeated and occupied by the Germans and even those French people who supported the Allies had comparatively little to offer the Allied war effort at that stage. Officers at Allied Forces Headquarters were angered by signs that Giraud, the man they had backed in the political squabbles in Algiers, was again proving difficult. He was ordering French troops into or out of the line in Tunisia without reference to the Allied command and neglecting problems of civil administration. But wearied by the bickering Eisenhower had been made to endure, the Americans were more or less resigned to having Giraud continue as senior French figure. However, France and its role in the continuing struggle against Nazi Germany loomed much larger in Churchill's political and historical perceptions.

Even after the Darlan deal, the British had continued to recognize General de Gaulle as the de facto head of state of a French government-in-exile. They had invested much prestige and a fair bit of money in his Free French movement. But they were in no position to impose him on French North Africa, where he at first had virtually no sympathizers in positions of influence. The existing Giraud-led regime was now very much in charge of the civil administration. What was more, Roosevelt still disapproved of de Gaulle. He still considered him a would-be tyrant, self-appointed to rule over France and favored by Churchill partly because he and the prime minister shared an interest in preserving the far-flung empires of their respective countries in the postwar world.

Nevertheless, de Gaulle continued to be popularly regarded both in Britain and the United States as the heroic voice of subjugated France. Newspapers and magazines recurringly recounted his creation of the Free French movement from scratch, his defiance of the death sentence imposed on him by the Vichy government, and his image as a beacon of light for the oppressed people of his occupied homeland. With little understanding of the various factions at play, Allied newsmen, newly arrived in North Africa and appalled at what remained of shabby Vichyite practices there, had taken to believing that virtually all French people who opposed such practices were Gaullists. When censorship on political reporting was relaxed, that was reflected in their reporting.

Now that plans were being made for what was to happen next in the war, Churchill persuaded Roosevelt that the time had come to resolve the discord over who should represent France in Allied councils. If that could be achieved, pro-Allied French forces could be better harnessed for the continuing struggle against the Axis powers. In addition, the Allied command in Algiers could be mercifully relieved of involvement in what remained of political infighting in French North Africa.

The Gaullist movement, exuding determination to free France from Nazi oppression, was beginning to establish a stronger toehold in Algeria and Morocco while Giraud, though still supported by the Americans for reasons of convenience, was proving too much of a narrow military man to govern the region effectively. Roosevelt and Churchill decided to bring Giraud and de Gaulle together in Casablanca while they were meeting there and let them sort things out between themselves. The president told the prime minister, "We'll call Giraud the bridegroom and I'll produce him from Algiers, and you get the bride, de Gaulle, down from London, and we'll have a shotgun wedding." Roosevelt's general approach irked some of the more somber figures in attendance. "His mood," Murphy thought, "was that of a schoolboy on vacation, which accounted for his almost frivolous approach to some of the difficult problems with which he dealt."

The Americans were able to produce Giraud easily enough. But de Gaulle presented a problem. The Free French leader had been waiting for two years for an invitation to Washington—an invitation befitting the leader of a great nation. He was bitter that the only time it had come, it had been rudely put off at the last minute. He did not object to meeting with Giraud. He thought little of him, believing him to have tarnished the prestige of France by kowtowing to the Americans. But he knew that Giraud was not personally tainted with the Vichy stigma. Indeed, de Gaulle had previously suggested a meeting with him. However, he angrily considered it beneath his dignity, and beneath the dignity of France, which he professed to represent, to answer this summons for him to meet, under the auspices of foreigners, with another French officer on the soil of a French protectorate state.

His refusal to go to Casablanca was deeply embarrassing to Churchill. Roosevelt commented mockingly on his inability to control his creation and "produce the temperamental bride." The prime minister was stung into warning de Gaulle that this petty act of defiance, from a man who owed his existence as Free French leader to Britain's generosity and support, could have serious consequences. He told him that the British government might find itself obliged to review its attitude toward his movement so long as he remained its leader; more bluntly, that it would insist on his replacement as Free French leader.

De Gaulle responded by bitterly complaining that the United States and Britain had decided to discuss important questions concerning France at Casablanca without consulting him. But urged by his advisers, who knew much could be at stake at Casablanca, he relented and agreed to journey there to meet with Giraud.

It was a stiff, formal meeting. De Gaulle was unbending in his wrath at the Americans and British for presuming to organize such political theater on French soil. They had even posted their own armed guards around the meeting place, compounding their presumption. Wanting only to command the forces that would liberate France and having been promised American arms for his troops, Giraud had no such qualms. He was prepared to welcome de Gaulle into the leadership of a provisional French government, but not to become his subordinate. De Gaulle's attitude was virtually the same. He rejected any deal that might dilute his authority. However, he was cajoled by Roosevelt into shaking hands with Giraud for the benefit of the news photographers and the two signed a brief communiqué in which, in general terms, they affirmed their commitment to Allied unity.

Though it was not apparent at the time and though the Americans still mistrusted him, de Gaulle's grudging presence at Casablanca marked the moment of emergence of this future president of France upon the world stage. Interestingly, a future president of the United States (Eisenhower) and a future prime minister of Britain (Macmillan) also attended the Casablanca conference, though in less prominent roles.

☆ 19 ☆

SETBACK

*The Americans had as yet no practical battle
experience, and it was now up to us to instill in
them . . . an inferiority complex.*

—FIELD MARSHAL ERWIN ROMMEL

What was happening in North Africa in the closing weeks of
1942 was laced with intimations of disaster for fascist Italy. As
Montgomery's Eighth Army began to push Rommel's German-
Italian forces back toward Tunisia and what was to be their doom,
Libya, the last remaining Italian outpost in Africa, was about to be
lost, probably forever. What was more, it was likely the Allies
would follow their North African victory by invading the nearby
Italian islands of Sardinia or Sicily. Italian mainland cities, rail-
roads, and military installations would then be even more exposed
to Allied bombing raids from captured bases a short hop away. An
invasion of the Italian mainland was likely to follow hard upon.

The Italian people were greatly disillusioned with Mussolini and
the promises he had made to them of greatness, glory, and a new
Roman Empire. *Il Duce* realized that the critical moment was
approaching. He warned his people that it would soon be decided
whether Italy must forsake forever his dream of empire and "resign itself to being a land of tourists, a large Switzerland."

Its own resources stretched to the limit, the Italian High Command pressed Hitler to strengthen his forces in North Africa to
prevent a total collapse there. But he had already done so and the
Germans now had comparatively few troops to spare. Western

Europe could not be denuded of forces in case the Allies seized upon his tribulations to launch their long-threatened frontal assault across the English Channel. Only from the Russian Front could any substantial number of troops be drawn to reinforce Axis positions in North Africa, and under the circumstances, they could not be spared.

In that case, the Italians said, the circumstances should be changed. They urged the Germans to find some way to negotiate peace terms with the Russians. To Hitler, that was unthinkable. He had always considered the eradication of Bolshevism a prime objective. To back away from it after having squandered hundreds of thousands of Germans lives would be more than an admission of defeat. It would fundamentally undermine his Nazi revolution. Besides, the Soviets were now going over to the offensive and were not likely to be receptive to peace bids. Even if they did agree to an armistice, Hitler knew it would be only until they could regroup their forces and gather further strength to inflict vengeance on the Third Reich for the tremendous suffering their people had endured at the hands of the Germans.

Though rejecting Italian urgings that he go hat in hand to Moscow, Hitler realized that the second front with which he was confronted in North Africa could not be abandoned without dangerous consequences. It would expose all of southern Europe to Allied attack and invasion. Montgomery's offensive was gathering momentum more slowly than expected but Rommel was being forced back to avoid total annihilation of his troops. Recognizing that his position was untenable, Rommel wanted to withdraw speedily across Libya all the way to Tunisia to join up with von Arnim's forces, which had halted the Allied advance there. He flew to Hitler's command post in East Prussia to present his case but was rebuffed by the German Führer, who would not countenance such defeatism.

Nevertheless, Rommel's supply situation was so precarious that on New Year's Eve, he was authorized to pull back toward Tunisia in slow, measured stages. Total British superiority in the air and on the ground, which Montgomery had insisted on before pressing home his offensive, permitted him no such luxury. He was down to little more than three divisions against the seven Montgomery could hurl against him. Against Montgomery's 450 tanks, he had only 36, plus 57 obsolete Italian tanks. By the end of January, just after the Allied summit conference at Casablanca had ended, most of his forces had been compelled to pull back behind French-built fortifications on the Mareth Line just inside the Tunisian border. The final contest for Tunisia was about to begin.

Though routed, Rommel's remaining troops were battle-hardened. Led by a resourceful, daring commander, they remained a formidable fighting force. To Eisenhower's despair, the same could not be said for American troops in North Africa. On visits to the front, he had seen for himself that they compared unfavorably to their British comrades-in-arms though many of those had also not seen battle before. Men of the U.S. 1st Armored Division—now in the line—had been shipped to Britain largely untrained. There they had received their equipment only shortly before they had embarked again for North Africa. Other U.S. units had been similarly ill prepared for combat.

Unlike British, German, and Italian troops, the American soldier was new to even the idea of soldiering. He brought with him a civilian mentality that, in the comparatively classless American context, recoiled against seemingly senseless orders. He was inclined to show little respect for the distinctions of rank. The spit-and-polish traditions and imperatives of traditional soldiering were foreign to him. This, as Eisenhower noted, was not merely in conflict with military standards but was being reflected in combat losses.

Men were negligent not only in minor soldierly observances but also in important duties that, in a military context, should have been almost reflexive. They disregarded the need for blackout lights at night. They failed to dig precautionary foxholes and slit trenches. Camouflage was neglected. Even officers sometimes showed a cavalier disregard for discipline. Most in the junior ranks had also only recently been drawn into uniform.

Of greater significance but not completely remote from lesser transgressions, errors in elementary battle tactics had resulted in unwarranted casualties. Frontal attacks had been made when enveloping movements were more appropriate. Planned advances were diverted by minor distractions or trivial obstructions. There were delays in establishing defensive positions in vulnerable terrain. The need for adequate reconnaissance was neglected. Communications were permitted to break down. Drivers in convoys made tempting targets for enemy aircraft by driving their vehicles nose to tail.

Eisenhower was depressed when he learned that mistakes made in maneuvers he had superintended in the United States nearly two years before, and recognized then as requiring immediate correction, were being repeated at the front "almost without variation." He issued stern orders that both training and discipline were to be tightened. He demanded frequent combat exercises down to company level, circumstances permitting. As for discipline, he ordered, "Every infraction, from a mere failure to salute, a coat unbuttoned, to more serious offenses, must be promptly dealt with; or disciplinary action taken against the officer who condones the offense."

But the Torch Supreme Commander himself neglected to deal promptly with the deficiencies of one of his senior officers. Visiting the headquarters of General Fredendall, whose Oran Task Force was now in the line as the U.S. II Corps, Eisenhower was greatly displeased by what he saw and heard. Fredendall's command post was in a deep underground bomb shelter more than sixty miles from the front. Two hundred army engineers had been employed blasting it into an almost inaccessible ravine. Drilling was still going on when Eisenhower reached there.

Perplexed, he asked whether the engineers had already helped construct front-line defenses and was casually informed by a young officer that the line divisions had their own engineers to handle that kind of job. It was the only time during the war that Eisenhower was to see a senior officer so concerned over his own safety that he had ordered an underground shelter to be dug for himself. General Bradley called it "an embarrassment to every American soldier." The Torch commander would later have reason to regret not having at once replaced Fredendall, who, according to General Truscott, was hardly the sort of man to leave in a position of great responsibility:

> Small in stature, loud and rough in speech, he was outspoken in his opinions and critical of superiors and subordinates alike. He was inclined to jump at conclusions which were not always well founded. He rarely left his command post for personal reconnaissances and visits yet he was impatient with the recommendations of subordinates more familiar with the terrain and other conditions than he was.

A commander of such qualities and such behavior could hardly be an inspiration to officers and troops already demoralized by finding themselves mired in seas of mud.

But the stalemate was demoralizing in other ways as well. As the advance into Tunisia had bogged down, national antagonisms had surfaced among Allied commanders in the field. General Anderson had initially been appointed to command all Allied forces advancing into Tunisia. Yet French units, which though poorly equipped had been sent into the line by Giraud, refused to serve under a British commander. Their officers warned that they would rebel if required to do so. At the same time, Fredendall made little effort to conceal his low regard for the British under whose command he was also supposed to operate.

For the sake of combat efficiency and in view of patchy communications, a system had been established for the British First Army, which had done most of the fighting, to operate on the left flank, the French XIX Corps in the center, and the American II Corps on the right, each to operate under its own national commander. Each of those commanders would be directly responsible to Eisenhower, who set up a forward command post at Constantine to oversee the situation. He left General Truscott in charge there most of the time because he himself was usually tied down at Allied Forces Headquarters in Algiers dealing with nagging political problems with the French and remaining in regular contact with Washington and London.

The tri-national battlefront in Tunisia was now a thin, broken line stretching four hundred miles from just west of Bizerte to the town of Gafsa—the ancient Roman town of Capsa—in the south. It included units that were confusedly mixed and for whom no reserves were available nearby. Efforts to remedy that situation and organize the battle line properly during the winter standoff were frustrated when poorly equipped French forces took a pummeling in mid-January. American and British troops had to be quickly dispatched to block what could have been a German breakthrough. General Anderson was then ordered to resume command of the entire battle line and try to inject a measure of coherence into it.

It was a temporary rearrangement. It had already been recognized that more basic adjustments to the Allied command in North Africa were essential. The British Eighth Army was closing in on

Tunisia from the east and Torch forces were preparing to renew their advance from the west once the elements permitted. It was clearly imperative to coordinate the various aspects of the final phase of the total Allied conquest of the region. At the January Casablanca Conference, the Combined Chiefs of Staff had acted to achieve that purpose.

The Americans had believed that the British might call for Eisenhower to be replaced. Many of them held him responsible for the stalemate in Tunisia. Even Roosevelt had his doubts about him and turned down Marshall's suggestion that Eisenhower be raised to full general until he had done more to prove himself worthy of the promotion. Marshall suspected the British Chiefs of Staff might try to lever the Supreme Commander out of his job and call for one of their own more experienced officers to take over from him.

But despite disappointment so far over Torch, the British had come to think highly of Eisenhower as a military administrator. He had forged, coordinated, and controlled a unique British-American Allied Forces Headquarters staff and had kept it functioning harmoniously. It had been an impressive achievement, particularly in view of the political pressures he had borne at the same time. His administrative skills were still needed and could be extremely useful in organizing the extended Mediterranean campaign that was being planned. Also, the British recognized the dangers of antagonizing the Americans by dumping Eisenhower.

However, the British High Command was in despair over his performance as a combat commander. The War Office would have been embarrassed if Montgomery's harsh judgment of him—"Nice chap. No general"—became known. But it did believe that a significant change in the Allied command in North Africa was essential. The problem was how to get agreement for that change without either humiliating the Americans, who would soon be providing most of the troops in the European Theater and who were already providing most of the equipment, or losing Eisenhower's valued services.

To that end, the British produced an eminently diplomatic solution. They proposed that the Allied Forces Headquarters in Algiers be strengthened at the deputy commander level. They suggested that General Alexander should leave his post as British commander in chief Middle East to assume command of ground operations under Eisenhower. Air Chief Marshal Tedder would be named deputy in charge of Allied Mediterranean air forces. Admiral Cunningham would remain as Eisenhower's naval deputy. Not only would Eisenhower remain Supreme Commander but Montgomery's Eighth Army would come under his command and he would have three greatly experienced, highly esteemed deputies—all British—working under him.

Marshall readily agreed to this change. There was no denying that the Allied Command needed modification and strengthening. He was relieved that the British had not sought to jettison Eisenhower, a move that would have been difficult to resist at that stage. General Brooke had no doubt that the changes being made, particularly the appointment of Alexander, would effectively serve the same purpose and, at the same time, would keep the Americans happy.

> By bringing Alexander over from the Middle East and appointing him as Deputy to Eisenhower [Brooke wrote in his diary], we were carrying out a move which could not help flattering and pleasing the Americans in so far as we were placing our senior and experienced commander to function under their commander who had no war experience. . . . We were pushing Eisenhower up into the stratosphere and rarified atmosphere of a Supreme Commander, where he would be free to devote his time to the political and inter-allied problems, while we inserted under him one of our own commanders to deal with the military situations and to restore the necessary drive and coordination which had been so seriously lacking.

Eisenhower was indeed flattered to be assigned such distinguished deputies, all of whom he regarded highly and with all of whom he got along extremely well. He readily conceded that they provided him with "needed machinery for effective tactical and strategical coordination." He could at last be relieved of day-to-day battlefront concerns and return to the job of Supreme Commander. However, he was offended by reports in some American newspapers that he was to become merely a figurehead while his British deputies would take over actual command.

He was already angry because of directives issued by the Combined Chiefs of Staff that appeared to diminish his authority. According to his aide, Captain Butcher, he was "burning inside . . . because the Combined Chiefs were attempting to issue directions as to how and what his subordinates were to do." Eisenhower complained to Marshall that the "responsibility to organize to win battles" was his and that no attention would be paid to moves to take it away from him. He did not intend to confine himself to such chores as squelching interservice and inter-Allied rivalries while Alexander, Tedder, and Cunningham, no matter how qualified, got on with winning the war.

Eisenhower charitably attributed the offending directives, which had been greatly influenced by recommendations from the British Chiefs of Staff, to an ingrained British affinity for running the war by committee rather than to a deliberate effort to ease him up and out of operational command, as had actually been the British intention. Once he had made it clear that his deputies would do their respective jobs while he continued to perform as their Supreme Commander, Eisenhower succeeded in putting the affair behind him.

In view of what had transpired and despite lingering resentments at the War Department, Allied Forces Headquarters in Algiers, with its mix of American and British officers, remained remarkably free of recriminations, rancor, and intrigue. The same could not be said for the enemy.

Hitler had grown increasingly disenchanted with Rommel. He was angered by Rommel's retreat out of Egypt and across Libya and he was exasperated by the general's readiness to contradict him on matters of strategy and tactics. The German Führer's new favorite in North Africa was General von Arnim, who had stopped the Allied forces from overrunning Tunisia and who was about to launch a new offensive against Allied positions in the Eastern Dorsal of the Atlas Mountains.

The Western and Eastern Dorsals traverse eastern Tunisia like the two sides of an inverted V, its apex just south of Tunis. In their earlier advance, before the Germans had been strongly reinforced, the Allies had rushed the passes through both Dorsals and had established supply depots and landing strips in the low ground between them. Von Arnim now planned to gain control of the Eastern Dorsal. He would thus dominate the plain west of it and neutralize those newly established Allied bases.

Allied Forces Headquarters had received advance notice of von Arnim's intentions. Intercepted enemy signals had been decoded by Ultra in England and, along with reports from other intelligence sources, had been relayed to Brigadier Eric Mockler-Ferryman, Eisenhower's chief of intelligence in Algiers. But Mockler-Ferryman's staff drew the wrong conclusions from the welter of detail provided. They passed word along that von Arnim could be expected to mount a major assault at Fondouk Pass in the Eastern Dorsal. Though reconnaissance strongly maintained that the Germans were concentrating their forces elsewhere, an ambush was laid for them at Fondouk. But on February 14, the enemy struck through Faïd Pass, thirty miles to the south, then split to envelop and destroy a Combat Command of the U.S. 1st Armored Division at Sidi-bou-Zid.

It was the first taste of combat for the Americans involved in this clash. They came under dive-bomber and fighter-bomber attack and then German artillery and armor went in against them. They had panicked under the onslaught. "There were notable pockets of gallantry," General Omar Bradley later recorded, "but for the most part our soldiers abandoned their weapons, including tanks and fled to the rear. . . ." The battlefield was left strewn with equipment, forty-four tanks among them. Additional American troops and tanks were rushed forward to break the grip of the pincer movement but, with little prior reconnaissance, they were battered as well. Von Arnim's forces then hesitated before pressing ahead, permitting other elements of the 1st Armored Division to race south fast enough to help save what was left of the defenders.

While that setback was in the making, Eisenhower accepted that it had been a mistake to try to operate on a forward line that "could not be held passively against any concentrated, determined attack." Fearing a German breakthrough, he approved Anderson's request to order a withdrawal that would set the Allied line back on the high ground on the eastern ridges of the Western Dorsal. Recognizing that the line was still thin, tenuous, and extremely vulnerable, Anderson sought to shift units around to brace particularly exposed positions. With communications unreliable, transport in short supply, and officers inexperienced, it was not easy to do. The danger of a major reverse had not yet been defused.

General Alexander was not scheduled to take over as Eisenhower's deputy commander in charge of ground forces for several days. The Supreme Commander had reason to regret that he did not yet have his services. The piecemeal response to the enemy offensive increased Eisenhouer's doubts about Anderson's command abilities. In addition, he had by then belatedly come to question the reliability of Fredendall, who, despite the critical situation, was involved in bitter rows with subordinates. They were angry that the II Corps commander was failing to maintain coordinated action among the Corps's constituent units and at the same time was improperly interfering in the operations of their separate commands, sometimes "uselessly shouting slogans and exhortations over the radio to units gone amok."

Drawing the Allied line back to the eastern ridges of the Western Dorsal was a prudent move under the circumstances. But the situation was turning critical. Rommel was casting a practiced eye over the terrain and assessing the possibilities. Troubled by stomach pain, low blood pressure, and dizzy spells, he was supposed to return to Germany for extended sick leave, having been instructed to hand over command of his forces to Italian Field Marshal Giovanni Messe. However, seeking to salvage his reputation as a victorious commander before leaving North Africa, he planned a last operation there, an exploit worthy of his reputation as a resourceful battle commander. As his parting shot, he intended to totally shatter the Allied advance into Tunisia.

On February 15, Rommel's Afrika Korps Combat Group had gone onto the attack at Gafsa on the extreme southern flank of the line. Over the next two days, it had swept northwest some fifty miles and had overrun the quickly abandoned U.S. airfields at Thélepte in the lowlands between the Dorsals, the best the Allies had in the region. If he could force his way through the Western Dorsal, he would be able to reach Tebessa where a massive Allied supply base had been established. Rommel would then be in a position to thrust northwest to the coast at Bône to cut off the British First Army and plunge deep into Algeria, driving the Allies into headlong retreat. That done, he would turn on the Eighth Army advancing on him from Libya, where Montgomery had paused a week at Tripoli to repair its smashed port facilities and make certain of his line of supply.

But Rommel had more than the Allies to contend with. He was limited in what he could do by having to share command in Tunisia with von Arnim and von Arnim had other priorities. Though no laggard himself, he considered Rommel's plan reckless. He knew Allied reinforcements were moving up from the west and that Montgomery would soon be closing in from the east. A reverse could seal the fate of the Axis powers in North Africa. Instead of freeing forces to assist Rommel's audacious thrust, he intended to employ them to launch probing jabs elsewhere on the line to disrupt expected Allied moves.

Aside from tactical considerations, von Arnim had no great fondness for Rommel, whose desert exploits had made him the most celebrated figure in the German Army. He was an ambitious man of Prussian military stock and was already bitter at having to deal with Rommel's presence in Tunisia. He recoiled at the idea of assuming a role that would effectively make him subordinate to this middle-class upstart.

Rommel, in turn, regarded von Arnim as an unimaginative hindrance, especially for refusing to transfer to him control of the 10th Panzer Division when he needed all the armor he could get for the campaign he had planned. Unable to gain his agreement for his audacious scheme, Rommel submitted it for approval to the Comando Supremo, the Italian High Command in Rome, to which both he and von Arnim were technically answerable. There its potential was appreciated and it was approved, but with an important tactical modification. Though von Arnim was now instructed to lend Rommel the assistance he requested, that modification was to save the Allies much grief.

Rommel had proposed sweeping through weakly defended Allied positions in a wide northwestward arc. He would overrun the major Allied supply depot at Tebessa, outflank gathering Allied reinforcements, and be well on the road to Bône before the Allies had any idea of what was happening. The plan might have worked. But instead of being permitted to implement it the way he proposed, he was instructed to surge north rather than northwest on his drive to the coast, aiming first for the towns of Thala and Le Kef. But though the Comando Supremo didn't know it, Anderson was concentrating some of the strongest forces at his disposal near Thala.

Being second-guessed when he knew he was right infuriated Rommel. Even more frustrating for him, von Arnim was taking his time obeying instructions to put all of the 10th Panzer Division at his disposal. Among the armor he was only belatedly releasing was a battalion of Tiger tanks to which Rommel had assigned a lead role in the assault. As a result, when the offensive was mounted at Kasserine Pass on February 19, it was not the concentrated onslaught Rommel had planned. Nevertheless, it was at Kasserine in the Western Dorsal, through which he launched his advance on Thala, that the U.S. Army learned what the British and Russians knew already, that the road to Berlin would be long and hard.

The Germans had seized the initiative. For troops of II Corps on the line, the situation was grave. After the beating they had taken at Sidi-bou-Zid on February 14 and the fallback to the Western Dorsal, there was little doubt that the enemy would strike at them again, and soon. But units that had been battered were still regrouping. Some had ceased to exist. Others had to be reequipped. Some officers had no instructions on where their troops were supposed to be and what they were supposed to do, though they all knew they were understrength and could be in serious trouble at any moment. It was cold and a drizzle fell intermittently as the men floundered about in fields and on hills of mud, wondering what was happening beyond the mist.

About to take over as Eisenhower's deputy in charge of ground operations, General Alexander grimly observed after a visit to the line, "General situation is far from satisfactory. British, American and French units are all mixed up on the front. . . . There is no policy and plan of campaign. . . . This is the result of no firm direction or centralized control from above." Alexander considered Anderson rather than Eisenhower to be primarily responsible. Eisenhower, he said, "could not be more helpful." But he was not being completely fair to the British First Army commander, who, whatever his shortcomings, had not yet been provided with the wherewithal—in air power, troops, and administrative backup—to achieve the mission to which he had been assigned.

Enemy probing action on February 18 indicated that the renewed enemy assault was likely to come through the village of Kasserine about five miles south of the entrance to Kasserine Pass through the Western Dorsal. The pass is less than a mile wide at its narrowest point. It is flanked by craggy mountains from which a strong defense could be mounted. The U.S. 19th Engineer Regiment had already laid almost three thousand mines at the sides of the road between the village and the pass before withdrawing through the pass and taking up positions to block passage by the enemy. But the engineers had never been in combat before and they and their officers had not been trained to serve as infantrymen. When they had come under fire during the enemy's probing action, some had fled helter-skelter to the rear.

Alerted by that enemy action, Fredendall telephoned Colonel Alexander Stark, commander of the U.S. 26th Infantry Regiment, at 8:00 P.M. on February 18 and ordered him to leave his position to the east and proceed immediately to the pass to take command there. Stark arrived at 7:30 on the morning of February 19 just as Rommel launched his attack.

Hoping to seize the pass by a battalion-strength surprise lunge through it, Rommel had withheld a softening-up artillery barrage. But having been anticipated and comparatively weak, the attack was driven back by Stark's men. But now German troops arrived in great numbers below the pass and began scaling the craggy slopes on its sides. It was apparent that the earlier raid was just a prelude to a major assault.

That assault was launched in the afternoon just as reinforcements urgently requested by Stark began showing up. It was brought to a quick halt by the troops who had dug in, the mines the engineers had laid, and the mud in which the German tanks bogged down. Unable to break through with a head-on assault, the Germans stepped up infiltration through the risings flanking the pass.

This attack at Kasserine was initially to have been only part of Rommel's assault on the Western Dorsal. He planned an accompanying breakthrough at Sbiba farther east. But that had run into effective resistance too. He therefore shifted the forces at his disposal there to the drive through Kasserine. On the morning of February 20, elements of the 10th Panzer Division, previously withheld by von Arnim, had finally shown up to bolster his strength. Rommel sent them roaring through the pass after unleashing the fiercest artillery barrage the Americans had yet faced, including sustained, terrifying fusillades of missiles from six-barreled German rocket launchers. This time the Americans were quickly overrun. They took heavy casualties and great quantities of their equipment were captured intact. A stubborn stand by a small British force that was patched together under the command of Lieutenant Colonel A. C. Gore, and sent to bolster the Americans and cover their withdrawal, was shattered as well.

Rommel then paused on his drive north and prepared to deal with an Allied counteroffensive. When none materialized, he resumed his forward movement. But by then, elements of the British 26th Armored Brigade, reinforced piecemeal by other British, American, and French units, had been assembled in his path under the command of Brigadier Cameron Nicholson. This "Nickforce" took severe punishment but, aided by Brigadier General LeRoy Irwin's U.S. 9th Division artillery, which arrived on the spot after a four-day, eight-hundred-mile forced drive from near Oran, it succeeded in halting the German advance. By the morning of February 22, Rommel realized he would not be able to achieve his planned breakthrough to the coast.

Had he been able to rely on von Arnim's unstinting support from the beginning of his offensive, he might have inflicted more serious punishment on the Allies. He would, however, still have run into difficulties. His supply situation had become perilous; his reconnaissance revealed that Allied reinforcements moving up to the line might close whatever gaps needed plugging, and that the Allied Command had developed a firmer grasp of what was happening. Marshal Kesselring, who arrived in Tunisia that morning aware of Rommel's victory at Kasserine and expecting to offer him hearty congratulations, found him ready to break off the battle and withdraw.

Rommel abandoned the Kasserine area without difficulty and was well into his withdrawal before the Allies, desperately regrouping, fathomed what was happening. He pulled back to the Mareth Line to prepare to receive Montgomery there. As he did so, von Arnim launched an offensive in the north to prevent the Allied forces from regaining their equilibrium and confidence after the Kasserine episode, and to cover Rommel's withdrawal. His troops made rapid progress. Had the assault been synchronized with Rommel's lunge through the Kasserine Pass, the Allies might have found themselves in very serious difficulties.

But though the British sustained heavy losses in this latest German operation, they brought it to a halt before they could be routed and then proceeded to drive the enemy back, inflicting heavier losses on them than they had taken themselves. Any hope the Axis command had of driving the Allies out of Tunisia was now lost. Von Arnim was left with no alternative but to confine himself to spoiling actions while adopting a defensive posture on a shortened front.

* * *

The battles of Kasserine Pass and at Sidi-bou-Zid six days earlier, as well as lesser setbacks in between, had staggered the Americans. They were among the worst and bloodiest thrashings the U.S. Army had ever suffered. American troops had finally met the Germans in combat and they had been mauled by them. II Corps had taken more than six thousand casualties, including three hundred dead and three thousand captured. It had lost almost two hundred tanks, a like number of heavy guns, and vast amounts of other equipment and supplies. A London newspaper reported that the Americans had been unprepared for battle, "misled by the stupidity of Hollywood's war films" in which James Cagney marched nonchalantly at the head of the marines, singing "some variant of Yankee Doodle Dandy." Less scornfully, another British paper observed, "The American troops . . . have bought their experience at some cost, but they had to buy it some day and might well have paid more for it." There could be no denying the shock that had been administered to them by the Germans.

> All our people from the very highest to the very lowest [Eisenhower wrote Marshall] have learned that this is not a child's game and are ready and eager to get down to the fundamental business of profiting by the lessons they have learned and seeking from every possible source methods and means of perfecting their own battlefield efficiency.

Eisenhower himself had learned important lessons as a result of the battle. He learned that much of the German equipment, particularly 88-millimeter guns that could knock out any Allied tank at a range of almost half a mile, was superior to the equipment at the disposal of his own troops. Washington was urgently asked to remedy that situation. He also was confirmed in his view that the level of training of American troops, demonstrated by their performance so far, had to be radically improved and soon. Though reluctant to do so before because of the danger of chauvinistic recriminations, he secured a team of experienced British officers to assist in training programs for them.

It was a delicate move because Eisenhower realized more clearly than before that relations between the British and Americans under his command could easily turn discordant and demoralizing when things went bad. The atmosphere remained harmonious at

Allied Forces Headquarters where differences were transcended by a sense of common purpose and the mood of camaraderie prescribed and promoted by Eisenhower. But elsewhere, the British made little secret that they had not been impressed with the fighting performance of the Americans at Kasserine, while among the Americans there were mutterings that the British had not done as much as they could while they fielded the worst Rommel could throw at them.

Relations between Anderson and Fredendall had also deteriorated to such an extent that the two senior Allied field generals, neither of whom had made much of an impression with his command skills, no longer bothered communicating with one another. Eisenhower finally decided that Fredendall had to be replaced as II Corps commander. Inspiring neither the confidence nor the aggressive drive of his officers, he had demonstrated that he was the wrong man in the wrong place. He was sent back to the United States, assigned a training command there, and promoted to lieutenant general! General Patton was brought from Morocco to replace him.

☆ 20 ☆

ENDGAME

We are masters of the North African shore.
—GENERAL SIR HAROLD ALEXANDER

As both Rommel's and von Arnim's offensives in Tunisia fizzled out, things began falling into place for the Allies. Montgomery, having completed his trek across northern Libya, was preparing to storm the Mareth Line. His line of supply was secure and his forces were rested and ready. Given momentary respite in Tunisia, Alexander had regrouped and reinforced front-line Allied ground forces.

Under Patton, troops of II Corps were being subjected to intensive training and a harsh regimen of discipline. General Juin's French XIX Corps, which had taken a severe beating defending its part of the line with antiquated weapons, was reequipped. Despite persisting doubts about General Anderson at Allied Forces Headquarters, he remained in command of the British First Army in the north although Alexander was keeping close watch on his performance. The outcome of the closing phase of the campaign was now beyond doubt, though the hardened Axis troops in Tunisia—more than a quarter of a million of them—did not give ground easily and the cold, wet, muddy winter was only gradually tapering off.

Once more Rommel informed the German High Command that the situation in North Africa was hopeless. He believed that to keep great numbers of troops there was "plain suicide." The major

Tunisian ports were still in Axis hands, and the Allies were not yet ready to launch a major offensive. It was not too late to execute a major evacuation of German and Italian forces. But Hitler refused to countenance such a move.

Rommel's final exploit in North Africa proved a limp gesture. He chose not to dawdle behind the Mareth Line defenses, which were not very substantial, while Montgomery deployed his forces to break through. Instead, he moved forward near the town of Médenine hoping to catch Montgomery, whose troops were far superior in numbers and equipment, unprepared. He didn't have a chance. His communications were intercepted by British intelligence. Montgomery was informed in advance where and when Rommel planned to attack. His assault was easily beaten back.

Rommel was in despair. No doubt his mood was influenced by his ailing physical condition. "Heart, nerves and rheumatism are giving me a lot of trouble," he wrote his wife. Whatever the reasons, he was more convinced than ever that maintaining a German army in Africa was suicidal. Three days after his defeat at Médenine, he flew to Hitler's headquarters to try to persuade him that North Africa was lost and that Axis forces there had to be withdrawn before they were lost as well. Hitler wouldn't hear of it. Tying up the Allies in North Africa would keep them from attempting an invasion of Europe. Instead of contemplating a withdrawal, the German Führer was fantasizing about launching a vigorous offensive a thousand miles to the west, in Morocco.

Having failed to sway him, Rommel tried to return to North Africa for the finale there. But Hitler wanted no defeatist on the spot; nor did he wish so celebrated a German warrior to be exposed to capture by the Allies. He ordered him to take extended sick leave. Rommel would later be implicated in the abortive plot by German officers to assassinate Hitler and agreed to commit suicide to save his family from persecution.

The weather cleared with the onset of spring and the endgame of the battle for North Africa began. The Allies enjoyed an ever-greater advantage. As well as troop reinforcements, vast quantities of supplies and equipment were reaching their forward positions while the Royal Navy reduced to a trickle the flow of supplies reaching the enemy from across the Mediterranean. The Allies were soon bringing up more equipment than the Axis forces originally had.

Under Patton, II Corps was rehabilitated. Revitalized after its demoralizing setbacks, it recaptured the lost forward airstrips in Tunisia, took Gafsa, and tied down German armor and reserves that would otherwise have been thrown against Montgomery's advancing troops. But the Americans were still committing tactical errors and the British still nursed doubts about them.

Alexander's plan for winding up the Tunisia campaign was to box Axis forces into the northern bulge of the country, sever their line of supply, and then demolish them piecemeal. To do otherwise—to split them in two before going in for the kill—would have meant II Corps playing a central role and Alexander did not have enough faith in U.S. troops to risk it. He reported to London that his "main anxiety is the poor fighting value of the Americans." The Americans, in turn, were inclined to believe that the patchy performance of Anderson's troops in the north had not exactly reflected glory on the British Army. The arrival of the Anglophobic Patton in Tunisia did nothing to improve British-American mutual respect, as was soon demonstrated.

A complaint from Patton's headquarters about the quality of air cover for II Corps troops drew a caustic response from Air Marshal Sir Arthur Coningham, chief of the Allied Air Support Command. Coningham defensively snapped that the Americans were resorting to the "discredited practice of using Air Force as an alibi for lack of success on ground." He said it had to be assumed from their grumbling that the American troops simply were not battleworthy.

Air Marshal Tedder, who had by then taken over as Eisenhower's deputy in charge of air operations, realized that this rebuke was "dynamite with a short, fast-burning fuse." He ordered Coningham to visit Patton's headquarters to apologize. At the same time, the fiery Patton was advised by Eisenhower, who was also trying to repair the damage, not to rebuff the apology. Peace was made between them but word of Coningham's jibe about the soldierly qualities of American troops had quickly found its way to command posts throughout region, compounding mutual recriminations.

The same effect was achieved later when General Sir John

Crocker, the British IX Corps commander, was reported to have commented acidly about the failure of the U.S. 34th Division to withstand an enemy attack. In fact, Crocker, an experienced officer, had responded privately with forthright bluntness to a request for advice on how the Americans might improve their performance. His analysis on what they were doing wrong, transformed into biting scorn, found its way into the press and into impressions of the fighting abilities of the Americans held by many of their British comrades. An Eighth Army gunner, passed on the road in southern Tunisia by U.S. troops, responded to their cheerful greeting with "Going to fuck up another Front, I suppose."

Eisenhower had forged a sense of kinship and harmony between the British and American officers at Allied Forces Headquarters. That he had been able to do so at a time when there was little to boast about at the front testified to his considerable leadership abilities. But he was much troubled by criticism of how the battle was being fought and by backbiting between the Allied forces in the field. In a moment of depression, he drafted a message to General Marshall suggesting that he be replaced because, he said, it was apparent that he could not control his commanders. He was persuaded not to send that message and that the situation was not as bad as it seemed.

But indignation at the War Department over the way the British appeared to be running the campaign continued to smolder. In its corridors, there were mutterings that Eisenhower had become merely a figurehead, that his British deputies were really in charge. The British undoubtedly wished that to be true. Macmillan, Eisenhower's British political adviser, told an associate, "You will find the Americans much as the Greeks found the Romans—great big, vulgar, bustling people, more vigorous than we are and also more idle, with more unspoiled virtues but also more corrupt. We must run [Allied Forces Headquarters] as the Greek slaves ran the operations of the Emperor Claudius."

At the Operations Division in Washington, the feeling lingered that "Ike had 'sold out' to the British—caved in on his commanders, caved in on Sicily." To add to Eisenhower's burdens, he had to respond to press reports that British troops were doing the real fighting in Tunisia; the Americans were said to be largely confined to cleaning up the battlefield afterward.

Marshall cabled Eisenhower that such stories generated public resentment in the United States, "with unfortunate results as to national prestige." Proof had to be provided that they were without foundation. The British were in no position to be overly critical. They had been humbled repeatedly by the reverses earlier suffered in the Libyan and Egyptian deserts by their now thriving Eighth Army. That was generously pointed out by Montgomery's chief of staff, Major General Francis de Guingand. But disparaging comments on the performance of the Americans continued to circulate.

Eisenhower conceded that the Americans still had not proved their worth in battle. But he knew it was essential to convince U.S. troops that they were capable of playing their full part on the battlefield. General Alexander, who had taken firm control of Allied ground deployments and tactics, also had to accept that. It was obvious after Kasserine that Alexander thought the Americans should leave the hard fighting to the British, helping out here and there when instructed to do so. Alexander's staff believed that much of II Corps should be ordered back into Algeria for intensive training well away from the front. Eisenhower would have been incensed had he known of a message sent by Montgomery to Alexander, casually dismissing the Americans as little more than a nuisance: "If my operations to break through the Mareth line are successful, I shall go pretty fast once I am through the gap. . . . I do *not* want the Americans getting in the way."

Eisenhower was also reluctant to instruct Alexander on how to deploy the forces under his command, and that included the U.S. II Corps. He believed a commander who had a situation under control should be free to get on with his task without intrusions from superiors. But prodded by Marshall, he felt obliged to explain to him what the Americans believed was at stake. He told him that if the British expected the Americans to do much fighting—indeed, *most* of the fighting—once Sicily and the European mainland were invaded, it would be a mistake to deny them battle experience and the confidence that would grow from it.

He said it would be wrong to use bits and pieces of II Corps to plug gaps in the line or tidy up where enemy resistance was known to be weak, rather than deploying it as a coherent whole so that it could prove its effectiveness. He warned that if the American people felt their troops had not been permitted to play "an effective part in the conclusion of the Tunisian campaign," their interest in the European Theater, while there was still a war to be won against Japan, might peter out.

> Success ... would give a sense of accomplishment to the American people that they richly deserved in view of the strenuous efforts they had made thus far in the war. Out of victory participated in by both countries on a significant scale would come a sense of partnership not otherwise obtainable.

None too subtly put, the message could not be shrugged off. Alexander had intended to shift one of II Corps's four divisions to the north to assist the British in the capture of Bizerte. Apprised of the strength of American feeling, he reluctantly permitted the entire corps—some 90,000 men—to shift across the First Army's line of supply into the northern mountains and assigned it the role of advancing on Bizerte in the windup of the campaign. Anderson's troops to their right would aim for Tunis while Montgomery's celebrated desert fighters, from whom the Germans were likely to expect the main thrust but who had run into some trouble once they had left the desert behind and moved into Tunisia's mountainous terrain, would be confined largely to diversionary feints.

Relentlessly pushed back, outnumbered and outgunned, the Axis forces, ordered to hold out till the end, stubbornly resisted in a series of furious clashes. The British were forced to take heavier casualties than they had in any other single encounter in the Tunisian campaign when their 78th Division overcame German defenders of the tactically important Longstop Hill. And the much-maligned American 34th Division won respect in storming and holding Hill 609 where German artillery had blocked II Corps's advance.

The resistance of the Axis troops merely delayed their final defeat. Supplies for them were rapidly exhausted. During the last two weeks of the campaign, not a single Axis merchant ship was able to break through the Allied sea and air cordon to reach Tunisia and make good their losses while supplies and equipment were now reaching the Allied troops in uninterrupted profusion.

The long-delayed end came with surprising rapidity. On May 6,

Axis forces were subjected across much of the line to a ferocious hammering from Allied aircraft and artillery. The way was blasted for both British and American troops to move forward toward their final objectives. On the afternoon of the following day, some German headquarters soldiers, wandering with their local girl-friends through the streets of Tunis, were amazed when British armored patrol vehicles cruised by them. They were followed soon after by troops of the Derbyshire Yeomanry and the 11th Hussars. Cheering crowds of French people greeted the British and what little resistance was met was quickly crushed. A few hours later, troops of the U.S. 9th Division entered Bizerte.

Both cities had already been largely evacuated by the enemy, mostly fleeing to Cape Bon Peninsula, protruding into the Mediter-ranean. But there was no way for the Axis troops to escape. With the Allies in control of the sea in the region and the skies above it, there could be no Dunkirk-style rescue for them. Their only option was mass surrender. Despite an order from Hitler for them "to fight to the last man," before another week had passed virtually all Axis troops who had not been killed had been captured. Fewer than a thousand escaped to Sicily in small boats. On the evening of May 12, 1943, a little more than six months after Operation Torch had been launched, Allied Forces Headquarters in Algiers an-nounced officially, "Organized resistance in Tunisia, except by isolated pockets of the enemy, has ceased."

Conflicting reports were submitted on how many Axis troops were taken prisoner. An official American account lists the num-ber at about 275,000. Other accounts list the total captured at closer to 240,000, most of them German. Long columns of men marched to surrender. Entire companies gave up en masse. Small groups showed up in a variety of vehicles sporting white flags. Some arrived on the backs of burros. One group turned up in an Arab cart pulled by plume-bedecked horses, cheering as if this were a holiday parade rather than their entry into captivity. In at least one case, German troops surrendered to American soldiers who had earlier been taken prisoner.

Circumstances did not allow for an accurate count of the cap-tives. Whatever the true figure, there could be no denying that the Axis powers had suffered a massive defeat. But the price paid by the Allies for their victory was not insubstantial. The total casualty figure for them was 71,810 dead, wounded, and missing, a figure that included casualties sustained in fighting the French before the cease-fire was declared in Algeria and Morocco. Those, mostly American, amounted to 1,469, including 530 killed and 52 missing. During the subsequent Tunisia campaign, the British First Army suffered 23,545 casualties (including 4,439 killed and 6,531 missing), the British Eighth Army 12,395 (2,036 killed, 1,304 missing), the U.S. II Corps 18,221 (including 2,715 killed and 6,528 missing), and the French 16,180 (1,100 killed, 7,000 missing). No accurate figures are available for the number of German and Italian casualties.

The Allies now had complete control of North Africa from the Atlantic to the Red Sea. Operation Torch's mission had finally been brought to a successful conclusion.

EPILOGUE

[I]t took an average of twelve divisions of the Western Allies some two and one half years to push about the same number of Axis divisions back from northwest Egypt to northeast Italy, a distance of some two thousand miles over terrain chiefly distinguished by its poverty of good communications and its frequency of highly defensible positions. At the end of several bitterly contested campaigns the greatest natural barrier in Europe, the Alps, still lay between the Anglo-American armies and the Reich. . . . [However,] following the Anglo-American landings in France on June 6, 1944, an Allied land force averaging fifty to sixty divisions attacked German armies of nominally the same number of divisional units, but in fact a great deal weaker in all respects. Within eleven months the Allied troops had advanced a distance of five hundred and fifty miles over a terrain notable chiefly for its comparative flatness, for a superb transportation network, and for the heart of the Axis war industry. At the termination of this type of campaign, undertaken in conjunction with the Red Army, there existed neither a German Army nor a German war economy.

—TRUMBULL HIGGINS

The Allied victory in Tunisia was received with jubilation in the United States and Britain. The *Chicago Daily News* crowed, "We came into North Africa on a shoestring when we waded ashore at Algiers six months ago. . . . [But] we entered Tunis on the tail of an avalanche." The London *Times* told its readers, "The Axis Powers have lost their gamble. . . . The allied triumph is

318

overwhelming." The successful completion of Operation Torch's mission was undeniable evidence that the Germans were finally on the run.

It was received with particular relief by the British, who, despite Montgomery's victory at El Alamein, had become used to setbacks. In London, Churchill observed, "there was, for the first time in the war, a real lifting of spirits." To mark the occasion, it was announced that horse racing at Ascot, suspended when the war began, would resume. London betting shops offered even money that Germany would be defeated before another year had passed.

The conquest of French North Africa was undoubtedly a major achievement, and not only because great numbers of Axis troops had been taken prisoner. Italy and Nazi-occupied southern Europe were now exposed to attack and vulnerable. The Mediterranean was freed to Allied shipping. Most important for morale purposes, the Germans had been stripped of their aura of invincibility. The war had entered a new dimension.

Messages of congratulations for Eisenhower poured in from Roosevelt, Churchill, King George, and other distinguished Allied figures. The man who twelve months earlier had been a behind-the-scenes War Department ideas man in Washington was now publicly deemed to be a military commander of historic consequence. For the moment, there was no hint of criticism or recrimination between the Western Allies. Some American officers would, like Patton, never overcome their distrust of and disdain for the British. Some of their British counterparts would, like Montgomery, never shed their conviction that the Americans had no understanding of how to fight a war.

But partly as a result of their North Africa experience, most American and British senior commanders in the European Theater learned to respect and like each other and to work congenially together under Eisenhower's leadership. Operation Torch ended with the certainty that though friction might still develop between the transatlantic cousins before Nazi Germany was crushed—as indeed it did—it would be transcended by mutual respect, mutual need, and a determination to resolve whatever differences were encountered along the march to victory.

Things were different in Berlin. Swiss correspondents based there reported that the defeat in Tunisia had a profoundly demoralizing effect in Germany, where news of the earlier German setbacks in North Africa had been largely suppressed. One Swiss newspaper reported that the people in the German capital were "walking around as though hit on the head." Coming soon after the German Army's disaster at Stalingrad, the Axis collapse in Tunisia lowered a shroud of foreboding over Berlin.

The Allies had learned important lessons in North Africa. Muddle and confusion would be a feature of other amphibious landings before the war was over. But never again would a major Allied seaborne operation be as much of a shambles as the initial Torch landings had been on the shores of Morocco and Algeria. Much was also learned between then and the Axis collapse in Tunisia six months later—by American troops in particular.

Much was learned about troop deployment for defense and offense, the value of aggressive patrolling, positioning of artillery to offer maximum support to infantry, procedures for seizing entrenched enemy positions and holding them, the value of concentrated as contrasted to dispersed armored assault, coordination of anti-tank defenses, the importance of trying to anticipate enemy moves, proper use of reserves, and countless other details only truly absorbable through combat experience. The crucial nature of air-ground liaison was grasped the hard way. Most important of all, soldiers discovered what it was like to be shelled, bombed, and shot at and yet fight on. Operation Torch was a massive exercise in on-the-job training. "In Africa," General Bradley later observed, "we learned to crawl, to walk—then run."

Operation Torch ruled out an early invasion of France, as General Marshall knew it would. That did not upset the British, who never wavered in their belief that such an invasion would have been calamitous. Lieutenant General Sir Ian Jacob noted that prior to Torch, "The Allies had no experience of carrying out large opposed landings under modern conditions. The technique of assault forces, of bombardment, of air support, of off-shore protection and of administrative organizations [had been] unknown and untried."

Some of the Americans, like Eisenhower, who had initially objected strenuously to the decision to mount the campaign in French North Africa, and thought the decision would be profoundly regretted, subsequently changed their minds about it. Nevertheless, long after the event, questions persist about whether Torch was the right operation, in the right place, at the right time.

The British accurately observed that an early invasion of France—Operation Round-Up in 1943—could not have been mounted because of a shortage of landing craft in the European Theater at the time. But that need not have been the case. Roosevelt had resisted domestic pressure to concentrate on defeating Japan first. But after the decision to launch Operation Torch had been made, officers well placed in the U.S. military command structure acted on their conviction that Torch was a costly irrelevance. The high priority placed at American shipyards on the production of landing craft was accordingly much reduced in favor of warships to meet navy requirements in the Pacific.

Even then, great numbers of landing craft were still being produced and could have been made available in Europe. But once the War Department had concluded that Torch ruled out an early cross-Channel invasion, most of them were diverted to the Pacific for operations there. British officers who visited Washington during the windup in Tunisia were "amazed to find how much more interested everyone was in the Pacific war than the Mediterranean."

Very much the same attitude applied to shipping. There is reason to believe that enough vessels could have been made available for an early invasion of France. German submarines prowling the Atlantic, and sinking great numbers of Allied cargo vessels, were a threat. Yet that threat, though still serious, was overstated. U-boats had already sunk a great volume of Allied shipping in 1942, but by August of that year, nine months before the proposed early cross-Channel invasion, the Allies had begun winning that Battle of the Atlantic. They did so by sinking increasing numbers of U-boats and through the increased ability of American shipyards to more than make good the heavy losses still being sustained.

As for aerial support, by the time an early invasion of France would have taken place, substantial numbers of Allied aircraft had been diverted to North Africa. Nevertheless, though exacting a heavy toll, the Luftwaffe was unable to prevent Allied bombers based in Britain from unleashing nightly destruction on German cities and strategic targets. All told, bomber and fighter resources were likely to have been adequate for pre-invasion softening-up operations. The Luftwaffe would have been torn between defending German cities and factories from air assault and coping with the invasion.

As for the availability of troops for an early invasion of France, little urgency was felt in Washington for shipping them across the Atlantic after the decision was made in favor of Torch. Many U.S. units earmarked for the military buildup in Britain prior to the invasion of France were sent to the Pacific instead. After Torch was launched, Marshall informed Eisenhower that no further American troops would be sent to Britain until approval was forthcoming for a cross-Channel operation that, in contrast to British wishes, "did not depend upon a crack in German morale." To Churchill's concern about this increasingly conspicuous shift in the American perspective, Roosevelt explained that Pacific operations had become more complicated and demanding than had been expected.

British calculations about the resistance Allied troops would have met in an earlier invasion of France were much inflated. Few of the German divisions guarding Hitler's Atlantic Wall at that time were top grade and none were at full strength. Shattering manpower losses on the Russian Front had compelled the Wehrmacht command to reduce the number of battalions in regiments from three to two. During 1943, when the Operation Round-Up invasion of France was to have been mounted and followed up, the Germans lost more than 2 million troops killed, wounded, or captured on the Russian Front. They were able to replace only about three quarters of that number, despite the urgent need to do so.

Many of the German divisions in the West at that time consisted of poor-quality troops, rejects from the front-line divisions in the East. Some were the surviving remnants—mostly service troops—of divisions that had been decimated by the Russians in their winter offensives of 1942–43. Also numbered in their ranks were troops sent to France to recuperate from wounds suffered in action. General Günther Blumentritt, chief of staff of the German army in the West, later observed that German divisions in France had repeatedly been "replaced by badly-damaged divisions from the Russian front. . . . The officers and men were mostly of the older classes, and their armament was on a lower scale than in the active divisions. It included a large proportion of captured French, Polish and Yugo-Slav weapons, which fired differing kinds of ammunition."

The British were not unaware of German weaknesses on the Atlantic Wall. Lieutenant General Sir Frederick Morgan, who was assigned the task of preparing for the eventual invasion of France, knew "the quality of the enemy's troops emplaced [at the time] on the Norman coast was not notably high."

Indeed, as historian Walter Scott Dunn, Jr., has described in detail, German forces were much weaker on Hitler's Atlantic Wall when the invasion of France promoted by Marshall and the U.S. War Department would have taken place than they were a year later when it was finally launched. During the months immediately prior to the eventual Allied Normandy landings in 1944, the Germans were able to create stronger new divisions for the defense of their Atlantic Wall.

These included recruits from the German Navy and the Luftwaffe, the usual roles of which had by then been greatly circumscribed by overwhelming Allied power. In addition, substantial numbers of able-bodied workers in Germany's war industries, who had previously been exempted from conscription, had not long before been replaced in their factories by foreign forced labor and drafted into uniform. Many of them were then assigned to units based in France. What was more, those strengthened German units in the West were being equipped with improved weaponry that Albert Speer, Hitler's war-production czar, was able to extract from factories he had only lately been given authorization to streamline.

As noted above, the Allied troops, and particularly the Americans, learned important lessons in North Africa and while subsequently struggling their way up the mountainous spine of Italy. If the cross-Channel invasion had taken place in 1943, they would have had to learn those lessons in France and certainly would have sustained heavy casualties in doing so. But even in North Africa, after their initial clumsy performance there, Rommel found "astonishing . . . the speed with which the Americans adapted themselves to modern warfare. In this," he said, "they were assisted by their extraordinary sense for the practical and material and by their complete lack of regard for tradition and worthless theories." After absorbing their initial lesson-learning punishment in France, the Allies would have been able to advance across less-difficult terrain—the mostly flat landscape of northern Europe—in which their endless flow of equipment and supplies and superior numbers could have been even more decisive than they were in the jagged topography of Tunisia and Italy.

Some American generals considered Churchill a cynical trickster for repeatedly voicing support for an early cross-Channel invasion while pressing for such an operation to be delayed. But the British leader genuinely did favor an invasion of the European continent without excessive delay. He was, however, a capricious strategist. His mind was continually seeking, and regularly finding, alternative plans for everything, a habit that irritated his chief of staff, among others.

> And Winston? [General Brooke asked in his diary]. Thinks one thing at one moment and another at the next moment. At times the war may be won by bombing, and all must be sacrificed to it. At others it becomes necessary for us to bleed ourselves dry on the Continent because Russia is doing the same. At others our main effort must be in the Mediterranean directed against Italy or the Balkans alternately, with sporadic desires to invade Norway. . . . But more often than all he wants to carry out all operations simultaneously. . . .

However capricious Churchill seemed, he could not put Britain's "lost generation" of young men out of his mind. General Sir Leslie Hollis, assistant secretary to the War Cabinet, said that the memory of one million dead in World War I "was the unseen visitor at every conference I attended." More recent experience, and fear of worse to come, was even more potent. Hundreds of thousands of British troops had already been killed, wounded, or captured since the outbreak of World War II. When it came to contemplating an early invasion of France, General Morgan observed, "certain British authorities . . . instinctively recoiled from the whole affair. . . ."

> We had sustained disaster after disaster, and the skin of our teeth was wearing a bit thin. Small wonder if those who bore the full responsibility were not over-enthusiastic about sticking their necks out further than they had ever stuck them out before.

The British people badly needed a victory. So did Churchill's generals. So did Churchill. What he and they dared not risk was another major reverse, with the English Channel running red with British blood.

The Americans were unable to share their concerns. They had suffered no great disaster in World War I and their certainty that an early victory was attainable had not been dented by defeat—except momentarily in the Pacific where they had been caught napping. The enormous manpower resources of the United States had barely been touched. And its industrial might was rapidly being harnessed.

Neither the exhilarating total triumph in North Africa nor the Soviet victory at Stalingrad purged the British of their fear that catastrophe awaited their troops across the English Channel. In May 1943, a few days after the victory in Tunisia, the question of timing for the eventual cross-Channel assault was again raised at a summit conference in Washington. Once more Churchill proclaimed his firm backing for such an operation and once more he qualified his commitment by saying it should take place when "a plan offering reasonable prospects of success could be made," as if anyone would suggest otherwise.

But now he was unable to persuade Roosevelt to see things his way. This time, the president backed General Marshall in his insistence that the assault on Hitler's Fortress Europe should not be further delayed. "The Americans," General Brooke observed at the time, "are taking up the attitude that we led them down the garden path by taking them to North Africa." Churchill was pressed by Roosevelt to agree that the cross-Channel invasion should take place the following year, in the spring of 1944. Lord Moran noted in his diary, "The P.M. is, I think, puzzled; he had not expected the President to lay down the law like this."

General Brooke was appalled. He insisted, "No major operations [across the Channel] would be possible" for another two or three years, "until 1945 or 1946." But apprehensive of the growing American exasperation, and anxious to overcome War Department reluctance to agree to an invasion of Italy after the Sicily campaign that was about to be launched, the British grudgingly accepted a spring 1944 deadline for the invasion of France.

Even then, Churchill attempted to insert ifs and buts. He told Roosevelt that his agreement to the timetable for a cross-Channel plunge should not be taken "rigidly and without review in the swiftly-changing situations of war." But at the Teheran Summit Conference in November 1943, both Roosevelt and Stalin denied him further room to maneuver. There, the British found the Americans "far more sceptical of [Churchill] than . . . of Stalin." Though still vainly proposing the possibility of new Mediterranean exploits instead, the prime minister finally felt compelled to accept that the cross-Channel invasion would definitely take place the coming spring. General Brooke was dismayed. Even on the day before the Normandy landings finally took place, he expressed the fear that they "may well be the most ghastly disaster of the whole war."

World War II would have followed a totally different course if Roosevelt had backed Secretary of War Stimson, General Marshall, and the War Department's Operations Division rather than Churchill in the debate over strategy. Despite the prime minister's forebodings, the British would have had no option but to acquiesce. Their ability to continue prosecuting the war depended on an unceasing flow of American supplies. Victory for them was improbable without the assistance of American troops. Roosevelt was in a position to issue an ultimatum to London, backing up his generals. But Churchill's extraordinary powers of persuasion were only partly responsible for his not doing so. The president was no pushover. He was motivated primarily by domestic factors and what he considered the best interests of the United States.

He agreed to Churchill's North Africa strategy in the summer of 1942 because he believed that to do otherwise was too risky politically. The American people wanted him to get on with winning the war. They were unlikely to look kindly on a huge and ever-growing U.S. army kept idle in Britain for the better part of a year until it was well enough trained and equipped to launch a successful cross-Channel invasion in 1943. Public, press, and congressional pressure—as well as demands from the navy and General MacArthur, now a popular hero—to deal conclusively with the Japanese first might have grown irresistible.

Unwavering in his conviction that Nazi Germany was the more dangerous adversary, Roosevelt believed an early demonstration of

U.S. troops in combat in the European Theater essential to focus the attention of the American public there. Marshall did not fully appreciate that. He later conceded that he "failed to see that the leader in a democracy has to keep the people entertained. . . . The people demand action." As a consequence, Marshall failed to recommend a credible combat "entertainment" against Hitler with which the president could capture the imagination and enthusiasm of the American people, without requiring them to wait for it. But Churchill was able to do so. For Britain's purposes, and for Roosevelt's, Operation Torch seemed eminently suitable.

Had Churchill agreed with Marshall that an early invasion of France should take place, Roosevelt would have found it difficult not to be persuaded as well and not to agree to an alternative "entertainment" for the American public while it was being readied. Although Marshall had earlier opposed the move for fear of wastefully dispersing American resources, some units of U.S. troops, accompanied by a corps of war correspondents, might have been dispatched to the Middle East to help the British Eighth Army fight back the Axis advance then in progress there. They would have given the required appearance of U.S. combat involvement against Nazi Germany. Meantime, the bulk of American troops and equipment might have been gathered in Britain to join British forces in the early cross-Channel assault the War Department had vainly promoted.

But nothing of the sort happened, and once French North Africa had been invaded, the commitment of Allied forces, and the Allied focus of the war in the European Theater, shifted to the Mediterranean. On July 10, 1943, two months after the end of the Tunisia campaign, Allied troops crossed the Mediterranean to invade Sicily.

Operation Torch was history, but Eisenhower remained Supreme Commander of the attacking forces involved. Alexander, Tedder, and Cunningham were still his deputies. Murphy was still his political adviser and would play a central role as a State Department trouble-shooter in Europe during the remainder of the war. Patton commanded the U.S. Seventh Army and Montgomery commanded the British Eighth Army in the conquest of Sicily. General Kenneth Anderson returned to Britain to command the British Second Army in training there. Clark, now commanding the U.S. Fifth Army, was preparing for the invasion of Italy.

That invasion was launched on September 3, after Sicily had been taken. By then Italy had surrendered. But the Allied forces had to fight their way up the narrow, mountainous Italian peninsula against determined German resistance. Nine months later, on June 4, 1944, they had gotten only as far as Rome after having sustained heavy casualties. Two days after that, and a little more than a year past the time initially proposed by Marshall, Operation Round-Up—renamed Operation Overlord—was finally launched. Allied troops crossed the English Channel to pour onto the beaches of Normandy, establish a bridgehead against fierce resistance, and advance across France, Belgium, and Holland toward the German heartland.

The liberation of Western Europe by the armies of the Western Allies was bloody and costly. But less than a year after the cross-Channel invasion was finally launched, Germany surrendered unconditionally, Hitler was dead, and Third Reich was a pile of rubble.

It is not unreasonable to suspect that much was lost that could have been saved and that much additional grief and destruction were suffered because the invasion was not launched sooner. It is not unreasonable to conclude that for all its merits, the primary achievement of Operation Torch was to delay the moment when the Allies were able to break through Hitler's Atlantic Wall, storm into Germany, and with the Soviets, go on to bring the most murderous war in history to a triumphant conclusion.

Acknowledgments

Thanks are due to many people for the assistance and advice they offered while this account of Operation Torch was being researched and written. They include members of the staff of the Military Reference Branch of the National Archives in Washington, where the knowledgeable Charles E. Taylor was particularly helpful; the equally astute and obliging Hanna Zeidlik and the staff of the U.S. Army Center of Military History; and the staffs of the U.S. Navy Historical Branch, the Library of Congress, and the main branch of the New York Public Library. Major Charles E. Kirkpatrick and Dr. Theresa L. Kraus generously provided me with copies of their incisive monographs on Torch preparations.

In London, I am much obliged to the staffs of the Public Record Office at Kew, the Imperial War Museum, the Royal Navy Historical Branch, the Reading Room of the National Army Museum, the London Library, the British Library at the British Museum, the Colindale Newspaper Library, and the special collection at the West Hill Branch of the London Public Library in Wandsworth.

Lieutenant General Sir Ian Jacob, who takes sharp exception to the conclusion I have drawn about the merits of Operation Torch, kindly shared with me some of his personal recollections of the period and its events and permitted me to read and quote from his diary of the war years. I am grateful also for the gracious hospitality he and the late Lady Jacob showed me. General Sir Charles Richardson was kind enough to recount for me some of his recollections of General Montgomery. I am obliged to the Ministry of Defence in London for agreeing to my request to release a classified file on Torch prior to its planned release date, though its refusal to release other classified documents no longer capable of damaging national security or interests seems wrong. The determination of officials to cling to outdated secrets is only slowly being eroded.

Thanks finally to Graham Hovey and Noland Norgaard for troubling to write to me about their experiences when they were news correspondents covering aspects of the campaign in French North Africa.

—N.G.

Endnotes

Abbreviations:

NA—National Archives, Washington

CMH—United States Army Center of Military History, Washington

USN—United States Navy Historical Center, Washington

PRO—Public Record Office, Kew, London

Full information on sources cited in brief will be found in the Selected Bibliography.

1: Operation Torch

15. "The job I am going on": Blumenson, *Patton Papers,* p. 92.

2: Genesis

17. "America has just come into the war": Moran, p. 16.

17. "[The president] has been completely": Stillwell, p. 41.

17. "would promptly take part": William Shirer, *The Rise and Fall of the Third Reich* (London: Secker and Warburg, 1960), p. 876.

18. "No American will": Churchill III, p. 539.

20. "My impression of Washington": Stillwell, p. 40.

20. "an undivided people": *Chicago Tribune,* December 9, 1941.

21. "death and destruction": *New York Herald Tribune,* December 9, 1941.

21. "like a kick in the stomach": Stillwell, p. 31.

22. "can best be settled": Gilbert, *Road to Victory,* p. 2.

22. "The whole plan": Ibid.

22. "Much of your time": Ibid., p. 143.

22. "wanted to show the President": Moran, p. 20.

23. "high British authority": London *News Chronicle,* December 23, 1941.

23. "made worth while": London *Daily Mirror,* January 19, 1942.

23. "We are entitled to ask": London *Daily Sketch,* December 17, 1941.

24. "a complete understanding": Churchill III, p. 555.

24. "The official reports": Ibid., p. 568.

25. "At present this country": Bryant, p. 292.

26. "the key to victory": Sherwood, *Roosevelt and Hopkins,* p. 445

27. "prove more difficult": Ibid., p. 446.

28. "concentrating exclusively": PRO. PREM 3/458/2.

28. "closing and tightening": *Foreign Relations of the United States: The Conferences at Washington, 1941–1942.* (Washington: U.S. Government Printing Office, 1968), p. 210.

29. "The potential front": Churchill III, p. 583.

29. "Plans should be set": Ibid., p. 577.

29. "invitation" from French officers: *Foreign Relations of the United States,* op. cit., p. 72.

30. "failure in this first venture": Pogue, *Ordeal,* p. 288.

30. "While the willingness": NA. RG 165, WPD 4511-45.

30. "entirely independently": Ibid., 4511-47.

31. "far more favorable": Ibid., 4511-37.

31. "so irrational": Ibid.

31. "too much anti-British feeling": Pogue, *Ordeal,* p. 264.

31. "just felt we weren't smart": Ibid.

32. "[He] has been completely": Stillwell, p. 41.

33. "kicked up a hell of a row": Sherwood, *Roosevelt and Hopkins,* p. 469.

33. "The Americans have got their way": Moran, p. 22.

33. "birthright for a plate of porridge": Bryant, p. 296.

34. "The President is a child": Diary of Lieutenant General Sir Ian Jacob.

34. "general dislike": Fraser, p. 230.

34. "military plans and ideas": Bryant, p. 415.

34. "God knows where we should be": Ibid., p. 299.

3: African Prelude

35. "[We] dropped like so many Alices": Pendar, p. 12.

38. "They [the Germans]": Langer, p. 154.

40. "The President wanted me": Leahy, p. 18.

41. "what practical form": Paxton, p. 77.

41. "second class Dominion": Ibid., p. 112.

42. "a complete opportunist": Leahy, p. 94.

42. "As one sailor to another": Ibid., p. 22.

42. "have 3,000 tanks": *Foreign Relations of the United States, 1941,* Vol. II (Washington: U.S. Government Printing Office, 1959). p. 189.

42. "skillful and determined": Charles de Gaulle, *War Memoirs,* Vol. II (London: Weidenfeld and Nicolson, 1956), p. 15.

44. "I didn't even know how": Coster, p. 104.

44. "Since all their thoughts": Smith, p. 39.

44. "the danger presented": Murphy, p. 121.

44. "One or two of us": Ibid., 121.

44. "We control officers": Pendar, p. 49.
45. "high society": NA. RG 226, Entry 99, Box 39.
45. "We soon began to collect": Pendar, p. 74.
45. "For the first time": Cline, p. 19.

4: Allies at Odds

46. "Allies are the most aggravating": Danchev, *Very Special Relationship,* p. 39.
47. "not above learning from us": PRO. CAB 65/25.
47. "65 reasons why": Stillwell, p. 49.
47. "All agree": Ibid., p. 45.
47. "an academic study": Matloff, p. 176.
48. "The greatest disaster": Bryant, p. 305.
48. "Was this some kind": Steele, p. 83.
50. "The struggle to secure": Matloff, p. 156.
50. "We can't win": Chandler I, p. 75.
50. "the shortest route": Cline, p. 156.
50. "We should at once": Matloff, p. 177.
50. "current commitments": Ibid., p. 179.
51. "The American": Danchev, *Establishing the Alliance,* p. 172.
51. "weakened in strength": Matloff, p. 179.
52. "we must turn our backs": Ibid., p. 182.
52. "going off": Stimson, p. 214.
52. Marshall Memorandum: Matloff, p. 184.
52. "It is the only place": Ibid., p. 185.
54. "be pulled to pieces": Stimson, p. 214.

5: Coup in the Making

55. "If you learn anything": Murphy, p. 96.
58. "we can achieve infinitely more": Smith, p. 33.
59. "arriving like jeunes filles": Ibid., p. 163.
59. "Agency Africa": See Slowikowski.
60. "Don't bother going": Murphy, p. 96.
60. "on some nice": Berle, p. 412.
61. "native population": Smith, p. 42.
61. "Nothing," he believed: Murphy, p. 212.
61. "however honorable": Coon, p. 23.
62. "mule turds were to be found": Ibid., p. 31.
62. "We will not find": Langer, p. 240.
63. "to prepare the ground": Ibid., p. 280.

65. "Whatever happens": Kersaudy, p. 78.

66. believed he heard "voices": Crozier, p. 184.

66. "help anyone impose a Government": Murphy, p. 133.

66. "so-called Free French": Churchill III, p. 591.

6: Pretense of Harmony

69. "I had to work by influence": Churchill IV, p. 289.

69. "somewhat addicted to freakish schemes": Fergusson, p. 119.

70. "dominated by a defensive": Truscott, p. 44.

70. "momentous": Greenfield, *Command Decisions*, p. 135.

70. "Western Europe is favored": Butler, p. 675.

72. "does not go beyond": Bryant, p. 358.

72. "[I]t was unlikely": PRO. CAB 79/56.

72. "They [the Americans]": Bryant, p. 355.

72. "With the situation": Ibid., p. 357.

72. "[W]e have lost a good deal": Kennedy, p. 198.

72. "had not fought as toughly": Ibid.

72. "the mockery of the world": Dilks, p. 433.

72. "Have you not got": Bryant, p. 330.

73. "returning to a concept": Wedemeyer, p. 105.

73. "residuary legatee": Pogue, *Ordeal,* p. 318.

73. ". . . a pleasant and easy man": Bryant, p. 354.

74. "What Harry and Geo. Marshall": Loewenheim, p. 202.

74. "still fearful": Moran, p. 35.

74. "I made it very plain": Sherwood, *Roosevelt and Hopkins,* p. 525.

75. "adept in the use of phrases": Wedemeyer, p. 105.

75. "reservations regarding this": Pogue, *Ordeal,* p. 318.

75. "march ahead together": PRO. CAB 69/4.

75. "entire agreement": Stoler, p. 41.

75. "real meeting of minds": Gilbert, *Road to Victory,* p. 91.

75. "I hope that": Chandler I, p. 260.

75. "nothing would be left undone": PRO. CAB 69/4.

76. "I was almost certain": Churchill IV, p. 289.

76. "Don't rush things!": Crozier, p. 107.

76. "We have not yet had time": Ismay, p. 250.

77. "Our American friends": Ibid.

77. "we might be ordered": Ziegler, p. 183.

78. "must not be permitted": Harrison, p. 11.

78. "The whole question": T. Morgan, p. 637.

78. "An agitation in the British press": Churchill IV, p. 757.

80. "in mind a very important": Burns, p. 232.
81. "this year": Ibid., p. 233.
81. "Full understanding was reached": Ibid., p. 234.
83. "Please make it": Pogue, *Ordeal,* 402.
83. "We are making preparations": Churchill IV, p. 305.
83. "preparations are proceeding": Ibid., p. 303.

7: Gathering Pace
84. "The British will never": Wedemeyer, p. 158.
85. "It is necessary": Matloff, p. 196.
86. "Now," General Albert Wedemeyer wrote: Wedemeyer, p. 136.
86. "certainly not of higher category": NA. RG 218, CCS 320.2, 6-24-42.
87. "nitpicking" operations: Wedemeyer, p. 120.
87. "sacrifical landing": Burns, p. 235.
87. "set out to educate": Moran, p. 34.
87. "a prime example of British cleverness": Wedemeyer, p. 144.
88. "His Majesty's Government": Churchill IV, 342.
88. "No responsible British military authority": Ibid.
89. "If disaster," it asked: Matloff, p. 242.
89. "brewing up together": Bryant, p. 402.
89. "not possible": Ibid., p. 403.
90. "I am ashamed": Moran, p. 38.
90. "Seasoned soldiers": Churchill IV, p. 343.
91. "pushed forward with all speed": Ibid., p. 344.
91. "things have gone badly": Hansard, January 17, 1942.
92. "too nervous and irritable": Harold Nicolson, *Diaries and Letters* (London: Collins, 1980), p. 225.
92. "incompetents, fools, log-rollers": London *Daily Mirror,* January 14, 1942.
92. "blimps, bullshit and brass-buttoned boneheads": Wykes, p. 41.
92. "Some good news at last!": Brittain, p. 157.
92. "faced with a major crisis": Ibid., p. 159.
93. "radical changes": *Times,* June 17, 1942.
93. "tribute to the heroism": Hansard, July 1, 1942.
93. "Considering," Churchill later wrote: Churchill IV, p. 353.
93. "suffered in both fields": Hansard, July 1, 1942.
94. "[W]e may lose Egypt": Ibid., July 2, 1942.
94. "The public are angry": Ibid., July 1, 1942.
94. "wins debate after debate": Ibid.
94. "If Rommel had been in the British Army": Ibid.
94. "habitual critics who": Ibid.

95. " 'stood when earth's foundations' ": Ibid.

95. "All over the world": Ibid., July 2, 1942.

95. "It would a deplorable disaster": Moran, p. 43.

96. "No responsible British general": PRO. CAB 120/410.

96. "This," he cabled him: Ibid.

96. "the safest and most fruitful": Loewenheim, p. 222.

97. "so laboriously accomplished": Library of Congress. Henry Stimson Diary, microfilm, reel 7, volume 38.

97. "these . . . decisions": Ibid.

97. "in wholehearted accord": Matloff, p. 268.

97. "If the United States": Ibid., p. 269.

98. "half-baked" schemes: Library of Congress. op. cit.

99. "with utmost vigor": Matloff, p. 277.

99. "get through the hides": Stimson, p. 220.

99. "If Sledgehammer cannot be launched": Sherwood, *Roosevelt and Hopkins*, p. 602.

99. "everything points to a complete": Gilbert, *Road to Victory*, p. 149.

100. "raised holy hell": Butcher, p. 20.

101. "was to be executed": Wedemeyer, p. 131.

102. "the blackest day in history": Butcher, p. 24.

102. "the least harmful diversion": Pogue, *Ordeal*, p. 346.

102. "All was . . . agreed": Churchill IV, p. 404.

102. "A very trying week": Bryant, p. 428.

103. "was now our principal objective": Matloff, p. 283.

103. "if it seemed clearly headed": Pogue, *Ordeal*, p. 349.

8. The Supreme Commander Takes Charge

106. "I am awfully sorry": Danchev, *Establishing the Alliance*, p. 197.

106. "idiocy": Eisenhower, p. 81.

106. "The decision to invade": Ibid., p. 80.

107. "From what our planners": Wedemeyer, p. 164.

107. "enthusiastically and effectively": Ibid.

107. "Planners who are responsible": Cline, p. 165.

108. "unless ordered": Danchev, *Establishing the Alliance*, p. 195.

108. "We are here": Butcher, p. 42.

108. "frequently seemed to retire": Stimson, p. 280.

108. "Torch offered as poor": Arnold, p. 186.

109. "nerve-wracking": Eisenhower, p. 86.

111. "to imperil any British troops": Howard, *Grand Strategy*, p. 115.

112. "departing from normal methods": Ibid., p. 120.

112. "Possibly they are beginning to realize": Ibid.
113. "within a month": Ibid., p. 117.
113. "stand or fall": Matloff, p. 288.
115. "Every movement at Gib": Butcher, p. 60.
115. "We shall appear": PRO. FO 371/31291.
116. "with the seriousness it deserves": Feis, *Churchill, Roosevelt, Stalin*, p. 72.
116. "It was . . . like": PRO. PREM 3/76.
117. Stalin offer to Hitler: *Time* magazine, October 1, 1990.
117. "a great many disagreeable things": PRO. PREM 3/76.
117. "I unfolded a map": Ibid.
117. "Stalin is a realist": Bryant, p. 460.

9: Time for Decision
120. "In the whole of Torch": Churchill IV, p. 488.
121. "It is more difficult": PRO. AIR 47/69.
122. "intervention of higher authority": Eisenhower, p. 90.
122. "that some form of operation": Clark, p. 51.
122. "[T]he chances of effecting": Chandler I, p. 471.
123. "still subject": NA. RG 165, OPD Executive Files, Box 2, Item 7.
123. "the time for analyzing": Chandler I, p. 476.
123. "that the operation": Butcher, p. 66.
123. "completely convinced": Clark, p. 52.
124. "unjustifiable hazard": Funk, *Politics*, p. 96.
125. "It would be an immense help": Loewenheim, p. 240.
125. "It would be quite impossible": Chandler I, p. 526.
125. "During this period": Clark, p. 59.
126. "within an hour": PRO. PREM 3/470.
126. "We agree to the military layout": Ibid.
126. "The highest military": Langer, p. 309.
128. "I was determined": Morison, p. 181.
128. "I received a weighty document": F. Morgan, p. 30.
132. "We tried to convince": USN. Admiral H. Kent Hewitt, Oral History transcript.
133. "I am of the opinion": Kraus, p. 3.
133. "actual friction": Ibid., p. 6.
134. "That gave them": USN. op. cit.
135. "possibly" to enemy action: Morison, p. 150.
136. "It was only possible": Ibid., p. 202.
136. "had in fact never seen": Maund, p. 111.

137. "torn between desire": Butcher, p. 58.
137. "of normal appearance": CMH. "Preparations for Torch." File 2-3, 7.
138. "They always give": Blumenson, *Patton Papers,* p. 85.
139. "the assault teams": Clark, p. 61.
139. "hire labor": CMH. op. cit.

10: Spies, Lies, and Conspiracies

140. "Eisenhower listened": Murphy, p. 136.
141. "misgivings" about the African venture: Ibid., p. 131.
141. "Why, Bob!": Ibid., p. 135.
142. Murphy "talked more like an American": Butcher, p. 91.
142. "The General disliked": Murphy, p. 136.
144. "I hated to do it": Blumenson, *Patton Papers,* p. 87.
145. "The enemy Intelligence": PRO. AIR 20/2508.
147. "to clean up the North African coast": Butcher, p. 77.
148. "The real triumph": Masterman, p. 110.
149. "The lack of coordination": PRO. DEFE 2/581.
149. "In spite of all difficulties": Ibid.
150. "Dammit, Lucian": Truscott, p. 87.
150. "were scattered up and down": Harmon, p. 77.
150. "If they can't find": Ibid.
151. "Having to use the incompetent": USN. Colonel A. T. Mason, "Special Monograph on Amphibious Warfare," p. 19.
151. "leave the beaches": Farago, p. 90.
151. "Never in history": Morison, p. 41.
151. "It is General Patton's view": PRO. DEFE 2/581.
152. "Information having been received": Murphy, p. 139.
154. "Do not try that!": Ibid., p. 144.
155. " . . . much as I hate [Darlan]": Eisenhower, p. 116.
155. "our principal collaborator": Howe, p. 80.
156. "practically without firing a shot": Ibid.
157. "This is great": Clark, p. 77.
159. "They talked of thick shore patrols": Ibid., p. 79.
159. "hardly ever been less certain": Ibid.
161. "I tried to keep": Ibid., p. 85.
162. " . . . the United States has no other thought": Funk, *Politics,* p. 156.
163. "The French were ready": Clark, p. 86.
163. "exceeded only": Ibid.
164. "How does this thing": Courtney, p. 46.
165. "All questions were settled": Clark, p. 92.

11: Torch Is Lit

166. "At last the hour": *Washington Post,* November 9, 1942.
167. "like a file of Indian squaws": Truscott, p. 90.
167. "the operation would not be practicable": Ibid., p. 91.
167. "individual and team techniques": Ibid., p. 90.
167. "that we are better": Howe, p. 70.
168. "the most valuable convoys": Roskill, p. 317.
169. "Batter Up": Howe, p. 45.
170. "Do you want a failure?": Interview with General Charles Richardson, October 30, 1990.
170. "Air raid after air raid": Rommel, p. 317.
170. "In the situation": Ibid., p. 321.
171. "All the information": Ciano, p. 509.
171. "the best jumping-off point": Warlimont, p. 267.
171. "the increased number of reports": Jacobson, p. 205.
172. "attacked and destroyed": Warlimont, p. 271.
173. "early in November": Murphy, p. 154.
174. "I am convinced": Ibid., p. 155.
174. "It is inconceivable": Chandler I, p. 651.
175. "Recommend Murphy be advised": Clark, p. 96.
175. "[T]he operation will be carried out": Murphy, p. 156.
176. "This is the first time": Eisenhower, p. 108.
176. "the most dismal setting": Ibid., p. 107.
176. "aircraft were stacked": Howard, *British Intelligence,* p. 59.
177. "a case of the jitters": Chandler II, p. 666.
178. "advised the reception committee": Courtney, p. 55.
181. "thrown his coat": Clark, p. 98.
181. " . . . KINGPIN [Giraud] refused": CMH. File 228.01. HRC J. Africa. 314.7.
182. "the governorship, virtually the kingship": Langer, p. 338.
182. "the difference between": Eisenhower, p. 112.
183. "Oh, no you won't": Clark, p. 101.
184. "From now on": Butcher, p. 145.
184. "Worries of a Commander": Butcher, p. 151.

12: Showdown in Algiers

201. "Here we are with a city on our hands": Tompkins, p. 79.
203. *Allo, Robert:* Murphy, p. 162.
203. "The entire town": Pendar, p. 104.
204. "you desire above all else": Murphy, p. 163.

204. "General Juin paced the floor": Langer, p. 346.
205. "If the matter": Murphy, p. 164.
205. "I have known for a long time": Ibid., p. 165.
206. "That moment has now arrived": Ibid., p. 166.
207. "Late at night": Pendar, p. 105.
209. "We received no opposition": Morison, p. 205.
211. "elastic but nonaggressive": Jones, p. 148.
211. "by its very nature": Funk, *Politics,* p. 224.

13: Oran
213. "This place gives me": Breuer, p. 134.
215. "[W]e beached very quietly": PRO. DEFE 2/581.
216. "No shooting thus far": Howe, p. 203.
219. "hare brained": Yarborough, p. 20.
223. "we were invading Africa alone": Ibid., p. 43.

14: Casablanca
225. "The grinding of ship's engines": Taggart, p. 15.
227. "We come among you": Langer, p. 365.
228. "On board ship": Morison, p. 67.
229. Sixty percent of landing craft: PRO. WO 204/10098.
230. "Well, Commodore": Truscott, p. 92.
230. "Boat crews were drifting": NA. RG 165, 381 Torch, Box 1296.
232. "combination of inexperienced": Morison, p. 123.
232. "stand by to move out to sea": Truscott, p. 97.
234. "I hope the Vichy people": Lacouture, p. 397.
234. "I cannot understand": Cook, p. 164.
234. "a good body disposal squad": Ambrose, p. 117.
234. "a little airplane incident": Ibid., p. 116.
236. "This is the largest landing operation": Speer, p. 246.
237. "powerful American armed forces": Warner, p. 321.
237. "It is with stupor": *Foreign Relations of the United States, 1942,* Vol. II, p. 431.

15: Negotiations
239. "Why do soldiers": Clark, p. 108.
240. "He is not your man": Sherwood, *White House Papers,* p. 646.
240. "I've promised Giraud": Chandler II, p. 667.
241. "This really messes things up": Murphy, p. 172.
241. "I am so impatient": Chandler II, p. 680.
242. "feeling of uncertainty": Clark, p. 107.

242. "Why do soldiers": Ibid., p. 108.

242. "Kiss Darlan's stern": Butcher, p. 251.

243. "big American who does nothing": Clark, p. 109.

243. "for psychological effect": Ibid., p. 108.

243. YBSOB: Murphy, p. 175.

243. Clark "quickly ran foul": Eisenhower, p. 117.

244. "What you propose": Clark, p. 111.

245. "In no circumstances": Clark, p. 114.

245. "like a king": Ibid., p. 115.

249. "I have never promised anything": Gilbert, *Road to Victory,* p. 254.

249. "The President of the United States": Arnold, p. 188.

250. "Neither the British": CMH. "Preparations for Torch," File 2-3.7.

250. "The planning of the operation": PRO. DEFE 2/581.

250. "No officer commanding": Morison, p. 32.

250. "The individual officer": PRO. DEFE 2/603.

250. "The entire operation": USN. CINCLANT, Serial 0014, January 9, 1943.

251. "It is my firm conviction": NA. RG 165, 381 Torch, Box 1296.

16: On to Tunisia

252. "I'm no reactionary": Macmillan, p. 221.

253. "national unworthiness": Morison, p. 241.

253. "close and friendly relations": Howard, *Grand Strategy,* p. 180.

253. "I now have a guardian": Eisenhower, p. 123.

253. "with all possible speed": PRO. WO 204/10329.

255. "First the Germans": Pendar, p. 118.

255. "traitor" to his face: Tompkins, p. 127.

255. "I tried to imagine": Murphy, p. 176.

256. "If they would only": Chandler II, p. 693.

256. "a bit of table pounding": Ibid., p. 698.

256. "None of you should": Cook, p. 163.

258. "The actual state": CMH. File 228.01. HRC J. Africa 337.

259. "As a result": Chandler II, p. 738.

260. "produced violent reactions": Thomas, p. 156.

260. "A permanent arrangement": Churchill IV, p. 568.

260. " . . . there is nothing": Alexander Kendrick, *Prime Time* (London: Dent, 1970), p. 254.

261. "Hitler's tool": Burns, p. 296.

261. a "stinking skunk": Langer, p. 370.

261. "The present temporary": Ibid., p. 371.

261. "[I]t is impossible": Burns, p. 297.

262. "a lemon which the Americans": Clark, p. 126.
262. "With our forces": Howard, *Grand Strategy,* p. 176.
262. "I can't understand": Macmillan, p. 221.
263. "my whole doctrine and reason": Chandler II, p. 962.
264. succinctly replied, "Shit": Pendar, p. 117.

17: Bog Down
265. "The dead were buried": Moorehead, p. 461.
265. "My forces available": Blaxland, p. 106.
268. "imbued with the will": Chandler II, p. 780.
268. "deeply disturbed" by what he saw: Tedder, p. 369.
269. "What are we saving them for?": Butcher, p. 174.
269. "semi-hostile": PRO. CAB 88/6.
269. "Arab leaders chosen": Pendar, p. 72.
270. "Through all this period": Eisenhower, p. 141.
270. "would undoubtedly stage": Ibid., p. 143.
271. "I think the best way": Chandler II, p. 811.
271. "as much as anything": Eisenhower, p. 137.
271. "less than two months": Chandler II, p, 867.
272. "Owing to the thinness": Howard, *Grand Strategy,* p. 182.
272. "News from Tunisia": Bryant, p. 534.
272. "I am most anxious": PRO. PREM 3/442/2.
273. "we were collaborating": MacVane, p. 78.
275. "fraternizing" with the Americans: Liebling, p. 187.
275. "Members of uniformed": Ibid., p. 190.
275. "a continuous parade of Very Important Persons": Murphy, p. 184.
276. "native population": Tompkins, p. 171.
276. "backwoods American generals": Macmillan, p. 292.
276. "Well-known German sympathizers": PRO. PREM 3/442/2.
276. "I think sometimes": Chandler II, p. 795.
277. "a certain lack of assurance": PRO. CAB 65/32.
279. "No one expects": Thomas, p. 168.
279. "London has been advised": Tompkins, p. 195.
280. "the act for which": Ledwidge, p. 141.
280. "Admiral Darlan's death": Clark, p. 130.
280. "please calm down": Berle, p. 430.
281. "trusted French agent": Butcher, p. 198.

18: Charting the Way Ahead
283. "We came, we listened": Wedemeyer, p. 192.
284. "I have never seen": Macmillan, p. 241.

285. "using the bases": Sherwood, *Roosevelt and Hopkins,* p. 674.
286. "springboard for a thrust": Harrison, p. 143.
286. "the Mediterranean as a kind of . . . dark hole": Diary of Lieutenant General Sir Ian Jacob.
287. "how best to tackle the Americans": Gilbert, *Road to Victory,* p. 293.
287. "They swarmed down upon us": Wedemeyer, p. 192.
288. "to improve their over-all Empire position": Ibid., p. 177.
288. "It is a slow and tedious process": Bryant, p. 548.
288. "must be made gradually": Bryant, p. 548.
288. "made particularly careful preparations": Harrison, p. 90.
290. "[I]f I had written down": Jacob diary.
290. "a 'Sledgehammer' of some sort": Churchill IV, p. 612.
290. "merely doing something," Ambrose, p. 158.
290. "One of the constant sources": Chandler II, p. 928.
292. "We'll call Giraud": Cook, p. 173.
292. "His mood," Murphy thought: Murphy, p. 208.
293. "produce the temperamental bride": Funk, *De Gaulle,* p. 68.

19: Setback

294. "The Americans had as yet": Rommel, p. 398.
294. "resign itself to being": Howard, *Grand Strategy,* p. 338.
297. "almost without variation": Chandler II, p. 905.
297. "Every infraction": Ibid., p. 904.
297. "an embarrassment to every American soldier": Bradley, p. 128.
297. "Small in stature": Ibid.
299. "Nice chap. No general": Interview with General Richardson.
300. "By bringing Alexander": Bryant, p. 556.
300. "needed machinery for effective": Eisenhower, p. 154.
300. "burning inside": Butcher, p. 223.
301. "responsibility to organize": Chandler II, p. 944.
302. "There were notable pockets": Bradley, p. 128.
302. "could not be held passively": Chandler II, p. 971.
303. "uselessly shouting slogans": Bradley, p. 128.
305. "General situation is far from satisfactory": Playfair, p. 304.
305. "could not be more helpful": Ibid.
308. "misled by the stupidity": London *Daily Herald,* February 23, 1943.
308. "The American troops": *Manchester Guardian,* February 25, 1943.
308. "All our people": Chandler II, p. 984.

20: Endgame

310. "We are masters": Churchill IV, p. 698.
310. "plain suicide": Rommel, p. 416.

311. "Heart, nerves and rheumatism": Ibid., p. 410.

312. "main anxiety is the poor fighting value": Blaxland, p. 168.

312. "discredited practice of using Air Force": Tedder, p. 410.

312. "dynamite with a short": Ibid., p. 411.

313. "Going to fuck up": Macksey, p. 261.

313. "You will find the Americans": London *Sunday Telegraph*, February 9, 1964.

313. "Ike had 'sold out' ": Bradley, p. 129.

314. "with unfortunate results": Chandler II, p. 1090.

314. "If my operations to break through": Nicolson, p. 181.

315. "an effective part": Butcher, p. 244.

315. "Success . . . would give": Eisenhower, p. 169.

316. "to fight to the last man": Macksey, p. 297.

316. "Organized resistance in Tunisia": *New York Times*, May 13, 1943.

Epilogue

318. "[I]t took an average": Higgins, p. 187.

318. "We came into North Africa": Butcher, p. 253.

318. "The Axis Powers have lost": London *Times*, May 13, 1943.

319. "there was, for the first time": Churchill IV, p. 698.

320. "walking around": New York *Herald Tribune*, May 11, 1943.

320. "In Africa," General Bradley later observed: Bradley, p. 159.

320. "The Allies had no experience": *The Economist*, September 28, 1946.

321. "amazed to find": Bryant, p. 614.

322. "did not depend": PRO. WO 193/101.

322. "replaced by badly-damaged": Liddell Hart, *Other Side of the Hill*, p. 386.

323. "the quality of the enemy's troops": F. Morgan, p. 158.

323. "astonishing . . . the speed": Rommel, p. 526.

324. "And Winston?": Bryant, p. 626.

324. "was the unseen visitor": Leasor, p. 329.

324. "certain British authorities": F. Morgan, p. 38.

325. "a plan offering reasonable prospects": Pogue, *Organizer of Victory*, p. 198.

325. "The Americans": Bryant, p. 619.

325. "The P.M. is, I think, puzzled": Moran, p. 96.

325. "No major operations": Pogue, *Organizer of Victory*, p. 200.

326. "rigidly and without": Higgins, p. 204.

326. "far more sceptical": Moran, p. 132.

326. "may well be the most ghastly": Arthur Bryant, *Triumph in the West* (London: Collins, 1959), p. 206.

327. "failed to see that the leader": Pogue, *Ordeal*, p. 330.

Selected Bibliography

Ambrose, Stephen E. *The Supreme Commander. London:* Cassell, 1971.

Arnold, H. H. *Global Mission.* London: Hutchinson, 1951.

Aron, Robert. *The Vichy Regime.* London: Putnam, 1958.

Bennett, Ralph. *Ultra and the Mediterranean Strategy.* London: Hamish Hamilton, 1989.

Berle, Adolf. *Navigating the Rapids.* New York: Harcourt Brace, 1973.

Blaxland, Gregory. *The Plain Cook and the Showman.* London: Kimber, 1977.

Blumenson, Martin. *The Patton Papers.* Boston: Houghton Mifflin, 1974.

———. *Rommel's Last Victory.* London: Allen and Unwin, 1968.

Bradley, Omar N., and Clay Blair. *A General's Life.* New York: Simon and Schuster, 1983.

Breuer, William B. *Operation Torch.* New York: St. Martin's Press, 1985.

Brinton, Crane. *The Americans and the French.* Cambridge, Mass.: Harvard University Press, 1968.

Brittain, Vera. *Diary.* London: Gollancz, 1989.

Brown, Anthony Cave. *The Last Hero.* New York: Times Books, 1982.

———. *The Secret Servant.* London: Michael Joseph, 1988.

Bryant, Arthur. *The Turn of the Tide.* London: Collins, 1957.

Burns, James MacGregor. *Roosevelt: Soldier of Freedom. London:* Weidenfeld and Nicolson, 1970.

Butcher, Harry C. *Three Years with Eisenhower.* London: Heinemann, 1946.

Butler, J.R.M. *Grand Strategy,* Vol. III. London: HMSO, 1964.

Chandler, Alfred, Jr., ed. *The Papers of Dwight David Eisenhower: The War Years,* Vols. I and II. Baltimore: Johns Hopkins Press, 1970–1972.

Churchill, Winston S. *The Second World War,* Vols. III and IV. London: Cassell, 1950–1951.

Ciano, Galeazzo. *Ciano Diaries, 1939–1943,* ed. Malcolm Muggeridge. London: Heinemann, 1947.

Clark, Mark. *Calculated Risk.* London: Harrap, 1951.

Cline, Ray S. *Washington Command Post: The Operations Division.* Washington: Department of the Army, 1951.

Cook, Don. *Charles De Gaulle.* London: Secker and Warburg, 1984.

Coon, Carleton. *A North Africa Story.* Ipswich, England: Gambit, 1980.

Cooper, Dick. *Adventures of a Secret Agent.* London: Frederick Muller, 1957.

Coster, Donald. "We Were Expecting You at Dakar." *Reader's Digest,* August 1946.

Courtney, G. B. *The SBS in World War Two.* London: Robert Hale, 1983.

345

Craven, Frank Wesley, and James Lea Cate. *The Army Air Forces in World War Two*, Vol. II. Chicago: University of Chicago Press, 1949.

Cray, Ed. *General of the Army*. New York: W. W. Norton, 1990.

Crozier, Brian. *DeGaulle: The Warrior*. London: Eyre Methuen, 1973.

Cruikshank, Charles. *Deception in World War Two*. London: Oxford University Press, 1979.

Danchev, Alex. *Establishing Anglo-American Alliance*. London: Brassey's, 1990

———. *Very Special Relationship*. London: Brassey's, 1986.

Davis, Kenneth. *The American Experience of War*. London: Secker and Warburg, 1967.

Dilks, David, ed. *The Diaries of Sir Alexander Cadogan*. London: Cassell, 1971.

Divine, A. D. *The Road to Tunis*. London: Collins, 1944.

Duff, Katherine. "Spain Between the Allies and the Axis," in *The War and the Neutrals* by Arnold and Veronica Toynbee. London: Oxford University Press, 1956.

Dunn, Walter Scott, Jr. *Second Front Now*. Tuscaloosa: University of Alabama Press, 1980.

Eisenhower, Dwight. *Crusade in Europe*. London: Heinemann, 1948.

Ellis, John. *Brute Force*. London: Andre Deutsch, 1990.

Farago, Ladislas. *Patton: Ordeal and Triumph*. London: Barker, 1966.

Feis, Herbert. *Churchill, Roosevelt, Stalin*. Princeton, N.J.: Princeton University Press, 1957.

———. *The Spanish Story*. New York: Knopf, 1948.

Fergusson, Bernard. *The Watery Maze*. London: Collins, 1961.

Foot, M.R.D. *SOE in France*. London: HMSO, 1966.

Frazer, David. *Alanbrooke*. London: Collins, 1982.

Fuller, J.F.C. *The Second World War*. London: Eyre and Spottiswoode, 1948.

Funk, Arthur L. *Charles De Gaulle: The Crucial Years*. Norman: University of Oklahoma Press, 1959.

———. *The Politics of Torch*. Lawrence: University of Kansas Press, 1974.

Gilbert, Martin. *Finest Hour*. London: Heinemann, 1984.

———. *Road to Victory*. London: Heinemann, 1986.

Greenfield, Kent. *American Strategy in World War II*. Baltimore: Johns Hopkins Press, 1963.

———. *Command Decisions*. London: Methuen, 1960.

Grigg, John. *1943: The Victory That Never Was*. London: Methuen, 1980.

Harmon, Ernest. *Combat Commander*. Englewood, N.J.: Prentice-Hall, 1970.

Harrison, Gordon. *United States Army in World War II: The European Theater of Operations.* Washington: Office of the Chief of Military History, Department of the Army, 1951.

Hayes, Carlton. *Wartime Mission in Spain.* New York: Macmillan, 1946.

Higgins, Trumbull. *Winston Churchill and the Second Front.* New York: Oxford University Press, 1957.

Hinsley, F. H. *British Intelligence in the Second World War,* Vol. II. London: HMSO, 1981.

Howard, Michael. *British Intelligence in the Second World War,* Vol. V. London: HMSO, 1990.

———. *Grand Strategy,* Volume IV. London: HMSO, 1972.

Howe, George. *United States Army in World War II: Northwest Africa.* Washington: Office of the Chief of Military History, 1957.

Ingersoll, Ralph. *The Battle Is the Pay-Off.* London: Bodley Head, 1943.

Ismay, Lord. *The Memoirs of General The Lord Ismay.* London: Heinemann, 1960.

Jackson, W.G.F. *The North African Campaign.* London: Batsford, 1975.

Jacobson, Hans-Adolf, and Jürgen Rowher, eds. *Decisive Battles of World War Two.* London: Deutsch, 1965.

Jewell, N.L.A. *Secret Submarine Mission.* Chicago: Ziff-Davis, 1944.

Jones, Vincent. *Operation Torch.* London: Pan/Ballantine, 1972.

Kennedy, Sir John. *The Business of War.* London: Hutchinson, 1957.

Kersaudy, François. *Churchill and De Gaulle.* London: Collins, 1981.

King, Ernest, and Walter Whitehill. *Fleet Admiral King.* New York: Norton, 1952.

Kirkpatrick, Charles. "Joint Planning for Torch: The United States Army." Paper presented at the Ninth Naval History Symposium, Annapolis, October 19, 1989.

Kraus, Theresa. "Joint Planning for Torch: The United States Navy." Paper presented at the Ninth Naval History Symposium, Annapolis, October 19, 1989.

Lacouture, Jean. *De Gaulle: The Rebel.* London: Collins, 1990.

Langer, William. *Our Vichy Gamble.* New York: Knopf, 1947.

Leahy, William. *I Was There.* London, Gollancz, 1950.

Leasor, James. *War at the Top.* London: Michael Joseph, 1959.

Ledwidge, Bernard. *De Gaulle.* London: Weidenfeld, 1982.

Liddell Hart, Basil. *The Other Side of the Hill.* London: Cassell, 1951.

Liebling, A. J. *The Road Back to Paris.* London: Michael Joseph, 1944.

Loewenheim, Francis, Harold Langley, and Manfred Jonas, eds. *Roosevelt and Churchill: Their Secret Wartime Correspondence.* New York: E. F. Dutton, 1975.

MacDonald, Charles. *The Mighty Endeavor.* New York: Oxford University Press, 1969.

Macksey, Kenneth. *Crucible of Power.* London: Hutchinson, 1969.

Macmillan, Harold. *The Blast of War.* London: Macmillan, 1967.

MacVane, John. *War and Diplomacy in North Africa.* London: Robert Hale, 1944.

Masterman, J. C. *The Double-Cross System.* New Haven: Yale University Press, 1972.

Matloff, Maurice, and Edwin Snell. *United States Army in World War II: Strategic Planning for Coalition Warfare.* Washington: Office of the Chief of Military History, 1953.

Maund, L.E.H. *Assault from the Sea.* London: Methuen, 1949.

Moorehead, Alan. *African Trilogy.* London: Hamish Hamilton, 1944.

Moran, Lord. *Winston Churchill.* London: Constable, 1966.

Morgan, Sir Frederick. *Overture to Overlord.* London: Hodder, 1950.

Morgan, Ted. *FDR.* London: Grafton Books, 1986.

Morison, Samuel Eliot. *Operations in North African Waters.* London: Oxford University Press, 1947.

Murphy, Robert. *Diplomat Among Warriors.* London: Collins, 1964.

Nicolson, Nigel. *Alex.* London: Weidenfeld and Nicolson, 1973.

Parrish, Thomas. *Roosevelt and Churchill.* New York: Morrow, 1989.

Paxton, Robert. *Vichy France.* London: Barrie and Jenkins, 1972.

Pendar, Kenneth. *Adventure in Diplomacy.* London: Cassell, 1966.

Playfair, I.S.O. *The Mediterranean and the Middle East.* London: HMSO, 1966.

Pogue, Forrest. *George C. Marshall: Ordeal and Hope.* London: MacGibbon and Kee, 1965.

———. *George C. Marshall: Organizer of Victory.* New York: Viking, 1973.

Raff, Edson. *We Jumped to Fight.* New York: Eagle Books, 1944.

Rommel, Erwin. *The Rommel Papers,* ed. B. H. Liddell Hart. London: Collins, 1953.

Roskill, S. W. *The War at Sea,* Vol. II. London: HMSO, 1956.

Sainsbury, Keith. *The North Africa Landings.* London: Davis-Poynter, 1976.

Sherwood, Robert. *Roosevelt and Hopkins.* New York: Harper, 1948.

———. *The White House Papers of Harry L. Hopkins,* Vol. II. London: Eyre and Spottiswoode, 1949.

Slowikowski, Rygor. *In the Secret Service.* London: Windrush Press, 1988.

Smith, R. Harris. *OSS.* Berkeley: University of California Press, 1972.

Speer, Albert. *Inside the Third Reich.* London: Weidenfeld and Nicolson, 1970.

Steele, Richard. *The First Offensive.* Bloomington: Indiana University Press, 1973.

Stillwell, Joseph. *The Stillwell Papers.* London: MacDonald, 1949.

Stimson, Henry L., and McGeorge Bundy. *On Active Service in Peace and War.* London: Hutchinson, 1949.

Stoler, Mark. *The Politics of the Second Front.* Westport, Conn.: Greenwood Press, 1977.

Strange, Joseph. "The British Rejection of Operation Sledgehammer: An Alternative Motive." *Military Affairs Magazine,* February 1942.

Strawson, John. *The Battle for North Africa.* London: Batsford, 1969.

Sweet-Escott, Bickham. *Baker Street Irregular.* London: Methuen, 1965.

Taggart, David, ed. *History of the Third Infantry Division in World War II.* Washington: Infantry Journal Press, 1947.

Tedder, Lord. *With Prejudice.* London: Cassell, 1966.

Thomas, R. T. *Britain and Vichy.* London: Macmillan, 1979.

Thompson, R. W. *Generalissimo Churchill.* London: Hodder, 1973.

Tompkins, Peter. *The Murder of Admiral Darlan.* London: Weidenfeld, 1965.

Truscott, L. K., Jr. *Command Missions.* New York: Dutton, 1954.

Tute, Warren. *The Reluctant Enemies.* London: Collins, 1990.

Verrier, Anthony. *Assassination in Algiers.* New York: Norton, 1990.

Warlimont, Walter. *Inside Hitler's Headquarters.* London: Weidenfeld, 1964.

Warner, Geoffrey. *Pierre Laval and the Eclipse of France.* London: Eyre and Spottiswoode, 1968.

Wedemeyer, Albert. *Wedemeyer Reports.* New York: Holt, 1958.

Wykes, Alan. 1942: *The Turning Point.* London: Macdonald, 1972.

Yarborough, William. *Bail Out over North Africa.* Williamstown, N.J.: Phillips Publications, 1979.

Zanuck, Darryl. *Tunis Expedition.* New York: Random House, 1943.

Ziegler, Philip. *Mountbatten.* London: Collins, 1985.

INDEX